TIGER WOODS
PUSHED TO GREATNESS
PRIMED TO FALL

*Controlled By His
Obsessive Father*

Linda Eckerson Grover

Copyright © 2016 Linda Eckerson Grover

All rights reserved.

No portion of this book may be reproduced in any fashion print, facsimile, or electronic, or by other method yet to be developed, without the express written permission of the author and publisher.

ISBN: 13:978-1536871647
ISBN: 10:153-6871648

TIGER WOODS

PUSHED TO GREATNESS PRIMED TO FALL

CONTENTS

Chapter 1	But He's Only a Kid!	1
Chapter 2	Practice, Practice, Practice	17
Chapter 3	Too Young To Be Perfect	25
Chapter 4	Pushed to Be the Best	35
Chapter 5	Controlling Tiger	45
Chapter 6	Coping With The Pressures	61
Chapter 7	Learning From Life	75
Chapter 8	Tough Lessons	91
Chapter 9	Big Changes For Tiger	107
Chapter 10	You Owe Me	117
Chapter 11	Seduced By Wealth and Fame	127
Chapter 12	Taking Charge of Tiger's Life	145
Chapter 13	It's All About The Image	165
Chapter 14	Defending Tiger	175
Chapter 15	Stealing Tiger's Spotlight	191
Chapter 16	Background Check	205
Chapter 17	Tiger's Out Of Control Father	215
Chapter 18	Playing The Fame Game	223
Chapter 19	Where It All Started	237
Chapter 20	Self-Serving Agenda	247
Chapter 21	Not The Best Image	253
Chapter 22	Hidden Family Ties	257

Chapter 23	Media Effects	269
Chapter 24	Family Matters	283
Chapter 25	Losing His Father	297
Chapter 26	Primed To Fall	315
Chapter 27	Destroying the Image	331
Chapter 28	Don't Blame Tiger	343
Chapter 29	Tiger's Struggle to Return	353

Determination becomes obsession and then it becomes all that matters.

- Jeremy Irvine -

1
BUT HE'S ONLY A KID

April, 1986
Navy Golf Course, Cypress, CA

THERE HE WAS. A golfer's worst nightmare - the dreaded kid on the golf course! He was a little over four feet tall and so thin he looked as if he could hide behind a two iron. He had shiny metal braces that blinded you as he smiled and large oversized glasses sliding down his tiny nose. The small carry bag on his left shoulder packed with only a few clubs was almost as big as he was. Worst of all, it looked as though this pint sized kid was walking toward the first tee to join our group. At that very moment, the only thought that came to mind was, "Oh, God, please tell me this kid is not playing with us."

I had never played with a child before and the closer this little kid got to the tee box the more I was regretting my decision to play this round. Our golf partner, Rick, had told us that we would be joining one of his friends and his son, but Rick obviously failed to mention that his friend's son was a "really young" son.

After struggling to secure his golf bag to the rear of the golf cart, "the kid" walked up on the tee box with his driver in hand and politely said, "Hi, I'm Tiger." His father, Earl, just laughed as he saw the expression of total surprise and apprehension on my face. Earl patted me on the back and said, "Don't worry, it will be fine. Tiger just might surprise you."

I leaned over toward my husband and whispered, "But he's only a kid!" With my husband feeling the same apprehension, he commented, "Well, we can't do anything about it now, so let's just wait and see."

Okay, fine.

So I decided I would temporarily put aside my aversion to kid golfers who, by the way, are usually only there to hack the ball around the course so they can pretend to play golf with their dad. The fact that Earl mentioned Tiger plays with his mother's clubs did not help my decision to be patient, nor did the fact that he was only ten years old. At this point, I'm thinking that "this kid" must be a really bad golfer. All I could envision was our having to wait on every hole for him to take three or four shots in the fairway to eventually reach ours. By now, I was telling myself that this could turn out to be a very long and tedious round, one we may soon regret playing.

After Earl, Rick and Ken teed off, Tiger and I both walked up toward the forward tees. Whether or not he was just being a young gentleman, I wasn't sure, but Tiger wanted me to go first.

As with all golfers on the first tee, my nerves caused me to tense up. With my first swing, I ended up topping the ball. Taking a mulligan, my drive made the fairway, but not far and not all that high into the air. Needless to say, I wanted to find the nearest hole and crawl into it. This was the 1980's and women golfers already had a bad reputation and men were not all that thrilled about playing with us. Well, I just proved their point as to why they hate playing with women.

But, worst of all, it was the little snicker that was coming from "the kid" standing behind me. When I turned around and looked at him, I really thought he was going to lose it. Thankfully, "the kid" muffled his mouth with his hand to prevent himself from totally breaking out in laughter. Then, of course, in my very mature and adult thinking, I immediately assumed this kid cannot be all that great either and maybe I would feel better after he tries to hit his drive. After all, I was convinced he was just here to knock the ball around the course with his dad.

Then it was "the kid's" turn to hit. He strutted up to the tee, steadied his stance, took his swing, and hauled off and hit the crap out of the ball. It was a perfect shot, a high draw that landed smack dab in the center of the fairway. After his perfect drive, "the kid" turned around with this cocky smirk on his face.

At that precise moment, I didn't know whether I wanted to applaud his shot or smack him for showing me up so badly. He's a kid for God's sake, and a short one at that. How dare he be that good!

Ultimately, I decided I would be nice and compliment "the kid" with, "great shot", after which I told him that he seemed to be a pretty good golfer. That was when "the kid" looked over at me, and with total composure, smugly remarked, "I know. It went exactly where I wanted it to."

Totally in shock with "the kid's" drive, I thought this had to be a fluke, just a one time lucky shot and we would probably never see another one for the rest of the round. However, to my surprise and disbelief, I later found that my assumption, or in this case, my wishful thinking, was totally incorrect.

I turned to Rick with a questioning expression on my face, wondering just who was this kid anyway? This was when Rick quickly responded with, "Oh, did I forget to mention that Tiger is actually the current Junior World Golf Champion for his age group? When I said we would be playing with Earl and his son, I guess I failed to include that little fact."

Tiger thought my reaction to the news about him was quite funny as he once again laughed at me, but he was also miffed that Rick had not told us about all of his wonderful achievements in golf. But it was his father, Earl, who could not understand why we had never heard of his son before. No offense, but at the time, Junior Golf was not popular or even all that newsworthy, so to hear the name Tiger Woods meant absolutely nothing to us.

As we all walked toward our carts, Earl commented, "He's good, isn't he. My son is the best there is. He's young now, but just wait until he's older. Some day he will take the world by storm. After all, I am creating a champion." I just smiled at Earl as I thought to myself, oh, sure, and that is really going to happen! Besides, to us he was just another kid golfer.

Tiger continued to play a good game of golf. He finished the hole with a bogie, which Earl stated was usually not normal for him. Then on the fourth hole, Tiger's tee shot landed on a slope, deep in the thick line of trees to the right of the fairway about one hundred and sixty yards to the green.

You could tell Tiger was not happy. In fact, I watched as Earl quietly talked with him before Tiger stepped out of the golf cart. Both Earl and Tiger carefully studied Tiger's very limited options, and the way they were discussing the lie, I just assumed they had no clue as to how he was going to get out of those trees as he did not have a perfectly clear shot to the green. To me, a lay-up in the fairway was probably his only recourse.

Tiger walked back to the cart, grabbed his five wood, walked up to the ball and whacked it as hard as he could. I just stood there in amazement as his ball dodged the trunks and branches of at least seven trees, narrowly missing the final two. After clearing all of the obstacles, Tiger's ball gracefully rolled up to about twenty yards short of the green.

How in the hell did he do that? First of all, he's only ten years old. Secondly, Tiger's shot looked to be humanly impossible. Of course, Ken, Rick and I all applauded his effort and yelled out, "great shot, Tiger." This was when Tiger turned around and calmly stated, "I know."

There is no way anyone could be so calm after a shot like that. To be honest, I think Tiger was in total shock that his ball hadn't nailed any of those trees and that it ended up landing so close to the green. Earl, of course, just sat in the cart with a proud, yet smug look on his face. He looked over at us and said, "Yep, that's my boy! He's phenomenal, isn't he?"

And how did the kid continue to play?

The first drive Tiger started out with and the one I thought was simply a lucky shot, turned out to be repeated on almost every hole. And even though Tiger had a great shot on the fourth hole, we did notice there were moments throughout the round when Tiger seemed to become extremely frustrated, and at times, even angry with himself.

On the par four, twelfth hole, Tiger over swung his drive, and once again push faded the ball well into the right rough. He immediately slammed the head of his driver into the ground and stormed off the tee box toward the cart. He then jammed his club into his bag, after which he threw himself into the cart, angrily crossing his arms as he began to pout. When Tiger mishit his shot, Earl scolded him by saying, "What were you thinking? You can't afford to miss shots like that." This comment probably did not help Tiger's mood and this made me wonder if Tiger was mad at himself or was he mad at his father's comment.

Then I heard Earl tell Tiger, "I understand you are upset, but you have to remember that you need to focus on where you want the ball to go. Getting angry is good, but you have to make the anger productive."

My husband and I just looked at each other, saying, "Whoa, what in the hell just happened?" Tiger's shot was not bad enough to warrant such anger, especially from someone his age. As we got back into our cart, we talked about the fact that we had previously seen some evidence of a temper on a couple of holes, but we never expected to see a demonstration of such bad behavior like Tiger had just portrayed. I had no idea what prompted Tiger's outburst and was a little surprised to see that Earl was actually condoning his son's behavior.

Apparently by the time Tiger reached his errant shot, he had shaken off whatever had been bothering him. Then Tiger grabbed a club from his bag, performed his normal set up and hammered the ball toward the green, landing about thirty-five yards short. Tiger proceeded to hit a great wedge shot and still made par on the hole. However, throughout the entire round it seemed like Tiger was never completely satisfied with whatever shot he made. For some reason, Tiger acted as though he should be perfect in his every stroke and that he was incapable of making any mistakes.

Earl's many remarks toward his son seemed to be demanding and full of expectations, such as when Tiger hit what seemed to be a good shot, Earl would tell Tiger that he could have done better. The tone of Earl's voice seemed just a little too firm. Also, throughout the round, Earl was constant with "you need to focus more", "you have to think the shot through," and "you didn't hit that shot perfect." It just seemed like a lot of directives for a young person to absorb while trying to concentrate on his own game.

Although Tiger's round seemed to be full of tantrums, his game still ended up being almost flawless, shooting a smooth seventy-nine. This was not good enough to beat Earl or Ken, but Rick and I sulked, knowing that we had just been brutally crushed by a ten year old kid. And, of course, Tiger made sure to make us aware of that fact, too. With his anger seemingly gone, apparently left back on the course, Tiger just laughed and giggled while rubbing in the fact that he had outscored us. Tiger thought it was so funny and got the biggest kick out of his teasing.

This had been an interesting round of golf. Not only did we make it through playing with a young kid, but we actually ended up enjoying ourselves and having fun.

After the eighteenth hole, we dropped our clubs off and we all headed to the clubhouse in order to allow some of us less perfect golfers to soothe our wounded egos with a couple of drinks, which I definitely could use after the way I had played.

As soon as we went into the clubhouse, Tiger immediately asked his dad if he could go outside and play while we all talked, but Earl insisted on him joining us. Tiger resisted by saying, "But I don't want to."

Earl promptly responded to Tiger, "I don't care because you know we have to discuss your game and where you made errors and where you could have done better."

Tiger whined, "Do I have to?"

Earl's voice got a little firmer, but still fatherly, when he said, "You know this is something we have to do if you want to be the best someday."

"But, Dad, I played really good today. Besides, you told me I'm already the best." Tiger interjected.

"No buts, just sit," Earl ordered. "Besides, you did not play all that good today and we will go over all of it in just a few minutes."

"Oh, all right", Tiger said in a sullen voice as he hung his head and shuffled his feet, sliding into the chair next to his father.

While sitting at the table with Earl and Tiger, we would soon find out this was the time and place where Earl regularly held court and it would be here when we would get our first glimpse into the relationship between this father and son. This was also the first real opportunity we had all day to truly get to know Earl and Tiger.

Earl came across as friendly and was very talkative, yet Tiger appeared to be fairly quiet. Of course, I just assumed this was because he really did not want to be there. Personally, it appeared to me that Tiger was extremely bored, but was pretending to be the dutiful son, yet still wanting to go out and play.

It was like, all of a sudden the laughing and child-like part of Tiger disappeared and a more obedient and mechanical person emerged. It was as though someone had turned the switch on, causing Tiger to seem more focused and involved in what his father was saying.

I had not yet decided if Tiger was just shy or if he was still upset with his dad for not letting him go outside and play. We would later find out that this reclusive behavior was quite normal for this young boy as it was part of his routine where he ended each round by silently mulling over his entire game, including each and every stroke he had taken.

Earl started off by reviewing Tiger's game with him, which seemed more important to Earl than how Tiger had actually scored. Earl wanted Tiger to be able to not only remember his shots, but to be able to explain the reasons behind each and every one of them. In Earl's mind, the thought process was as important as the execution.

We listened intently as Earl spoke slowly and precisely to Tiger as he critiqued each and every shot. Tiger sat there totally mesmerized by Earl's every word, almost as though he was in a trance. Earl spoke in a very calm, monotone voice, causing me to wonder if he was doing this because we were there or was this, in fact, his normal manner.

Then we noticed how Earl's demeanor started to change as he continued to talk to his son. He was now criticizing Tiger's game in a more blunt and direct manner, only occasionally sharing encouraging words. Earl would ask Tiger why he chose certain clubs for various shots and what was his thought process before and during each shot. He then criticized Tiger for making wrong choices when picking his clubs and making so many mistakes in hitting his shots.

Then Earl asked Tiger if he was able to "see the line" while he was putting. Tiger responded by saying that he saw it only part of time as he was unable to grasp it on many of the greens. This was when Earl basically scolded Tiger by telling him he has to focus more. Earl repeated himself one more time, making sure that Tiger fully understood the importance of focusing.

Earl once again changed his tone and calmly told Tiger, "Clearing your mind and focusing on each and everything you do will make you better than everyone else. Remember, you have to push yourself to be the best and if you cannot be the best then there is no reason for you to continue playing golf." Tiger just hung his head as though he was embarrassed and ashamed of the way he had played. You could tell Earl was disappointed in his son and Tiger knew it.

I just sat there quietly watching the interaction between the two of them and it was quite obvious that Tiger was absorbing each and every word that was coming out of Earl's mouth, asking few questions until it was time for him to speak. I also remember thinking that it appeared Tiger had succumbed to his father's lecture instead of supporting his own decisions.

Personally, this seemed to be way too much criticism without enough praise to give to such a young child who had actually performed amazingly well.

After Earl finished his session of reviewing Tiger's round, I asked Tiger, "You seem to be very good at golf. How long have you been playing?"

Before Tiger could open his mouth to answer my question, Earl quickly chimed in and told us how Tiger took his first swing at eighteen months old. He explained to us how Tiger used to watch him practice while Tiger was still in his high chair. Earl told us that even though Tiger was so young, he still knew Tiger had a natural ability for the game. This was when he decided to get Tiger into golf and has been teaching him ever since.

Earl continued by bragging, "I'm grooming him to be a star. I mean with his talent and with enough pushing, I know I can get him to the top. After all, I'm creating a great golfer here. And since he is black, it won't be easy for him. It will be hard for him to be accepted and I don't want his color to hold him back. Besides, I know how that feels, but that's a story for another time."

Rick saw where this conversation was heading, so he quickly interjected with, "Tiger even appeared on the television show, "That's Incredible", when he was only three years old."

Earl demanded, "You must have seen Tiger on the show!" Again, Earl acted a little miffed that we still did not know who his son was or what he had accomplished in golf.

I responded, "No, sorry, we never saw him." I turned back to Tiger and asked, "Did you have fun on the show and being on television?"

After mulling it over for a moment, Tiger answered, "I don't remember being on TV because I was too little. My dad put me on the show to let everybody see how good I was."

This was when Earl reminded Tiger that he was also on the Mike Douglas Show and hit the ball around the putting green with Bob Hope. Tiger looked at his father with a confused look on his face, "Pop, I told you before that I don't remember who that man was."

This was when Earl started bragging about Tiger's early accomplishments in golf and some of the tournaments he had won. He proudly stated how Tiger had already won two Junior World Championships and would be playing in his third in a few months. Earl continued to tell us that Tiger is so good he doesn't even play in his own age bracket in Junior Golf.

After learning that Earl and other various swing coaches had been teaching Tiger to play golf for several years, I asked Tiger, "How did you get to be such a good golfer?"

Tiger shrugged his shoulders and responded, "I don't know. I just see what I want my ball to do and then I just hit the ball and it's supposed to go where I want it to."

Earl once again interrupted his son by saying, "Tiger has this natural ability to see the shot he wants to make and then he's able to make his body do it. There is very little mechanics to his natural swing. Unfortunately, Tiger has not trained his body to always perform the way I feel he should, so there will be times when he gets frustrated when he is unable to execute his shots correctly. But he is learning and with enough coaching, some day Tiger will be an amazing golfer. Actually, he is already an amazing golfer, but some day, with enough pushing, he will be the best golfer ever."

I was surprised to hear Earl's next statement when he added, "It will take some pushing to get my son there and to keep him interested in the game, but I know I just have to do it. Besides, some day when Tiger is rich, he can pay me back for all the hard work I put in to get him there."

After hearing Earl's comments, I thought to myself, yes, the kid is good, but how can anyone think that a ten year old kid will grow up to beat the likes of Nicklaus and Palmer. I understood how proud Earl was of his son, but the best golfer ever? This was a little hard to believe especially since Tiger was so young and so inexperienced.

Who knew that someday I would be so wrong!

I decided to ask Earl why Tiger got so mad whenever he was a little off line on any of his shots or when he didn't hit the ball where he wanted. Earl eagerly explained, "I have always tried to teach Tiger that he needs to be perfect in order to get better in golf. I truly believe that his anger makes him try harder and I know it will help him become a stronger and more focused golfer as he grows into the sport."

I then commented, "But it seems Tiger is too young to have such a nasty little temper."

Earl shot back, "It's something he will eventually grow out of, but in the interim, it will help him to be a better person as well as a stronger golfer."

After listening to the various comments Earl was making, I was somewhat surprised that a father would allow, and especially encourage, his young son to show so much anger, thinking that a child would actually benefit from the results of that anger. Besides, how does someone "grow out" of being so angry all the time especially if it was instilled in them so early in life?

But, of course, I just met Earl and Tiger, so who am I to judge his parenting and coaching skills.

For some reason, Earl then wanted to critique my game. This was when I looked over at Tiger and watched as he rolled his eyes, almost like saying, "why bother." I could also tell that Tiger had now reached the point of total boredom and wanted to leave. He put both elbows on the table and braced his head with his hands as he let out a huge sigh, trying to stress his desire to leave to his father.

Ignoring his son's antics, Earl continued to evaluate my game.

Once he was finished with his assessment, Earl offered to give me private golf lessons. He told me if I was really serious about getting better at golf, I would definitely benefit from his teachings if I was willing to work with him a couple times a week. Earl also explained how he does not teach anyone else other than Tiger, but for some reason he felt compelled to help me improve my game.

This was when Tiger interrupted, "But Dad, I thought I was the only one you give lessons to. Are you going to give lessons to her instead of me?"

Earl looked over at Tiger and very calmly explained, "No, Tiger. I would simply give her lessons after you and I are finished with your session. You know how important our time together is to us."

I immediately jumped in, "Thank you so much for the offer, but I don't want to inconvenience you and Tiger. Besides, I have a ten year old daughter and I need to be there for her after school."

It was then when Earl reassured me that giving me lessons would not be an imposition as he would already be at the golf course working with Tiger after school. Earl then suggested I bring my daughter to the course and she and Tiger can spend time together while we work my golf game.

This was when Tiger's little ears perked up and a big smile emerged. All of a sudden it seemed as though Tiger was actually excited about his Dad giving someone else lessons when he quickly chimed in, "That would be cool. She and I could play."

After some encouragement from Earl, and even a little bit from Tiger, I finally decided to take a chance and accept his offer to give me golf lessons.

On the drive home from the golf course, my husband and I found ourselves discussing Earl and Tiger as we attempted to understand some of the events that took place during and after our round of golf. I guess I was just so surprised to see such a wicked temper come from such a young child. It was sad to see Tiger filled with so much frustration and anger and I was curious as to why. I thought it might be possible that Earl was putting too much pressure on his young son and Tiger's anger was the result of his reacting to those pressures. I also thought Earl's comments to his son, both on and off the course, were just a little too harsh for a young kid who was trying to get better at a sport. It was as though Earl was going to push his son to be great whether Tiger wanted it or not.

I was also surprised how Earl actually believed that Tiger's tantrums were justifiable and he was defending his son's negative actions, thinking Tiger would become a better person because of those actions. In regard to our conversations with Tiger, it almost seemed as though Earl was controlling Tiger, especially when he kept jumping in and would not let his son talk or answer anything on his own.

It appeared that much of the "fun" and "just being a kid" in Tiger was not always allowed. He seemed to be a good kid, and very smart, but in just the short time we were with Earl and Tiger, I wondered what kind of a person Tiger would grow up to be, especially being taught some of the lessons Earl was promoting in his son and stifling his youth and his fun at the same time.

I guess only time will tell.

2
PRACTICE, PRACTICE, PRACTICE

EARL AND I WERE meeting in the afternoon twice a week at the Navy Golf Course for my golf lessons. In the beginning, I found taking lessons from Earl to be extremely intimidating, especially since his ten year old son, Tiger, was an incredible golfer and far better than I was, or rather, far better than I could ever be. I mean, we wouldn't even be in the same universe if we compared our golfing abilities.

When it came to Tiger's lessons, the training was very intense and regimented, but there were occasions when Earl and Tiger made it a point to have some fun, keeping a small portion of their time together somewhat light and void of all the strict demands. The time Earl spent with his son was not only centered on his golf as it was also about the bond they had formed and the special connection that existed between the two of them. This father and son would spend their many countless hours together, not only to work on Tiger's golf training, but they were also able to expand that time to share their thoughts, feelings and the whatever's. These were some of the many incredibly wonderful moments that existed between father and son; moments that were valued as they focused on the many lessons of life.

Each time after I arrived at the course for my lessons, I would stand nearby and watch as Earl would finish up his practice session with Tiger. Many times, I would arrive early simply to watch the father and son duo go through their many and precisely orchestrated practice routines and I found it captivating every time Tiger exhibited such tremendous skill and natural ability in each and every stroke. I found I was learning so much about the game of golf simply by just listening to the conversations, questions and critiques that occurred between Earl and Tiger.

Tiger's golf swing was so smooth and so effortless and I was always amazed at how this young person could be so perfect. This was Tiger's time, and it was through these lessons he would dream about his goals and his career in golf. It would be the results of these lessons that would someday make Tiger a truly great golfer. I just knew that the hard work and constant dedication he was putting forth would hopefully one day lead him to an unimaginable future.

After all, Tiger was working hard to become the best. But it was Earl who was pushing his son to be the absolute best.

I continued to be amazed at the progression of talent Tiger repeatedly and effortlessly demonstrated whether it was seeing him shoot his first scratch game or watching as he continuously hit seemingly impossible shots unknown to most humans. I remember always thinking that kids aren't supposed to be like this, to have such ability and talent. But Tiger was just that kid. Simply speaking, no adult was safe around Tiger as he would single handedly destroy any confidence one might have in their own game of golf.

As Tiger's coach and instructor, Earl was always relentless. He had created a well-organized training format for Tiger, complete with drills, repetition, concentration and hours of dedication and hard work. One of the many precision drills Earl would have Tiger practice was sticking two tees into the ground, no wider than the head of Tiger's driver. Tiger would address the tees, ready his stance and then he would proceed in taking numerous swings, never once touching either tee. To me, and to most golfers, this would be an impossible task, but Tiger did it with such consistent ease and perfection that he made it look extremely easy.

I remember the time when Earl had me attempt the same drill, but after taking one of the tees out with my every swing, Earl immediately removed that drill from my lessons.

There was this one time when Tiger was so frustrated with my inability to master the technique that he stepped up to the tee to demonstrate how simple it actually was. After several perfect swings between the tees, Tiger turned around, and in his normal, but cute and cocky tone, snipped at me, "I don't know why you're having trouble with this. See how easy it is? If I can do it, so can you."

Yeah, right, only in my dreams. I was never blessed with the same natural ability and perfect swing as Tiger.

When it came to his putting, people often wondered what made Tiger so good and why it seemed so natural for him. One reason was Tiger literally spent many endless hours perfecting his putting stroke, as he felt putting, along with his short game, was the most important part of his game. Over the years during his practice sessions, Earl would pick out several spots on the green from various distances. From each location, Tiger would have to make ten to twenty consecutive putts before moving to the next distance. During this drill, if Tiger missed just once, he had to start all over again with ball number one at that distance.

However, when Tiger was unable to use an outside green for his regular practice, he would often practice at home and use the leg of the coffee table as his target and the same ball repetition. Even after Tiger turned pro, he would use this same routine in his hotel room between rounds at a tournament.

These were only a few of the many drills that Earl gave Tiger and after watching him, it showed me why Tiger was already such a good golfer at his young age. Of course, the natural ability he possessed didn't hurt either.

My own lessons from Earl were not simply going to the driving range and just hitting balls. It turned out to be real work and almost like having a drill sergeant teach you how to play golf. After all, Earl was a former Lieutenant Colonel and a Green Beret, and I think it was his strict military background and training that caused him to be so forceful and disciplined in all of his drills and instruction. This applied not only to Tiger, but also with me. The regimentation just came naturally for Earl and he demonstrated that trait often.

And if I thought he was tough on me, I can only imagine how Tiger felt. I remember so many times when I would see Earl's demanding firmness with Tiger. Earl had this unyielding need and obsession to make sure Tiger was beyond perfect and it showed most of the time in Earl's coaching.

There were several times during my lessons when Tiger would stand nearby and watch as Earl put me through some of the same regimented drills that he went through himself, albeit, my were not as intense has his own. Having Tiger observe my progress was quite interesting at times.

Although Tiger was young, there were some occasions when he would see a glitch in my swing that Earl had not noticed. This is when Tiger would immediately chime in and give his critique on how to change it. He would notice that I was not taking the club back correctly or that my hands were not facing the target on my follow through.

It was such a strange feeling to have a little kid tell you what you were doing wrong and then actually give accurate advice on how to correct that part of your swing. To further batter my already injured ego, sometimes Tiger would teasingly cough or drop something in the middle of my swing, feeling that since his dad did the same thing to him in order to help him focus, it was only fair he did it to me.

Gee, thanks, Tiger!

Each time Tiger would give his input or play one of his tricks on me, I would turn to Earl and we would just smile at each other approvingly as we enjoyed allowing Tiger to share his opinions and advice with us.

When I first started taking my lessons from Earl, Tiger was only ten years old, and yet he had the confidence to tell his dad how to teach someone else to play golf. Tiger's input into my lessons and my golf game continued over the next couple of years, and each time Earl and I would get the biggest kick out of Tiger's unsolicited help. And because of the way Tiger acted, I wondered if he was simply a grown-up disguised in a kid's body as he was so knowledgeable and so astute, and way beyond his years.

Simply put, Tiger was such a "joy" to be around, and I don't always mean that in the most complimentary way.

As my lessons continued, Earl would have me work on my chip shots around the greens. Earl was relentless when it came to perfection as he taught me to chip with almost every club in my bag.

But it was young Tiger who once again inserted himself and explained, "Your short game is the most important part of golf and it can make or break your score." Earl would later tell me that I should listen to Tiger as he definitely knows what he is talking about. My response was, "But Earl, he's only a kid!"

I remember the time when Tiger asked me if I wanted to have a putting contest with him. Noticing the impish and calculating gleam in his eyes immediately led me to believe that Tiger was most definitely up to something and I decided I wanted no part of it. Also knowing the way Tiger putted, I was smart enough to figure out that I would certainly come out on the losing end. I politely made an excuse and passed on his offer. Hey, I'm no fool. And besides, my ego just could not handle another beating from this kid.

Eventually, Earl had me move on to the dreaded sand traps. I hated it when Earl would tell me, "Do it like Tiger. Just hit the ball out of the bunkers with total ease and grace."

Trust me when I say that it took me a long time before the ease and grace part of it ever happened and it was never, ever like Tiger.

But it was when I watched Tiger take his practice shots out of the traps that I would just stand there feeling totally deflated. I remember thinking, why can't I do it that way? Each time Tiger would position himself in the sand while perfecting his stance, and with each effortless swing, he would gently and precisely place the ball on the green. He would do this over and over and over, seldom ever missing his target area. To watch Tiger's continuous perfection became rather monotonous.

I noticed that over time Tiger's lessons became more intense and serious with less fun shared between father and son. Tiger may have been taking private lessons from a professional golf instructor, but Earl was still providing Tiger with his own personal instructions. Earl would never relinquish his hold on Tiger as he felt it was necessary that he always remain an integral part of Tiger's learning process. Of course, Earl always believed that he could teach Tiger better than anyone else. After all, in Earl's mind, look what he had already done for Tiger. Over the years, it was Earl who took all of the credit for training and coaching Tiger, but much of the credit should go to the professional golf instructors who spent so much time with him.

There were so many times when I saw the playful and fun side of Tiger. His teasing and laughter. But over time, the jovial part of Tiger slowly diminished. Young Tiger was now turning into a mechanical and stoic figure, someone who had become overly focused on his long term goals. Everything in Tiger's life was now about golf and about being perfect and being the best. It was Earl who was now making sure Tiger was getting down to even more serious business when it came to his growth in golf. Earl had begun the process of pushing Tiger even harder in order to ensure that Tiger would be able to win every tournament he played in.

Sadly, the fun was now gone, as was the child and his needs.

3
TOO YOUNG TO BE PERFECT

EARL WOULD INVITE ME and my husband to play golf with him and Tiger at Navy Course several times over the next few years and we reciprocated by inviting them to play with us at Los Serranos Golf Club in Chino, California. This would be the course that Tiger would eventually play in his attempt to qualify for the PGA Tour's Los Angeles Open at Riviera as a young teenager. During these outings, I had the opportunity to watch Tiger's game improve over the years, but unfortunately, I was also able to see his temper and attitude progressively change, and not always for the better. Throughout each round, Tiger would show signs of a temper, but it appeared to be more like frustration and maybe even embarrassment from playing with adults. I also wondered if Tiger was starting to feel the pressure of trying to be perfect.

Tiger would get so upset if his drive was five yards left or right of where he was aiming, meaning if his golf shots were not absolutely perfect and did not completely meet his own personal standards and expectations, he would become angry with himself and with his game. Tiger would get so aggravated because he knew what he wanted his shot to do, but he was not always successful with the result. In Tiger's mind he could envision the shot, but at times he was unable to make his body do what he expected it do.

Over the years, we would watch as Tiger would slam his club on the ground, stomp his feet, yell at himself and even become quiet by sulking. Sometimes Tiger would get so upset that he would just quit playing and walk off the course.

In many cases, Tiger's anger ended up affecting his ability to play. However, a time finally came when Tiger was able to control his game and mental ability enough where his play level was not always affected by his outbursts and anger. As he grew and developed mentally, he was able to focus in a way that helped him to control his mindset. Unfortunately, this did not stop his outbursts of anger on the course.

In the early years, I had thought Tiger was just too young to have developed such a bad temper and an overly arrogant attitude, but I also felt that because Earl was teaching Tiger he could be, and should be, perfect, Tiger had come to believe that anything less was unacceptable. Earl was also creating an environment for Tiger where he was never allowed to fail and it was all about being the absolute best.

So now, not only did Tiger display bouts of anger, but he was combining this with his ever growing arrogance and feeling of superiority.

Over time, I realized it was Earl who was teaching Tiger to act superior and demonstrate these arrogant traits. Earl also made it a point to reassure Tiger that he would someday benefit from his actions. In fact, I was surprised to learn that, as a father, Earl was actually creating and endorsing Tiger's attitude and bad behavior, feeling his son was rightfully entitled to all of these actions, simply because of his superior talent in golf. Unfortunately, Earl believed that because his son was so very special, Tiger was allowed to feel superior to everyone else.

I found that it was always so awe-inspiring to see Tiger play such amazing golf at his age and to be able to witness the dramatic improvements that developed within him and in his game over the years. However, I do remember this one particular day when we played a round of golf with Earl and Tiger at the Navy Course.

Everyone was playing pretty well and then Tiger had a bad hole. When Tiger was in the fairway to take his second shot, he topped his three wood and the ball moved forward about sixty yards landing in the fairway bunker. You could tell that Tiger was fuming when he just dropped his club to the ground, stomped his foot and yelled. From the way Tiger acted, you knew he wasn't sure what he had done wrong and for Tiger, that's not good because then he can't fix it.

Earl had to calm Tiger down by explaining what caused his missed hit. Tiger slammed his club into his bag and then threw himself into the golf cart and began to pout. I'm sorry to say that

Tiger's unpleasant behavior was something I had witnessed quite often throughout the years.

Tiger was able to hit his next shot out of the sand trap and made a bogey on the hole, but he ended up quitting the round after only eight holes. Earl told me Tiger quit because he was upset with our play level and because he thought we were playing below his standards. Of course, Earl was once again making excuses for Tiger, basically trying to cover up for Tiger's poor play and bad attitude by using our play level as an excuse.

I just looked at Earl and said, "Seriously? We have played with you two for quite some time now and you want me to believe that statement? Tiger is just a little too young to have such high standards, don't you think? Besides, since when does a twelve year old child feel he has the right to judge my game or anyone else's for that matter? And then he uses our playing as an excuse to quit!"

This was when Earl finally chose to be truthful and explained to me that Tiger actually quit because he thought he was not playing up to his own standards and true ability. I knew that Tiger could be hard on himself during a round of golf, but today just seemed a little over the top, even for Tiger. The tantrums I was used to seeing, but now using others to justify your poor play? That is going a little too far in my opinion.

At this point, I suggested to Earl that Tiger needs to be made aware that not everyone can play golf like he does and as he grows he will need to be more considerate to that fact and not act so superior to others, no matter how they play. While I understand that competing in a tournament is a completely different story altogether, when playing with others just for fun, he needs to reevaluate his attitude and standards.

Earl once again made another excuse for Tiger, justifying his son's rude and arrogant actions. Earl tried to explain how Tiger is so competitive that it is extremely difficult for him to play with people who do not create a challenge for him. To me, this was just another lame excuse on Earl's part. However, making excuses for Tiger was just something Earl did on a regular basis. It was almost as though Earl made it convenient for Tiger to act any way he wanted, whether it was good or bad.

Not long after we had this conversation, Earl mentioned to me that he did in fact have a discussion with Tiger. He explained how he was trying to teach him that quitting in the middle of a round should never be an option, no matter the circumstances. While I believed that Earl may have had a conversation with Tiger about quitting, I don't think Earl ever talked to Tiger about his attitude, because, in reality, Earl was doing what he thought he had to do in order to train Tiger to be a champion.

Earl honestly believed that Tiger's superior attitude and over the top arrogance was necessary in order for him to believe in himself one hundred percent of the time that he could one day be the best. I could understand Earl's theory, but I was just afraid that what Earl was actually teaching Tiger may come back to bite him in the butt some day. I found it difficult to believe that in order to be a champion, Tiger needed to have such an over the top attitude and nasty disposition.

Besides, what did Earl know about training someone to be a champion in golf? Earl was only a recreational golfer himself and was definitely not a professional golf instructor. He had only been playing golf for two years when Tiger was born. The only thing Earl truly knew was being in the military, and to me, it looked like Earl was using his military experience to train Tiger in golf.

Okay, I guess that sort of makes sense! Golf. Military. Nope, I can't see any similarities there.

Each time we played with Tiger, I noticed there was a definite growing consistency in his golf game, but there was also a varied inconsistency in his temperament. Many times, I thought Tiger was simply reacting from being pushed too hard by his father. But then there were times when I wondered if Earl got so wrapped up in training Tiger to be perfect and to be the best that he forgot that Tiger was just a child, especially since his training was like a mini boot camp. The strict disciplined regimentation that Earl was dispensing to Tiger was in addition to his school, homework, professional lessons and tournaments, so it seems that it would be normal that a child felt the need to resist, resulting in his acting out. Tiger was just a kid, not a robot.

I remember when I would bring my daughter, Michelle, to my golf lessons, and after Tiger was done with his session, the two of them would go off hand in hand to play. Each time we would arrive, Tiger would look over and see Michelle standing nearby. This was when Tiger would get distracted and tell his dad he wanted to quit his lessons right then and there so he could go play.

Earl would not hear of it. Earl sternly insisted that Tiger needed to finish what they had started and only then could he go play with Michelle. Every time, Tiger would moan and groan because he wanted to quit and his concentration and desire to practice became almost nonexistent. This showed me that playing and having fun took precedence over working on his golf game.

I learned a lot about Tiger from Michelle. They would play together and, of course, talk a lot, the way most children do. Then on the way home from my lessons or at some later time, she would tell me all about her conversations with Tiger and everything they talked about. She was still young, too, so she was at that age where she would share everything with me.

Of course, in a couple more years that would change and I wouldn't be able to get a word out of her. You know, the dreaded teenage years.

I remember one particular conversation. Michelle blurted out, "Mom, did you know Tiger gets mad at his dad?"

Curious about what this was about, I asked, "No, I didn't. Why is that?"

"Because he never lets Tiger play with any of his friends. And Tiger also told me that he can't bring his friends with him when he plays golf. He said his dad is really bossy."

I immediately responded, "That's not a very nice thing to say. Are you sure Tiger really said that?"

"Oh, yes, and that's not all. Tiger also told me that his dad makes him do golf things all the time even when he doesn't want to do them. That's when his dad gets mad at him because Tiger wants to do something else."

Hoping the answer would be no, I carefully asked, "Does Tiger's dad yell at him?"

"Nah, he just makes Tiger do it and tells him he knows what is best for him. His dad is always telling him that."

"Does Tiger ever tell his dad he doesn't want to do some of those things?"

"Yeah, but Tiger said his dad never listens to him. Tiger wants to do other things, but his dad keeps making him do those golf things. Even in the garage, he has to always practice."

I responded with, "I know Tiger practices a lot because he wants to be a professional golfer when he grows up. He needs to practice a lot so he can get better. I thought he really loved to practice all the time?"

"That's what Tiger told me, too. His dad said he has to be the best and he has to be better than everyone else. Practicing and playing golf is all he ever does and he doesn't want to do it all the time. But Mom, he's my age and you don't make me do things like that. How come?"

"Do you want me to?"

"Oh, no, please Mom, don't be like Tiger's dad!"

Out of the mouth of babes. That was from a young eleven year old girl who appeared to be somewhat perceptive as to the grueling work Tiger was being put though. She had always been allowed to be just a kid but, sadly, Tiger wasn't.

I was aware of how obsessed Earl was about Tiger's golf and I knew he was pushing Tiger, but it was a shame how he would not listen to how his own son felt. I knew that Earl and Tiger were extremely close and talked all the time. Earl always made sure that Tiger could talk to him about anything, especially during their "special" father and son talks. But I also knew how determined Earl was to make sure his son was the best golfer and Earl was going to do anything it took to make that happen. It was also obvious that Tiger needed the interaction with kids his own age outside of his golfing program and school. It was almost like Earl wanted Tiger all to himself.

Earl and I had discussed this topic numerous times and each time Earl would deny that he pushed Tiger into doing something he didn't want to do. But I saw firsthand how Earl coached Tiger and the manner in which he talked to him. Earl's coaching was strong and sometimes relentless. But their conversations varied as there were many times when Earl's tone would be caring and encouraging but then there were many times when Earl's tone was firm and quite demanding. It was almost like a sales pitch where Earl was trying to convince Tiger that he knew what was best for him.

Most people have been led to believe that it was Tiger who has always expected perfection from himself. But in reality, it was Earl who made the demands and continuously drilled into Tiger's head that he had to be perfect in every aspect of his golf game or else he would fail and face unacceptance. Earl expected perfection from his son, and would settle for no less. Personally, I always felt Tiger's desperate need for perfection would someday affect him in his golf and in his personal life. Nobody is perfect and Earl should have made Tiger realize that he could still be successful without always expecting to achieve the impossible.

Not only was Tiger continually putting excessive pressure on himself, but both of his parents were also contributing additional and unwarranted pressures by always pushing him to practice more in order to be perfect and telling him he would always have to be perfect in order to excel and to be accepted. They wanted their son to someday be a big star. Frankly, I believed what they were teaching Tiger was quite a lot for a young person to deal with at such an early age and to have to grow up believing, thus always expecting total perfection from one's self throughout life and yet never being allowed to have any middle ground.

Additionally, over the years, both of his parents did their best to convince Tiger that he was better than everyone else, not only in golf, but also as a person, resulting in his superior, "and better than you" attitude. When you think about it, Tiger had, and still has, such an over the top superiority complex and his drive for perfection has caused him to continuously display moments of being dissatisfied with himself.

The drive for perfection that both Earl and Tida had instilled in Tiger and the arrogantly superior attitude that they promoted in their son would, Earl believed, give Tiger the necessary edge to become a champion. In order to make Tiger be great, Earl knew, especially from his military tactics, that he would have to mentally prepare Tiger and this was part of the training.

Earl also knew that he needed to have control over Tiger and to accomplish this, he had to create trust and dependency from Tiger. This was when I noticed how Earl's methods had evolved, but Tiger's own evolution was being stunted by his father's increased control. Earl had already established his influence on Tiger with his fatherly advice and militaristic training, so as Tiger grew, Earl realized that he needed a new game plan in order to maintain control of his son.

4
PUSHED TO BE THE BEST

EARL ALWAYS KNEW TIGER would be great at golf, but for Earl to see his own son continually excel during each and every round, made him truly ponder what his son's future could be and how much Tiger could actually achieve in the world of golf. Earl never questioned Tiger's ability to go far. He just questioned how far.

There was this one time I will always distinctly remember when Tiger, Earl, Ken and I were all playing a round of golf at Los Serranos Golf Club in Southern California. This particular day just happened to be an extremely cold morning in December with the temperature reaching an abnormally low twenty-three degrees, and we were scheduled to be one of the first groups to tee off. All of us were so bundled up with multiple layers of clothing and jackets that we questioned how we were going to move, much less hit the ball. There was so much frost on the ground that after every hole we had to scrape off the thick ice that had collected in the spikes on our golf shoes; otherwise we would end up slipping and falling as we walked on the cart paths.

Being a kid, Tiger decided to take advantage of the ice and "skate" on some of the cart paths. I remember he was having so much fun slipping and sliding as Earl repeatedly told him to stop for fear of his falling. Tiger would just object, "Oh, Pop, I'm just having some fun." Then he would run and slide down the cart path again and say, "See, I'm not going to fall."

Just then, and to everyone's surprise, Tiger's feet came out from underneath him, immediately landing him directly on his rear end. Tiger's expression was completely priceless as he showed a look of total shock and embarrassment. I don't know what hurt more, his pride or his bottom side. Looking down at Tiger, we all wanted to laugh because it really was funny, but the adult in all of us made our concern for Tiger's well-being our main priority. Tiger was starting to cry, but his father's firm words kept the tears from coming. And of course, Earl gave Tiger a lengthy lecture on being more careful.

Showing little sympathy, Earl immediately scolded Tiger with, "You have to be more careful, Tiger. What if you broke your arm or your wrist? Do you know how long you would be laid up and wouldn't be able to play golf? Months, that's how long. You know better than to be so careless. I never want to see you do something like that ever again, understood?"

After Earl's comments, Tiger wasn't able to hold back the tears. Quickly, he wiped them away, trying to prevent anyone seeing him cry. You could tell he was embarrassed because he had been scolded by his father in front of others. We all really felt sorry for Tiger because he was just a little kid. And then hearing what Earl told him, I couldn't quite decide if Earl was worried about his son or was he more concerned that Tiger might permanently injure himself and prevent him from having a career in golf.

As we continued with our round, our hands and feet were so cold that we found it difficult to hold on to our clubs, which was also preventing us from taking a proper swing. It appeared that Tiger struggled more than anyone else. He just wasn't used to it being that cold, especially since he seldom ever played golf that early in the morning. Throughout the morning, we all did our best to make it through the entire eighteen holes. By the time we had finished, it was still cold outside, but at least it had warmed up into the mid-forties.

After the round, and to get out of the cold, we all hurried into the warmth of the clubhouse where we adults immediately sought warmth through some hot and "spirited" drinks and Tiger warmed up with several cups of hot chocolate. Tiger was so cold that his teeth continued to chatter for what seemed like an eternity. The entire time we were in the clubhouse, he had both hands clasped tightly around the mug of hot chocolate and just sat there shivering as he tried to get warm. I swear his eyes were frozen wide open because it seemed like it was forever before I actually saw him blink. He just stared straight ahead with this strange blank look in his eyes. Eventually, though, he did begin to thaw out and he was able to function much better, thanks to the hot chocolate and the heat from the nearby fireplace.

Since it had become a traditional routine for all of us, we once again quietly listened as Earl held court and critiqued Tiger's round.

After Tiger warmed up and was finally able to talk without his teeth chattering, I remember him asking his dad, "How can any golfer ever play his best in this type of weather?" explaining how cold he was while he played his round. Tiger told us that his hands and feet were freezing and were almost completely numb to the point of hurting. Tiger was extremely frustrated because he had never been exposed to this type of weather before.

Earl responded with, "That's what makes the game fair. No one can ever play his best in this or any other bad weather, but you have to learn to be able to play better than anyone else, no matter what the weather conditions are." Earl continued to console his young son by saying, "No one can play his best in inclement weather, but whoever can handle the conditions the best, wins."

Years later, Earl told me about the time when Tiger was at Stanford, and was at the driving range hitting golf balls in the cold, pouring rain. When Earl asked him why in the hell he was practicing in such miserable weather, Tiger simply replied that he remembered the story from years earlier when Earl had told him about winning in bad weather and that if he wants to win, he has to be the best in any kind of weather. So, Tiger further explained to his father that the only way he can be the best is to practice in all the various weather conditions, and that day just happened to be the pouring rain.

Earl got the biggest kick out of his son and the fact that Tiger thought about that particular story so many years later. Earl told me, "I guess my kid does listen to me after all. I really didn't think he ever listened to a word I ever said!" Personally, I believe Tiger remembers every single word that Earl has ever spoken. But of course, Tiger listened to his father because sometimes when Earl talked, he had this mesmerizing tone to his voice that was so convincing, no matter what subject he was talking about. It always seemed like he was preaching, and you were unable to resist what he was saying.

By the time Tiger was eleven years old, he had become an incredible golfer, playing in many junior golf tournaments and beating most adults. He excelled significantly in his abilities and his focus and his talent was undeniable. But for years, Tiger was still unable to beat his father, who was a proficient golfer in his own right with a solid two handicap. Earl always knew that because Tiger was becoming a very skilled golfer and possessed tremendous talent, the day would eventually come when he would match his father's play level, even possibly beating it. Well, that day came, but it was obvious that Earl wasn't as prepared as he thought he would be.

When Tiger was just one month shy of being twelve years old, he was playing with his dad at the Navy Golf course in Cypress, a course they had played regularly over the years. They had already completed the front nine and Earl was ahead of Tiger by one shot. However, part of the way through the back nine, Earl glanced down at the score card and after scanning each score, he noticed Tiger was ahead of him by one shot. He immediately thought, "When did this happen? How was it that I didn't even notice this?"

Earl loved his son and wanted him to win, but Earl's own ego got the best of him as he proceeded to do everything in his power to better his pace and try not to lose to his son. It wasn't long before Tiger also became aware of his score and realized that he was ahead of his father. This was when Tiger decided to alert Earl to that fact, thinking his dad hadn't yet noticed their scores.

Tiger started to tease Earl unmercifully, which of course, put even more pressure on Earl, who was now desperately trying to outscore his eleven year old son. By the end of the eighteenth hole, Earl finally gave in to the reality that he had just lost to Tiger for the first time in his entire life.

Earl was beyond proud of his son, but yet at the same time, he was royally pissed. Earl described it to me as being like a double edged sword. He so badly wanted Tiger to excel and to eventually play better than him and surpass him in his scoring, but when that day finally came, Earl admitted that he was simply not prepared, and in the end he could not believe he had just been beaten by an eleven year old kid. It didn't matter that it was his own kid, because as he saw it, he was still out played by a kid, and he was pissed at himself for letting it happen. Earl never beat Tiger again.

It wasn't very long after that victorious day of beating his father that Tiger became a scratch player at Industry Hills in Southern California. Shooting scratch golf was something Earl rarely accomplished, so it was an end to an era when the father was a better golfer than his son and could teach him new things. It was now time for the father to take note and learn from his son.

Winning was beyond important for Tiger. I had never seen anyone who had the same kind of drive and fortitude as Tiger. Whether or not it was instilled or was simply re-enforced by Earl, Tiger showed extreme dedication and laser focus toward only one eventual and attainable goal and that was to always win. To Tiger, a win was a win, period. In his mind, there was no second place for him. Simply put, he had to be the best and coming in second during any tournament play meant that he had failed.

In Tiger's mind, this would mean that he did not meet the goal that he had set for himself. Tiger is the type of person who just does not settle, as his main focus and objective is to beat anyone and everyone who crosses his path. When you think about it, in a way, Earl had most definitely taught him well.

Tiger believed the only way he could ever be the best was to be perfect in every aspect of his game. Through this belief came his mental toughness, his incredible concentration and his extremely strong inner drive. These attributes were necessary in order for Tiger to handle the many challenges that he would be faced with and, therefore, overcome the obstacles that life and golf would present.

If Tiger has a bad shot and he ends up behind a tree, this becomes the obstacle. From here he must face the challenge by focusing on making his next shot a viable one and not losing a stroke by being foolish. He must focus, and in his mind see the shot and the desired outcome. Then he has to execute the shot with total precision in order to attain complete success from his attempt. All of these actions are continuously demonstrated by Tiger throughout his game and it comes from years of hard work and his determination to continually excel in order to always be the best.

A perfect example of Tiger's determination and need to win occurred when he was about thirteen years old and was attempting to qualify for the Los Angeles Open at Rivera Country Club as an amateur. This would have made Tiger the youngest player ever to participate in a PGA event. Qualifying rounds were held at our home course, Los Serranos Golf Club. Tiger had played this course with us on several occasions, and each time we cautioned him about the par five eighteenth hole on the South Course. The first time Tiger played this hole, we told him he was not long enough to attempt to clear the water and make the green in two. It was necessary for Tiger to lay up and rely on his short game to make birdie or even par. Each time he played this hole, Tiger would lay up accordingly and because of that, he did make a small percentage of birdies.

However, in the qualifying round, Tiger hit a good drive on eighteen and he knew that in order to catch Mac O'Grady and to qualify, he needed to make eagle. In his desperate need to win, Tiger, of course, pulled out his three wood and went for it. The result: Tiger dumped his shot into the water, made bogie and failed to qualify. This incident never really tempered Tiger's need and desire to sometimes attempt the impossible.

I remember when Earl told me how shortly before Tiger turned pro he had realized his constant demand for perfection from Tiger may have been a mistake. Earl knew he had drilled the need for perfection into Tiger, truly believing it would make him stronger and a better player. However, Earl's lessons came with consequences and he eventually realized how much Tiger had actually been affected by his constant need to seek perfection. Earl thought about trying to correct the situation by having Tiger face the fact that he cannot always be perfect, but Earl decided against it. He knew the damage was already done and the lessons he had taught Tiger were so far ingrained in him that Earl's efforts to reverse them would be futile.

Although Earl tried to have Tiger understand that success was measured only by doing his very best and, even if he didn't win, but he did his best and tried as hard as he could, he would still be successful. However, according to Earl, Tiger, of course, did not see it that way. Unfortunately, Earl's earlier misguided lessons regarding perfection had already made a strong impact on Tiger. Being a true perfectionist, Tiger believed that second sucked and success to him was only if he won.

All of the lessons Earl taught Tiger from the time he was a young child have been so deeply embedded that after he turned pro, Tiger remained unflappable and unstoppable. It is Tiger's own drive and ambition that has continued his relentless pursuit for perfection and for his next win. Whether it was in junior and amateur golf or as a professional, Tiger has always had this tremendous need to feel that he is perfect and that he can be, and will be, the absolute best.

5
CONTROLLING TIGER

THE FIRST FEW TIMES I was with Tiger, I thought that he was somewhat shy and reclusive, especially since he always seemed to be so very moody, quiet and even a little distant at times. However, after I had the opportunity to be around Tiger and share more time with him, I realized that whenever he was quiet, he was either deep in his own thoughts and in his own zone or he was just pouting over one thing or another. There were even times when Tiger appeared to be under a spell which usually occurred when his father was present and most often when Earl was talking to him.

Although I tried on many occasions, I found it quite difficult to actually penetrate Tiger's space, finding that Earl was usually the only person who could truly affect him. When I was around Tiger and when he was in his zone, it wasn't like he was being rude or unfriendly. There were times when Tiger simply did not feel like talking to anyone and, therefore, would seldom share in any of our conversations. Of course, since Earl had a special knack of monopolizing most of our conversations, none of us, including Tiger, rarely got a chance to talk. But when it came to Tiger, it was as though he was waiting quietly for a special signal from his father to let him know that it was okay for him to finally say something.

On a few occasions, Tiger would actually join in when we were discussing golf, but most of the time Tiger just would not talk. We would all try to encourage him to join in, but to no avail. Tiger either wanted to just sit and pout because he wanted to do something else, or he would simply go off into his "zone". Then again, there were times when Tiger just did not want to be there.

I could understand why Tiger was so quiet all of the time. Tiger was a child being forced to sit around with a bunch of adults and listen to conversations which he had absolutely no interest in. Tiger was simply getting bored and wanted to do something more to his liking. Although Tiger wanted to be with his Dad, what kid wants to be around adults all of the time? This was nothing new since Earl always took Tiger with him, especially when he was going to be with his adult friends.

I remember Earl telling me that Tiger hated being around adults and how he never felt as though he fit in. Sadly, Earl would continue to force Tiger to participate with all of the adults. Fully knowing how uncomfortable his son was with these situations, I never could understand why Earl would intentionally subject his son to them. Earl would always justify Tiger's presence with such comments as, "When Tiger is older he will be more grounded and will have learned to interact with people better," or "This will be such a great learning process for him. Tiger has the ability to learn so much from being around adults." It was almost as though Earl was pushing Tiger into adulthood and forcing his social skills to match his golf talent. Earl kept ignoring the fact that Tiger was just a kid who simply loved to play golf.

The one thing that bothered me the most was why it was so important for Earl to always have Tiger around him. I knew Earl and Tiger were close, but did they have to be together all the time, even when Earl was with his own friends? According to Earl, Tiger loved him so much that it was actually Tiger who always wanted to be around his father. Earl said he was simply doing what his son wanted, however, over time, I became aware that Earl was actually trying to maintain his strong and constant bond with Tiger in order for him to continue manipulating his son.

This allowed Earl to maintain his persuasive influence over his son. No matter what excuse Earl conjured up, he still should have recognized the signs that Tiger may have wanted to do other things like playing with kids his own age instead of being around Earl and all of his friends. But once again, Tiger was forced to abide by his father's requests.

I was around Tiger and Earl for many years and from what I witnessed, I highly doubt that it was Tiger who preferred to hang around the adults. Many times, Tiger would get antsy and throw a tantrum, as though he was bored and wanted to leave. After Tiger played his round of golf, he just wanted to go home so he could be a normal kid and do normal kid things. Unfortunately, Earl would not give in to Tiger's tantrums and demands as he expected him to sit with the adults.

However, as Tiger got older, Tiger also changed. Earl would finally give in to what Tiger wanted and agreed to let him leave. At this point in Tiger's life, Earl feared that too many demands and restrictions might interfere with Tiger's desire to continue with his golf. Earl most definitely did not want to ever disrupt the flow of progress and a potential golf career.

Earl created an environment where everything focused on golf and revolved around golf. Earl was the one who made golf Tiger's number one priority. Sadly, Tiger, as just a regular kid, was not Earl's number one priority.

As he grew, Tiger became more proficient at golf, but his moods and the "in his zone" moments remained the same. The only difference was that as he got older his thoughts became more focused and more mature, as did his ambitions in life. But one thing that always remained a constant in his life was his father. Earl had created a life for Tiger in which he relied on his father for everything, thus Earl was able to keep Tiger close at all times. It was Earl who needed to insinuate himself into every aspect of Tiger's life, resulting in an extremely close bond that created the dependency Tiger continually relied on.

Tiger had tremendous skill and talent for golf and from an early age, many people were hoping Tiger would one day be a truly good golfer, possibly even a great one. Earl, on the other hand, always knew Tiger would be one of the greatest golfers in the history of the sport. After all, Earl spent years grooming, rather pushing, Tiger to be just that and had instilled in him to believe that he could go after and break the records of some of the greatest golfers ever.

Forgetting about the long term toll all of these pressures might take on Tiger, Earl tried to do everything in his power to convince Tiger that he was the best in golf. This caused Tiger's egotistic and arrogant attitude to explode where he eventually reached a point in his life when he no longer just believed that he would be the best; Tiger *knew* that he would be the best and it wasn't long before he demonstrated that very fact.

Tiger's enormous passion for golf, along with his training and pressing to be the best, was so intense and determined that some people were concerned that he could possibly burn out at some point early in his career. Tiger loved his golf, but had it become a detrimental addiction that was consuming every facet of his life while pushing to be the absolute best? Personally, I always wondered how long he could handle the continuously regimented life that had been carved out for him at such an early age by his father. After all, Earl had been pushing Tiger since he was two years old and more so as he grew.

I also thought that maybe his parents, Earl and Tida, were not giving Tiger the opportunity to be just a kid, even though on several occasions, Earl tried to convince me that it was Tiger who always wanted to play golf and didn't care about anything else. But over the years, it became quite obvious that it was Earl who was programming Tiger and pushing his son to all new heights. It was also Earl who was instrumental in making sure Tiger put golf first and foremost in his life, setting aside and ignoring any other needs or wants he might have.

It had reached a point where Tiger would basically eat, drink and sleep golf throughout his young life, unwilling to experience many of the things that a normal life could offer a child. Tiger's life had become so absorbed in golf that he was never expected to do any household chores or even hold down a job as he became a teenager. This caused me to wonder what important parts of his life Tiger would be missing out on as he grew into an adult, such as learning responsibility, interacting with others and learning to treat people with kindness.

I watched as Earl not only permitted, but also encouraged Tiger's egotistical and selfish behavior toward others, believing those traits were totally acceptable and even necessary in a true champion. It seemed to me that the traits Earl created for his son were wrong and I worried about the long term effect it might have on Tiger.

Earl and Tida always portrayed themselves to be loving and devoted parents, but ever since they realized their son might eventually be great in the world of golf, they saw future dollar signs and a better life for themselves through their son. This was when they decided it was necessary to get an early start by creating a future direction for Tiger. Helping to guide a child in choosing a path in life is quite normal for most parents. However, when it came to Earl and Tida, I honestly believe they had become so fixated on their son's extraordinary talent and his potentially prosperous future in golf that they went to extremes in pushing their son.

There were many times when Earl insisted on Tiger going to his practice sessions even though Tiger didn't want to. Tiger would try to object, but because he was just a kid, he ended up obeying Earl and doing what his father wanted. Each time, Earl tried to convince Tiger that sometimes you have to do things you don't want to in order to excel in life, thus forcing Tiger to conform to Earl's wishes. Earl's goal was to teach Tiger true discipline, believing it would be necessary if he were to succeed in golf. Many of Earl's tactics were similar to the discipline that he was required to maintain in the military. But Tiger wasn't in the military. He was just a kid who loved to play golf.

Because of Earl's efforts, he created a life for Tiger where he was always telling his son what to do and how to act. Earl ended up controlling Tiger and there were many times when Earl made Tiger participate in things he really didn't want to, even though Tiger tried to voice his objections. An example would be when Earl would tell Tiger they would be playing golf on such and such day and Tiger would get all excited and actually looked forward to playing. His mood would be very upbeat. Then there were times when Earl would tell Tiger that he would have to do an interview with a newspaper reporter or would have to make an appearance somewhere and this would be when Tiger's attitude immediately changed to frustration and resistance, and his response was usually, "Aw, Pop, do I have to?" or "I really don't want to." Unfortunately, Tiger's unwillingness to participate occurred often and was simply dismissed by Earl. But because of his father's strong hold, Tiger was once again forced to abide with what his father wanted and whatever plans he had made for him.

An important question is, did Earl push Tiger too hard and did he forget to see Tiger for the child he was and address his true needs? Sadly, Earl created a situation that eventually caused Tiger to disregard his own personal needs and wants, and in turn, disregard the needs of others.

From the time Tiger could walk and take his first swing of a golf club, Earl chose to start the controlling process so he could gain the necessary trust from Tiger in order to be able to permanently implant his influences on him early on. Through his father's manipulation and domination, Tiger eventually became the perfect and obedient son. Earl used to describe Tiger as being very special, respectful and well-trained. Sadly, many would call it being controlled.

Simply put, Earl believed that he was the one who had to make the decisions and choices for his son and do whatever was necessary to reach his son's ultimate goal, no matter what Tiger actually wanted. I am not saying that Tiger didn't want to play golf. I just feel that Earl initially pushed Tiger into golf and ended up pushing him too hard, thus sometimes creating an extremely stressful environment for Tiger.

Besides, if Earl had not taken up golf two years prior to Tiger's birth, who's to say that Tiger would have ever turned out to be a golfer. He only started to play golf because he saw his father hitting golf balls in the garage.

Over the years, Earl and I had many conversations regarding the approach he took in raising his son. Whatever questions were brought up regarding Tiger's upbringing, Earl would always defend himself, basically stating that he was doing what he felt was right for his son. He honestly believed that he needed to push Tiger so he could excel. But then there were conversations when Earl would contradict himself by stating that it was Tiger who always wanted to play golf, and as a father, he was just doing what his son wanted. Of course, I reminded him of the many times when Tiger was younger and he tried to resist what Earl had wanted him to do. But as Tiger grew and his father's influences became more embedded, Tiger stopped resisting and simply accepted Earl's "guidance" and complied with Earl's wishes and demands.

Luckily, in spite of Earl's pushing, Tiger ended up loving golf and grew up wanting to be the best in the sport. However, when he was just a little tyke, how did Tiger know what he really wanted? And why did Earl push Tiger in that direction at such a young age?

This discussion came up several times, and each time Earl would answer my questions, it usually ended with the fact that he didn't push Tiger. Frankly, Earl could care less what anyone else in this world thought. He told me that as Tiger's father he was going to raise his child his way and that included making sure Tiger became the best black golfer in the sport's history.

There were times when I thought Earl's intentions and efforts were very commendable, but when I became more aware of Earl's ongoing control, I came to realize that Earl had truly become overbearing and fanatical when it came to Tiger's golf career. Earl was controlling so much of Tiger's life, it was almost like Earl was the puppet master, pulling all the strings, and Tiger was just his puppet.

From the many and various conversations I had with Earl, it came to light that Earl's obsession stemmed from his own life experiences with racial discrimination. When Tiger first entered junior golf, Earl had reacted to the fact that Tiger was the only black child playing golf in all of the junior tournaments and Earl had convinced himself that Tiger would never be given the same opportunities as the other kids who were also trying to excel in that sport. Earl knew Tiger was good at golf, but he was afraid Tiger still might not be accepted because of his color. This was when Earl determined that for his son to be truly accepted, Tiger not only needed to be a good golfer, but he would have to be the absolute best.

Simply put, in Earl's mind, Tiger was going to be the first black golfer with the potential to succeed and Earl was going to make sure that Tiger was successful and popular, no matter what he had to do to achieve it. It was also Earl's goal to make sure that Tiger was so great that he would never fail in the eyes of the public or the media, therefore, guaranteeing him total acceptance. Sadly, because of Earl's pressure, Tiger was also forced to be so great that he would never fail in Earl's eyes.

It was Tiger's early talent and ability in golf that prompted Earl to start marketing and promoting him from the time he was just a little boy. He honestly believed that Tiger's talent could one day bring fame and recognition to his family, and realizing the full potential of that talent, Earl chose to take advantage of the opportunity to make Tiger into a celebrity. Earl wanted people to know about Tiger and did everything he could to promote him to a celebrity position.

In addition, Earl believed he had to continually put Tiger's name and face in the media to ease him into acceptance. As Tiger excelled and began to participate in the Junior World, U.S. Junior Amateur and the U.S. Amateur, Earl once told me that he was determined to have people accept Tiger as a great golfer, even if he had to force feed Tiger to them.

The only problem was that in the early years, Earl was the only one who believed that Tiger was special and he could never understand why others were unable to view his son the same way. Unfortunately, and contrary to Earl's efforts, Tiger never wanted all of the attention or the hype that came from Earl's promoting. Thus, it is quite possible the temper and anger Tiger continuously displayed most likely came from the frustration he was experiencing due to his father's actions and his constant control and demands. Many times, Tiger tried to refuse to give in, but was unable to reject his father's demands and expectations.

Simply put, Tiger did not want any part of the media and, against Earl's pushing, Tiger also never wanted to be placed in the spotlight. Remember, the Tiger we are talking about is a quiet and somewhat reclusive person who was always content with being in his own "zone".

So in reality, it was always Earl who was forcing Tiger into the forefront and the spotlight and made sure to do everything he could to keep Tiger there. The only thing Tiger really wanted was to play golf and, of course, win. Because he was young and naïve, Tiger was unable to envision what his future could really be like, and he was put in a position where he had to go along with, and trust, his father's advice and direction.

It's funny, because I remember the time when there was all this media hype about Michelle Wei and Earl was literally outraged at her parents and what they were doing to market and promote her in order to gain recognition and popularity for their daughter. Earl and I were sitting in Earl's living room watching a report about Michelle Wei on television and all Earl could do was rant about how ridiculous it was to promote someone like that, especially since she was an unknown and had no golfing history to substantiate all the hype. Earl also stated how wrong it was that all the special treatment and the exemptions into professional tournaments and events were just handed to her on a silver platter. Earl said that when Tiger was her age, Tiger was never given any special opportunities. Tiger was forced to qualify to gain entry into tournaments and had to earn his own exemptions.

Although Earl showed so much jealously over Michelle's parent's success at getting her media attention, it was Earl who forgot that he tried to do the exact same thing with Tiger. Fortunately, Tiger's eventual outcome in professional golf was more successful than Michelle Wei's. It just shows that Earl was the type of person who would ridicule someone else for what they did, but he would turn a blind eye to his own actions when it pertained to Tiger or his golf. Even though I brought this fact to his attention, Earl still refused to believe there were any similarities between him and what Michelle Wei's parents were doing for their daughter.

In order for Tiger to understand and appreciate the status Earl had created for him, even from a very young age, both of Tiger's parents continually told him how perfect and great he was and how much better he was than anyone else in golf and in life. In their eyes, Tiger was perfect and he should be worshiped and cherished by the entire world, as their son could do no wrong.

Over the years, Earl truly believed that he was only giving his son loving words of encouragement while helping him to shape his life. But in reality, he was teaching Tiger to set his expectations of himself so high that he was never allowed any room for error

Earl and Tida even placed Tiger so very high up on a pedestal making him, at such a young age, feel superior to all others and above it all simply because of his special talent. The error in their thinking was Earl and Tida put Tiger up on the pedestal *only* because of his talent and his ability to play golf. Sadly, the placing of Tiger was not because he was just Tiger, great kid or because he did well in school. It strictly pertained to his golf and all of his accomplishments on the golf course and especially who he could someday become.

Earl had three other children who were never interested in golf or good at any other sport, so Earl had basically removed himself from their lives as they grew up. When any one of his other children were young, never once did Earl attach himself to them or try to insinuate himself into their lives, much less try to influence them. So why was Earl so attached to Tiger? What made Tiger so different from his siblings? Was it only because of his golf and the eventual recognition, status and wealth that Earl himself would attain through his son? Most definitely!

Ignoring his son's personal needs and desires, Earl continued to steer Tiger's potential career and celebrity status by contacting the media for coverage and exposure, making early connections with various sponsors, and always trying to put Tiger in the spotlight, forgetting that Tiger was only a kid and was only human.

After realizing everything Earl did for Tiger, many people, including myself, wondered how long Tiger would be able to maintain the lofty expectations Earl had set for him. What Earl did for Tiger could either make a champion or eventually break him. At the time, only the future would tell.

Both Earl and Tida were constantly involved in every aspect of Tiger's life, especially his golf. Being an only child, he was never allowed the freedom of being away from his parents and it appeared as though they were acting like typical "stage" parents, rather than regular "sport" parents, always sharing the moments and the spotlight with their son. Earl, Tida, or both of them, would always be present at each of Tiger's lessons, tournaments, appearances, interviews, and award functions, while continually demanding special treatment for their son and for themselves. Their constant presence in Tiger's life continued throughout Tiger's amateur and professional career. Over time, they started to believe that since they have a son who is special, then they must be special, too.

Although Earl defended his many actions, he spoke often about how he thought everyone had a misconception as to the way he was raising Tiger. On one hand, Earl would state that he didn't care what anyone else thought about his fathering techniques and then he would turn around and immediately make up a million excuses as to why he was raising Tiger this way.

During our twenty year friendship Earl continuously tried to justify his behavior to me and made excuses for the things he had done, stating they were all for Tiger. But, no matter how Earl tried to explain his involvement in his son, I still had a difficult time believing he was doing everything only to benefit Tiger. I knew how preoccupied and obsessed Earl had become with Tiger's golf and his potential career. It had reached a point in Earl's life where absolutely everything was about Tiger's golf and it was Earl who went completely overboard with his own actions and behavior. I knew Earl had an agenda that he had put into action when Tiger was young and I wasn't sure what the eventual outcome would be. But one thing I did know was Earl would most likely reap the rewards.

Over the years, I watched as Earl's misguided obsession for Tiger's golf and potential stardom grew and how it progressed into control and manipulation of his son and his life. Earl was now the leader and Tiger had become his follower. Earl created a protective circle around Tiger where Earl was now in total control of his son. At times, I likened it to a cult and Earl was the leader and head of the family and the chosen people were sucked into the circle, me included.

6
COPING WITH THE PRESSURES

WHEN YOU THINK ABOUT IT, how does a very young child, especially a child around the age of two, three, four or even six or seven, truly know what they want in life? They don't even know about life or what life is much less what life has to offer. I don't care how smart a child is. There is just no way that any child can know if they have goals to attain in life and whether or not they can be great at something. How can they know if the talent they possess can take them far in life? They do not even understand the true meaning of being perfect, much less what it means to fail.

Young children are usually playing cowboys and Indians or focusing on their video games or simply playing with their friends. Most children think they want to be a policeman or a fireman or even an astronaut when they grow up, and then two weeks later they change their minds and want to be something else. How can someone so young know what they truly want in life?

Many people know that a child's attention span is not fully developed and it is not proficient enough to understand life in general, thus the parents become instrumental in making the choices for them, believing they know what is best for their child. This child eventually ends up being pushed in a direction the parents have already chosen for them and many times it will be a direction that is not necessarily what the child wants.

When children are young, they are concentrating on their education, which Tiger did do, but they are still just being a kid. Although Tiger was a smart kid and did well in school, his parents steered him toward golf, starting long before he was ever in school. A child simply does not pick up a golf club at eighteen months old and asks his dad, "Daddy, teach me this," or "Daddy, I want to be a star some day." There has to be someone who places that club in his hand, tells him what the club is for and how to use it. Even then, the child does not have a clue what everything is all about. To the child, it is simply fun to him and it means that he can act grown up and be like his daddy, thus creating a situation where daddy can spend time with him. Just like the kiddie tool boxes or doctor's bag or the little girl's play cooking stove or sewing kit. It's all about playing, having fun and acting like grown-ups and mimicking mommy or daddy.

Tiger was no different than any other child his age. How does any two year old or even a five year old know what they want, much less what they are doing? It is almost as though the child has to perform or be in the spotlight in order to fulfill the parent's own past dreams or aspirations, which is something the parent always wanted for themselves. By making their child popular and in the forefront also allows the parent to share in the spotlight, creating their own self-importance. As everyone knows, the parent ends up living vicariously through their own child. Many times, the child can reach a point where they have had enough "fun" and they no longer want to participate. Unfortunately, they are told by the parent that they have to keep going and quitting is not an option. They must continue to work hard at what they are doing, causing the child to be unhappy and frustrated and possibly negatively affecting them for many years to come. But in the end, the parent gets what they want and need. The same was true of Earl and Tiger.

The situation with Earl and Tiger was similar to that of a typical little kid beauty pageant where the child really has no desire to prance around in a beauty contest, but is pushed by the mother. The mother is constantly defending her actions by saying, "but my daughter wants it so bad," or "she loves doing this so much," all the while the little child is in the corner screaming at the top of their lungs, "I don't want to do this anymore." Sadly, it is actually the parent who is pushing her child to do it as she continually puts pressure on that child to perform.

There were many times I saw Tiger become unhappy and frustrated mainly due to the additional pressures and stress placed on him by Earl as he always forced him to be on display and perform above what should have been expected of a child. Earl always said that he was doing what Tiger wanted, but was Earl truly listening to Tiger or was he simply doing what he wanted for his son and for himself? Like a pushy "stage" father, Earl did everything he could to promote Tiger when he was just a little kid including calling local and national television shows such as the Mike Douglas Show, That's Incredible, and many other television news shows, so Tiger could perform in front an audience and be seen on television by millions.

I am sure at three years old Tiger did not ask his father to call these shows so he could be on them. I am also sure that Earl didn't care how Tiger felt about being on display. Besides, at such a young age, I often wondered how Tiger was affected by all of the expectations that had been placed on him. Can you just imagine what it was like for a shy little kid to have to perform on television in front of a huge audience? But then again, at three years old, Tiger most likely did not have a clue as to what was going on. It was all show for Earl's sake so he, himself, could be on television and be seen. It was Earl who was getting his fifteen minutes of fame

There are a lot of fathers and mothers out there who have raised their children to either succeed in their profession or become famous. But you never hear about them writing books about their children and themselves, or marketing and promoting their child the way Earl had done with Tiger from the very beginning at such a young age.

There have been a lot of children who could hit the golf ball like Tiger, but they were never promoted and put on public display by their parents for the world to see. Generally speaking, a parent has the tendency to shield their child from such public exposure and to allow them to experience a normal life and grow into their potential stardom.

However, from the time Tiger first started playing junior golf, Earl had resorted to continually contacting the local newspapers and well-known Los Angeles based television sports broadcaster, Jim Hill, in order for Tiger's accomplishments to get as much media attention as possible. Even though Junior Golf was not newsworthy and no one had ever heard of Tiger Woods, except in Southern California, Earl would still do whatever was necessary to promote and market his son. Of course, it was always Earl who would give the information on Tiger to media and tell them what to say about his son.

Tiger was just a little kid, and I knew how Earl's actions were unnecessarily putting many additional pressures on him and his performance, thus creating such grand expectations which Tiger would continually have to live up to. Everything Earl did to promote his son ended up affecting Tiger in one way or another and many times it was not always for the best. Sadly, it forced Tiger to conform to his father's demands at a very young age.

As Tiger grew and excelled further in golf, Earl continued to contact the local newspapers and television stations in order to showcase his son. Tiger could never understand why he had to be subjected to the media especially since he felt so uncomfortable when doing interviews. Tiger hated the attention that being in the spotlight gave him and he hated being on display. There were times when Earl had told me how Tiger was extremely opposed to the exposure he was creating for him. However, this never stopped

Earl as he was completely convinced he knew what was best for his son.

Earl honestly believed Tiger would eventually understand the purpose of the press and all of the coverage, and a day would come when Tiger would appreciate what Earl had accomplished for him. Earl's attitude was, "Trust me. You will learn to love it." As always, Earl would once again be convincing, causing Tiger to give in to his father. Unfortunately, Tiger never could get comfortable doing interviews or being in the spotlight. In fact, he later learned to distrust the media and their intentions, believing the media's stories were not always accurate and the supposed facts they reported were sometimes fabricated or slanted.

Another pressure situation Tiger was subjected to was having to play golf with adults. Since Tiger was taught to play golf by his father, and as he learned and as he played, Tiger was continually pitted against the adults. Since Tiger always played golf with Earl and since Earl always played golf with his friends, the foursome would always include Tiger and three adults. When Tiger was a child and even as a young teenager, it must have been difficult for Tiger to feel like he fit in with the grown-ups.

I always wondered what it would be like to be a small child and always have to play a round of golf with adult friends of your father. For most children, it would be fun, going out on the course and having a great time just being with your dad. If you mess up in your game, oh well, who cares? Many children are not able to take the game seriously, rather they have no real desire to take the game seriously. They are simply going out to the course to have a good time and just be a kid. But with Tiger it was different.

Tiger was being trained and coached to be a truly good golfer and he was not simply going out to the golf course to have fun. Tiger was taught to take the game quite seriously and his long term ambitions, or rather Earl's ambitions for Tiger, were very different from the other children his age. Now, when Tiger was four years old, I had a difficult time believing that he was really concerned about the success of his game, but as Tiger grew, I could see where he eventually gained tremendous interest in the outcome of his play.

When I started playing golf with Tiger, he was only ten years old, and I noticed that he was able to be somewhat focused in his game. I mean at least as much as a ten year old can stay focused on any one thing. However, over time and as he matured, I could see a transformation taking place in him as he began to take the game more seriously and became more competitive and confident.

Since the majority of the time Tiger was playing golf with adults, I thought about the pressures it would have on him and how it could possibly affect his mentality toward the game. The adults are bigger and stronger and they are hitting all of their drives and fairway shots considerably longer than him. They have the ability and concentration to be more consistent in their game, even around the greens. They have more strength to hit the ball out of the long grass in the rough or when their ball is in a trouble spot.

Over all, an adult's strength, play level and mental ability are usually far better than that of a child, even Tiger's. Thus, playing with adults, Tiger was always forced into a position where he had to push himself even harder than most children.

As a little kid, Tiger was good, but to hear Earl tell it, Tiger was a superb and an exceptional golfer possessing a tremendous talent that could beat any and all adults. Earl actually believed Tiger was the only kid in the entire world who possessed such a talent.

It's true that Tiger was able to hold his own with the adults as he got bigger and stronger, but when he was young and small in size, there was just no way that he could compete with any adult, much less have to be placed in a position where he felt he should have to. But once again, having Tiger play with the adults gave Earl the opportunity to put Tiger on display and show off the great golfer Earl had created. Of course, this made Earl look good to all of his friends.

It had to have been difficult for Tiger to feel that his drives were inadequate when measured against an adult's because sometimes he would have to take two shots to reach an average adult's drive, even when he played from the forward tees. Earl always believed he did the right thing by subjecting Tiger to an adult environment from a very early age. Earl's thinking was that Tiger would grow up being a stronger and more focused competitor. Sadly, Earl never took into consideration just how this would affect Tiger's personal growth and what would result from it as Tiger matured.

Again, there was Earl who was constantly telling Tiger that he could beat these grown-ups, which was adding more pressure on Tiger's performance. The problem is that children feel things differently than adults and if Tiger failed in his attempts to outscore someone, how did that make him feel? He certainly did not want to disappoint his father nor did he want to embarrass his father in front of his friends by failing. Then you wonder if Tiger actually felt like a failure or was he able to simply shrug it off and try harder the next time? According to Earl, Tiger was able to shrug it off. But, if that was the case, then why was there a temper and why did Tiger act otherwise. Many times I saw a young boy who acted embarrassed and disappointed in himself, simply because Earl's expectations for Tiger were set far too high.

Each time Tiger played, whether it was with us, Earl's regular foursome or in one of his tournaments, Tiger would try to do everything in his power to not look bad in front of the other players, many times causing him to quit in the middle of a round or demonstrate his erratic moods and tantrums. This made me question if Tiger would grow up putting excessive pressures on himself unnecessarily in order to be the best. Many times I questioned why Earl put Tiger in so many unrealistic situations including playing with the adults. Tiger's young psyche had to have been affected by the excessive pressures and tremendous expectations from his early years in golf. As Tiger grew, his ability and focus had matured, but what lingering effects still existed from his earlier years?

It makes me wonder how Tiger would have turned out if he had not been pushed so hard by his father and if he had been encouraged to simply go out and play golf. What if his parents had told him that being the best in the world was not important and they would still love him anyway, whether he broke records or not? What if they had told him to just do his best in a sport he truly loved? What if they had told him they just wanted him to be happy doing something he loved? If that had happened, who would Tiger be today? He would still be a champion, but with a better attitude toward life and people. And maybe even happier within himself.

Over the years and as he grew, I had noticed many changes in Tiger that included a more strenuous regimen as he demonstrated even more ambition and a stronger drive toward his golf. When you are young, you want to win and beat the other kids, but as you get older, your sense of winning changes altogether. And as Tiger went on to play in junior and amateur golf, Tiger became stronger and even more focused and determined in his efforts to excel as a winner. Of course, that is the difference between being a small child and growing up experiencing more of life.

Another difference in Tiger I had noticed was his intolerance for mistakes. It had reached a point where Earl had set Tiger's standards so high that he was now expecting such a level of pure perfection from himself and he wasn't allowing himself any room for error. Although his main purpose in life was to be the best golfer in the world, Tiger had become so completely addicted to the game of golf that it was difficult for him to think of anything else.

The older Tiger got, the closer he was to reaching his ultimate goal, and that was not only to be a professional golfer, but to be the absolute best professional golfer. He wanted to go out on tour and win every tournament and break every record he could. But the closer he got to that goal, the more pressure he began to place on himself. After all, Tiger had been raised with pressure all his life and was constantly told how great he was and how great he would be and how perfect he had to be in order to succeed. In Tiger's case, failure was not an option. This was when Tiger started to believe in himself even more which caused his self-confidence level to go completely off the charts, thus creating a huge ego and removing any sense of uncertainty that he once had.

In addition, Tiger was pushed to believe that he truly was the best. Over the years, Earl did everything he could to convince Tiger that he could beat anyone. He made Tiger understand that he had to go out on the course and beat everyone in the field. Earl didn't give up until Tiger truly believed that no one else was better than him in golf. Earl had convinced Tiger that he was invincible and that no one could ever touch him.

Earl did not simply build up Tiger's confidence; Earl ended up forcing Tiger to have impracticable beliefs. In order to save face, each time Tiger played in a tournament, he knew that he always had to win, not just because he wanted to, but because he had to. Tiger knew that he was expected to win. After all, Earl had drilled into Tiger's head that he had to win in order to be the best. And if people were going to like him and accept him, he had to win.

But the problem was that just "being the best" for Tiger was never good enough. It seemed as though Tiger was never satisfied with himself and his performance, as he always felt he could have done even better. Earl used to tell Tiger. "You're good, but you can always be better."

And because of all the great things that had been told to him by his parents and others to reaffirm his tremendous ability and talent, Tiger believed that he must never fail, because if he did, he would let so many people down, including himself. Tiger now had the added stress of not wanting to disappoint anyone, especially his parents.

Then the day came when Tiger finally decided to join the pro circuit and Earl couldn't have been prouder. Now the entire world would have the opportunity to know and love the Tiger who Earl had worked so hard coaching and training to be the best. This was the very moment Earl spent years grooming Tiger for, to be a professional golfer, a player on the PGA tour. But it also meant that it was time for Earl to let go and let Tiger be his own person in the world of golf. Unfortunately, although Tiger had grown into a man, Earl was still a constant in Tiger's life as Earl was unable to relinquish his control over his son.

As a rookie on the PGA tour, Tiger not only had to go out and win in order to prove all of the hype that had been written about him, but he also had to satisfy his sponsors, parents, and agents. No other golfer came out with so much pressure to perform. At this point, the demands on Tiger were hefty, to say the least. But Tiger had always been told that he was incapable of failing because he was just too good for that to ever happen. So, in a way, he grew up thinking that it would be impossible for him to ever fail at anything, especially his golf.

According to Earl, Tiger's thinking was, "Okay, I'm too good to fail, but if I don't win, then I fail. What then?" Unfortunately for Tiger there was no middle ground and he would never settle for being second best.

It was difficult for Tiger to go out in front of thousands of spectators and perform to his own perfectionist standards. Even though Tiger was extremely good at playing golf, being on the PGA tour was a lot of pressure in itself. So why did Earl, who was supposedly a loving and devoted father, add so much more on Tiger, such as building his celebrity status and creating a role model image, constantly exposing him to the media, instigating instant contracts with sponsors, and even forming the Tiger Woods Foundation. All this was on top of Tiger having to go out on tour as a rookie.

Earl forgot to look at the big picture and see that he was placing far too much on Tiger's shoulders, almost to the point of pushing Tiger too hard, too far, and too fast.

Earl should have given these things to Tiger in very small increments over a longer period of time, or not at all. But Earl persisted and decided to lump everything together and pile it on Tiger all at once, making his already pressured life even more burdened. With Earl controlling Tiger's life, he was now forcing Tiger into a very awkward and untenable position where he was unable to reject his father's actions and intentions. Just like when he was a kid, Tiger was still being controlled and manipulated by his father.

Although when Tiger came on tour as a rookie with a tremendous amount of additional pressure, he was still able to come out with total conviction and resolve, unlike so many other rookies who are completely unprepared and are extremely nervous about playing in their first professional round of golf. But what made Tiger so different than all of the other newbies? It was years of his hard work, dedication and a huge superiority complex. The confidence level Tiger possessed was simply the part of Tiger that had been instilled in him by his parents since day one, along with his own drive and fortitude.

Frankly, I don't know how any person could have so much confidence in himself that he actually thinks he is completely infallible and void of any failure. To my way of thinking, you are simply setting yourself up for many huge disappointments. Surely Tiger did not think that he was going to come out as a rookie on the PGA tour and start winning each and every tournament he played in. But to my surprise, Earl told me that both he and Tiger felt confident enough that he could actually go out and win every tournament because Tiger was that good. With that kind of mentality, it's obvious why Tiger gets so upset when he doesn't win a tournament. Tiger truly expects to win.

Tiger always goes out and plays each tournament with complete and total determination and conviction to win. Tiger's theory is, why should anyone go out and play for second or third? If you don't play to win, then why play at all. Tiger had always been taught to believe that he is the best and is capable of always winning.

If Tiger is the best, then what about the many golfers who have defeated Tiger over the years? Doesn't that make them one of the best golfers, too? After all, they did beat Tiger Woods.

7
LEARNING FROM LIFE

TIGER'S LIFE WAS ALL ABOUT learning, adapting and accepting the changes in life and what was yet to come. For Tiger, every single day was a learning process, as it is in everyone's lives, but for him he had the added pressures of learning to not only be a golfer, but to be the best. Tiger didn't need to be perfect in all aspects of his life. He only needed to be perfect in golf, always coming out above the rest.

From the time he was just a little boy, Tiger's life was full of lessons, whether it was from his golf game, school, coaches or from his parents. Although the direction of Tiger's life had already been mapped out for him by his father, there were still many other areas of life that would have to be addressed along the way in order for Tiger to eventually attain his goals in golf, primarily the hope of becoming a professional golfer.

Tiger's parents, Earl and Tida, always wanted everyone to believe that Tiger had two great parents who chose to dedicate their lives to help guide and direct him throughout his entire journey to greatness. They honestly believed they were an integral part of Tiger's life and they thought they were continually teaching certain life lessons and solid values to their son as he ventured through life. Earl led people to believe that it was he, himself, who made sure the game of golf was always more important to Tiger than anything else in the world. Earl and Tida also tried to convince the public that they knew it was imperative that Tiger be raised with true family values and the importance of honesty and integrity. With this, they were hoping Tiger would grow into a good, sincere and well respected person.

But sadly, it was Earl and Tida's warped sense of values and their own self-serving agendas that diminished their ability to transform their hopes onto their son.

Earl and Tida were, in fact, good parents, but their actions and behavior over the years definitely proved otherwise. Even when Earl wrote his slanted and overly embellished books about raising Tiger, he led people to believe he and his family were perfect and had impeccable values and everything was about helping Tiger through life.

But how can Earl state that he always wanted Tiger to remain humble when, in fact, Earl was training him from a young age to have a so-called "killer instinct" and forced Tiger into believing he was superior, especially in golf? Also, Earl taught Tiger that acting superior and believing he was entitled was his right because he was so special and better than everyone else.

Realizing Tiger's future potential triggered Earl's greed and his own need of self-importance produced a less friendly, overly arrogant and somewhat ruthless son. In the end, Tiger might be respected for his ability, but few people respect him for his attitude.

Earl's obsession and his need to dominate his son caused him to be Tiger's only real "teacher" throughout his son's life. Earl also made sure he had a tremendous influence on Tiger as he grew up. Earl accomplished this by becoming Tiger's friend, mentor and confidant, and as owner of these various positions, Earl basically controlled Tiger's upbringing and was able to manipulate every aspect of Tiger's life and thought process. Ultimately it was Earl who taught Tiger about life by exposing Tiger to Earl's own personal feelings, opinions and experiences. Some of these were good, but many were very tainted.

Earl's problem was that he had his own strong opinions and viewpoints about life and how one should live it, often standing quite firm and steadfast in his beliefs. In his mind, he knew everything and seldom needed anyone else's advice or input. And according to Earl, these convictions were only given to Tiger in the form of advice and recommendations, many times by simply giving suggestions to Tiger so that he could supposedly process the information and make his own decisions.

However, even though Tiger "thought" he had reached his own conclusions, Tiger would still discuss the outcome of his reasoning with Earl before he would act upon it, essentially leaving the final decision to be made by his father. This form of manipulation also allowed Earl to retain control of his son. Earl described this process as making himself available for his son, but what Earl was doing was only creating a situation where Tiger would rely and depend on his father, thus becoming a crutch for Tiger throughout his life and preventing Tiger from ever standing on his own.

Through their "special" father and son relationship, which had been carefully and purposefully orchestrated by Earl, an extremely close and very special bond was formed between Earl and Tiger. And from that bond, a lifetime of endless love, trust and respect ensued. Because of this connection, Earl and Tiger were able to talk to each other about absolutely anything and everything, never fearing judgment or resentment from the other. Tiger never had the need to hide anything from his father as he was always confident that he could discuss all facets of his life with Earl, thus creating their special and insightful father and son talks. It was so strange how Earl actually believed and even stated that:

"I have become such an important part of Tiger's life, that through our father and son talks, I have become part of Tiger's conscience and Tiger will always feed off of my mere presence. Tiger will be a better person with me in his life."

There were many occasions when I was able to witness Earl and Tiger's father and son's talks. One particular conversation I remember was regarding an incident that occurred while Tiger was playing in a Junior World championship. When Tiger was much younger, he was still quite small for his age and many of his competitors were somewhat bigger than him and during many of the tournaments, the other players were simply older. Of course, from the time Tiger turned ten years old, he was usually playing in the next age bracket because his talent and ability far exceeded the others in his own age group.

During this one particular tournament, Tiger was playing a match with a boy who was almost six feet tall and weighed close to one hundred and eighty pounds. Tiger told his father that he was afraid of him because he was really big. Since Tiger had already beat the boy in match play, Earl tried to convince Tiger that size has absolutely nothing to do with one's ability to play golf and just because he might be bigger, it does not make him better. This was when Earl reminded Tiger about all of the adults he had played with, so size shouldn't matter. But to Tiger, size did matter. He explained to his father that those adults weren't playing in a tournament nor were they his age. Tiger was really bummed out because he always wanted and expected to win. Then Earl's next comment was cut and dry. He told Tiger, "Since you are so good and I have trained you so well, you will always be better than everyone else you play against. You never have to worry about someone's stature or feel intimidated by anyone for any reason."

This sounded more like Earl's ego talking rather than giving soothing advice to his son. However, this incident, along with a few others, helped Tiger learn at a very young age not to be afraid or nervous simply because of the way someone else looks. Tiger learned that size does not determine a winner and this helped Tiger to grow up with less fear toward others. Over the years, and as Tiger matured, he was able to gain tremendous strength of mind, never again allowing himself to be intimidated by anyone.

As Tiger got older and was preparing to eventually play on the professional golf circuit, Earl felt it was necessary to pass on a few words of advice to his son about the professional world of golf. I remember when Earl decided to warn Tiger about the various women who would hang out around the golf courses during tournaments.

Earl tried to tactfully describe them as "golf groupies" who had only one main objective, and that was to meet and marry a rich golfer. He told Tiger these women are basically out to get your money and that is not a good thing. There are even people at the tournaments who would make the necessary connections and then introduce these women to the pro golfers. Earl explained how the women would walk around the course during the tournaments, check out all the players and then they would pick out the pro they wanted to meet. At this point, the "contact person" would make the required arrangements and the introduction between the "golf groupie" and the pro golfer would be made.

Earl told Tiger to avoid those women at all cost as he was too good for them. Earl explained how Tiger would have to be careful because some day he will be a star and he does not want to get mixed up in that kind of mess. Tiger listened with piqued interest as he was quite surprised to learn that golf groupies and the meeting process actually occurred at tournaments. After their talk, Tiger vowed to heed his father's words and advice.

Another father and son talk I recall was when Tiger asked Earl if fame would have any effect on his future with women. Tiger knew there might be a chance that some women would only be dating him because of his money and status, but he wanted to know if he would ever be able to tell the difference between those particular women and the ones who were truly sincere. He needed to know if he would be able to recognize if a woman is real or just after him for his money.

Earl told Tiger that unfortunately he would never really know for sure. He further explained that the problem with women is they will always say whatever they think you want hear, so it might be difficult to know if they are being truthful or feeding you a line of bull. Many women want to be a trophy wife and are out to marry only for the money and fame, and since he would definitely have both, Earl warned Tiger that he would always have to be extremely cautious whenever he dated any woman. Earl suggested to Tiger that he could try dating someone who was introduced to him by a close friend or someone he felt he could trust, but unfortunately, that too may not garner the results he would like. Earl continued to share with Tiger that, in all honesty, he will never really know for sure about any woman or their true intentions. Sadly, this would be the price he would have to pay for his fame and for being wealthy.

Since Earl and Tiger were always so close, Earl had a tendency to share almost everything with Tiger, including his thoughts on the subject of marriage, including both of his own. Since Earl's first marriage was a mistake caused by his youth and since he fell out of love soon after his second marriage to Tida began, Earl's opinion on the subject was never really positive in nature.

Throughout their frequent father and son talks, Earl felt confident Tiger would understand his parent's relationship and the fact that he did not love Tida, Tiger's mother. Over the years, I always wondered how Earl and Tida's relationship, rather the lack thereof, affected Tiger as he grew up. Of course, I always believed Earl should have shielded his young son from such personal information about himself, but Earl always claimed these talks would make him closer to Tiger.

But then I wondered how can a child grow up well adjusted when he knows his parents are only together because of his future potential in golf and not because they love each other or even him? I mean it would have to affect Tiger's values growing up and when he eventually got married himself. After all, the example Earl and Tida were setting for Tiger was not one based on true family values.

Sadly, because of his parent's loveless marriage and having been given this information, Tiger felt so much additional stress and pressure. Earl even admitted to me that Tiger thought that if he was more perfect and played better golf that maybe his parents might stay together. After all, Earl had always told Tiger that his parents would be separating the minute he turned pro. Imagine the pressures that were being placed on Tiger just because of his parents. Not only did he have his future career to consume him, but also the knowledge that someday his parent's marriage would come to an end.

Apparently, Earl was also comfortable and was able to speak quite freely with Tiger whenever they discussed women, especially when it came to the typical father and son "sex" talks. When Tiger was in his late teens, Earl tried to have another one of their little "sex talks". This was when Tiger told his father no thanks and that he would just go it alone from here on out and do it his way. When Earl shared this with me, he just laughed and proudly stated, "That's my boy!" He then commented that apparently Tiger no longer needed any coaching on that subject.

Frankly, this was way too much information for me, but it did make me wonder if either of them knew about each other's "habits"! Although they were close and were comfortable talking about everything, maybe this is a part of their personal lives they preferred not to share even with each other. After all, some secrets need to stay private.

Earl knew that because of the plans that had been made prior to Tiger becoming a professional golfer, and knowing he would be successful in winning tournaments, Tiger's life would forever be changed as he would now be more visible to the media. It would be an entirely different level of existence for Tiger.

Shortly before Tiger turned pro, Earl preached to Tiger to stay squeaky clean as he would always be in the public's eye and, unfortunately, his always being on display would be like living in a fishbowl. Earl explained to Tiger that in order to keep the public's respect and to be able to maintain his position in the golf world, staying on the straight and narrow would be an absolute necessity. He stressed to Tiger that there would always be someone out there who will try to find something on him in order to make him look bad.

Earl's advice was to never do anything that might give them any ammunition toward you or your family. Earl tried to express the importance of keeping his personal life and professional life separate, thus encouraging Tiger to safeguard his private life with total secrecy. Earl wanted to make sure Tiger understood that he needed to prevent the media from ever knowing anything about his personal life and that he needed to protect his golf image at all cost. Earl warned Tiger that he needed to be cautious as to who he talked to and what he says to people as not everyone could be trusted. Obviously, Tiger took what his father said so much to heart that he even named his one hundred and fifty-five foot yacht "Privacy".

A perfect example of his distrust occurred soon after he joined the PGA tour, when Tiger met and became friends with this one guy who was about the same age as himself. They were actually developing a friendship and Tiger was feeling comfortable sharing many aspects of his life with him. One day when they were meeting up and they were both sitting in Tiger's limousine, the guy started asking Tiger certain personal questions which soon made Tiger feel somewhat uncomfortable and a bit suspicious. After Tiger quizzed him as to why he was asking these questions, the guy reluctantly revealed that he was actually a reporter.

This really pissed Tiger off and the fact that he had allowed himself to be set up in such a way. From that day forward, Tiger never again allowed anyone to ever take advantage of him nor was he able to trust very many people after that incident. Tiger became ruthlessly cautious when it came to letting anyone ever get close to him again. Trust soon became a huge issue with Tiger and even continues to this day.

Of course, because of Earl's own ego and feelings of his own superiority and importance as the father of Tiger Woods, Earl had already created the "inner circle", known to many as the "Woods'

Camp". For Tiger and Earl's so-called protection and trust, only the chosen people were allowed in and if you said or did anything wrong, you were out.

An example of this was when Tiger fired his caddy, Fluff. I asked Earl what had happened to cause such an immediate action, especially since it had not been that long since I had read an article about Fluff in one of the major magazines. Earl explained to me that Fluff had become a little too "loose lipped" about Tiger's private life and was giving away far too much information to the wrong people, meaning the media. Earl's actual words were, "Fluff was flapping his damn gums to everyone. Just because he was Tiger's caddy, he thought he was hot shit."

Tiger's policy was if you work for him, you keep your mouth shut and say nothing. Apparently Fluff did not abide by the rules, so he was let go. And these rules hold true for anyone in Tiger's "camp". Earl further explained how each and every member of Tiger's inner group must keep absolutely everything a secret and reveal nothing to anyone. There are no exceptions to this rule. Trust and loyalty is crucial and means everything to Tiger. Over time, I realized how true this was and how many stories and secrets I, too, was forced to keep.

The same secrecy was basically true of Earl. He constantly cautioned members of his own personal staff and all employees of the Tiger Woods Foundation that loyalty to the Woods family was essential. Anyone caught talking to the media or anyone else for that matter, would be terminated immediately. Even though this sounded like paranoia, to Tiger and Earl it had just become a way of life.

But again, why? Why was it so important to Earl that he felt they had to keep so many secrets? Why did they feel the need to actually create the illusion that there may be secrets? Tiger was only a golfer and the illusion that he was someone important was simply created by his father, his agents and the media. Yes, Tiger is a great athlete but he certainly isn't the president of the United States or anyone else with such prominence, so why go to all of the trouble to create such a high profile status for him? Simply put, by creating this distinction, Tiger became more newsworthy and his sponsors sold a lot more products.

I remember this one conversation with Earl regarding Tiger's employees, including his agents. Earl stated, "Tiger thinks he can trust everyone in his camp, but what Tiger forgets is that everyone is greedy and they are only in it for the money. It is only a job to them and they are only looking out for themselves." Earl continued by saying, "Trust me, if those people weren't getting a slice of Tiger's earnings then they would never be there for Tiger and their loyalty would never exist."

Because of Earl's strong feelings on this subject, he was always skeptical about anyone, other than himself, having Tiger's best interest at heart. Earl stated, "And we are supposed to believe these people just because they say so?" Earl was unable to trust a lot of people and because of Earl's own paranoia and distrust, Tiger also became cautious when it came to people trying to get close to him.

Tiger experienced many new life lessons after he turned pro, both on and off the golf course. One particular story that Earl shared with me was the time when Tiger won the Masters again in

2005, beating out the defending champion, Phil Mickelson. Earl had called me immediately after Tiger won the tournament and after the green jacket ceremony was over. He said, "You won't believe what just happened when Mickelson put the green jacket on Tiger." Earl explained that Tiger had just called him with the news of what had just occurred while he and Phil were on television. Earl said that as Mickelson was putting the green jacket on Tiger, he whispered to Tiger in a very nasty tone, "You don't f_ _king deserve this. Next year, it's mine." Mickelson said it just close enough to Tiger's ear and soft enough so the microphones could not pick it up.

Earl and Tiger actually had a good laugh over it and felt it was just so childish of Mickelson to say such a thing, especially at that very moment. Of course, everyone knows there has never been any love lost between those two golfers and hasn't been for years.

It is a well-known fact that when Phil Mickelson came onto the professional golf scene, he was to be the new up and coming "chosen one", but unfortunately like so many other rookies who had preceded him, Mickelson did not perform to the standards that were expected of him. Then along came Tiger, who now was to be the new up and coming "chosen one", and Tiger did, in fact, come out and prove himself to be the best. According to Earl, this caused Phil to feel threatened and more animosity and resentment ensued between the two of them.

During Tiger's career on the pro circuit, there were many times when he was very sick, either with a high temperature, the flu, a serious cold or even an injury, but each time Tiger was determined to hide this information from the press. I know this to be true because I would be at Earl's house watching Tiger on television or I would be on the phone with Earl, at which time he would inform me of Tiger's illness or injury.

Even the media and the golf analysts were oblivious to what was happening with Tiger. In Tiger's upbringing and his in-depth training, Earl had taught Tiger to never let the media know he was ill or injured during any tournament as he felt it was a sign of weakness and vulnerability. Earl implored Tiger that he can never use anything as an excuse if he was playing poorly, especially since he knew the media would blow the facts totally out of proportion and possibly use it against him.

Over the years, Earl taught Tiger that he must always have the fortitude to play in any situation and to never use anything as an excuse, especially his health. From this, Earl had convinced Tiger that quitting was never an option, no matter the circumstances.

Thus, Tiger never revealed anything when it came to his own physical condition, just as Earl did in regard to the seriousness of his own illness in 2005, when we discovered his cancer had returned. It had become known that Earl was ill, but no one knew to what extent or the nature of his illness. Tiger chose not to reveal any additional information regarding his father, mainly because it was no one's business. Secondly, Earl had a fear that the media would have used his condition against Tiger should he have had a bad round of golf and blamed it for his poor play.

Fortunately, Tiger showed great strength and determination when he played in his first Masters tournament as a professional in 1997. Earl had only been out of the hospital for a little over two months after having open heart surgery. This was another medical incident involving his father that put additional mental stress on Tiger's ability to play golf. But Tiger proved to himself and to everyone else that he had the fortitude, ability and mindset to overcome the obstacles. Tiger was basically still a rookie since he hadn't been on tour that long, actually less than a year, but he still came out and won by a record breaking twelve strokes.

And, of course, Earl was there on the sidelines to witness the magical moment unfold. Although Earl was still recovering from his surgery, he was there on the eighteenth hole to witness his son fulfill his dream of winning his first major tournament, the Masters at Augusta. This was the very moment that was shared by father and son with the now famous hug.

It was through these years when Tiger learned to endure so much in his life. Unfortunately, Tiger never knew the detrimental effect his own father had on him and how much his life would be changed because of it.

8
TOUGH LESSONS

FROM AN EARLY AGE, Earl consistently protected Tiger when it came to racism. This was one topic that was discussed numerous times between father and son throughout Tiger's life, especially since it had been a distressing subject for Earl as he had endured a lifetime of prejudices and bigotry. Color should never have been an issue in anyone's lives, but unfortunately it was; and Earl and Tiger had to learn to tolerate such indifferences and cope with the results. Sadly, Tiger once made the statement, *"I don't want to be the best black golfer. I just want to be the best golfer."* There aren't very many golfers on tour that can make a statement like that, since their statement would only consist of, "I want to be the best golfer." It's such a shame that Tiger would be forced to add a preface to that comment with a statement about color.

There was this one particular father and son talk when Tiger asked his father, "What if I am not good enough or what if they don't like me because I am black?"

This had always been a very sensitive subject for Earl, but one that he answered with great pride and confidence. He told Tiger, "If you are perfect and you are the best, they will like you no matter the color of your skin."

Basically, Earl was telling Tiger that he "had" to be the best in order to be accepted. He was also telling Tiger, indirectly, that color did, in fact, matter.

Whether Earl's statement was right or wrong, I really don't know, but I did feel what Earl was telling his son would have a tremendous amount of additional pressure put on him, especially when he started out on the PGA tour as a rookie. Not only did Tiger have to cope with his playing ability as a rookie, but he also had to be concerned about what the people would think about his being black. It's too bad that Earl didn't let Tiger feel that he could be accepted for just being Tiger.

People became a fan of Tiger, first because of all the hype that came along with his coming out as a rookie and then because of his ability and great play. There was not as much of a color barrier when Tiger came on to the PGA tour. The majority of the golfing fans did not care if he was black, white, green or purple; they just wanted a winner, a true champion to root for. Even if Tiger had come out as just a struggling rookie golfer, not ever winning very many tournaments, I think he still would have been accepted. Tiger had the charisma and the fist pumping personality that people liked.

Because of Earl's over the top obsession for his son and his potential in golf, Earl had made the decision that he wanted Tiger to grow up and become a black role model in the world of golf and Earl's desire was discussed many times between father and son. As Tiger grew and his talent became more apparent, Earl tried to impress upon Tiger that he would eventually need to accept the responsibility and the position of a role model, and for the most part, to inspire all children in the world. During Earl and Tiger's many conversations on the subject, Earl had considered the possibility of having golf clinics and doing what they could to help children learn about and appreciate life through golf. Earl wanted Tiger to pass on Earl's own values to the world. After all, Earl believed he had so much to pass on to the entire world, so why not do it through his son. This was when Earl made the decision to create the Tiger Woods Foundation and later the Tiger Woods Learning Center, all to benefit children.

Over the years, and as Tiger got older, he felt obligated to go along with his father's wishes and accept that position, thus causing him to dedicate his life to being a great role model for everyone. I remember when Earl told me how Tiger had initially resisted his idea of creating a foundation and having Tiger be the role model. He explained how Tiger just wanted to play golf and not be bothered with anything else, especially a foundation. But over time and after quite a bit of convincing, Tiger eventually gave in and accepted his new challenge.

Unfortunately, not everyone was a Tiger fan, and soon after he turned pro, Tiger began to constantly get hate mail and death threats before and during each of the tournaments he was playing in. Earl was enraged that the threats were directed at Tiger and especially at his race. Tiger himself could not understand why someone would target him simply for playing golf. After all, there had been other African American members of the PGA, such as Lee Elder, Calvin Peete and Jim Thorpe, but Tiger was the first African American superstar. Then, of course, there is currently Vijay Singh who is from Fiji and is popular and respected on the tour.

When Tiger first went out on tour, he knew that he would have to fight some racism, but Earl was hopeful that because of Tiger's tremendous talent and abilities he would be able to break through the color barrier. At first, Tiger tried to ignore the threats, actually hoping they would eventually stop, but over time the threats had become more numerous and frequent and Tiger was forced to have security around him at all times. I had a difficult time understanding these threats, especially since there are thousands of African American athletes in this world, many of whom are great stars in their sports. Earl explained to me that unfortunately golf was different from the other sports. Sadly, discrimination still existed in golf and especially on many golf courses. However, Earl honestly believed that Tiger could make a difference and to the majority, he ultimately did.

In order to help alleviate the security problem, Earl even took it upon himself to contact the PGA and course officials alerting them to the fact that since the spectator crowds were increasing in numbers, the need for extra security on the tournament courses should be considered. Over time, security was beefed up at each tournament, especially for Tiger, who had become a fan favorite and garnered the largest following. The need for Tiger's personal body guard was no longer necessary due to the improved crowd control and the security that became present at each tournament course.

However, sadly, the hate mail and death threats continued, but at least Tiger finally reached a point where he could once again feel safe while playing on tour.

People have always questioned why Tiger blows through autograph lines or will not stop and talk to spectators or even give a high five on his way to the next hole. As Earl explained to me, they want to protect Tiger from getting too close to anyone fearing one of those hateful people could be lurking in the crowd and might harm Tiger. As Earl once put it, it's better to be safe than sorry.

Tiger continued to learn from his experiences in life, both before and after turning pro, and unfortunately he made a few mistakes along the way. But there was one experience that proved to be an extremely profitable decision.

Most people believe that Tiger decided to turn pro strictly because of the money Tiger would earn on the PGA tour and the endorsement deals he had signed with various sponsors. And then when Tiger made the decision to turn pro, Earl led people to believe that it was based solely on Tiger winning his third U.S. Amateur tournament and had absolutely nothing to do with the money. In fact, the decision to turn pro had already been made long before the tournament regardless of its outcome. According to Earl, the real story for Tiger turning pro was mainly because of an incident that occurred with the NCAA.

Earl told me that while Tiger was attending Stanford, he was invited by Arnold Palmer to join him for a casual dinner. There was absolutely no reason in the world for Tiger to turn down such an opportunity that was a completely harmless social meeting. But due to the fact that Tiger did not pay for his own dinner, the "powers that be" at Stanford and the NCAA saw this to be an unauthorized aid to a scholarship athlete and in violation of their rules. They blew the situation so far out of proportion that they were threatening to take away Tiger's scholarship.

Earl was so angry with the ludicrous accusations Stanford was making about his son that Earl decided to tell Tiger to walk away from Stanford and his future college degree and just join the pro circuit. Of course, it probably did not hurt their decision making process that Earl had already established a relationship and a commitment to have Tiger sign with a sports agent at IMG and from that commitment, several sponsors were waiting in line with extremely lucrative deals to sign Tiger up the minute he turned pro.

I remember back when Tiger made a huge mistake when he was supposed to play in the 1996 Buick Challenge, just a couple of months after he joined the PGA tour. The fact that Buick was not one of Tiger's major sponsors at the time meant that Tiger was committed to play in their tournament because of any sponsor relationship. Since Tiger was still new on the tour and he had claimed he was mentally and physically exhausted from his busy schedule, Tiger decided to simply withdraw from the tournament and go home. At this time, Earl was having some health problems stemming from a mild heart attack and his medical situation was weighing quite heavily on Tiger's mind. Everyone, including his father, questioned Tiger's decision to withdraw, especially since he was still a new rookie on the tour. Besides, how tired can a twenty year old get?

Then, to add insult to injury, Tiger made the decision not to attend the awards banquet that evening, which was being held in his honor. Tiger was to be presented the Fred Haskins Award for top collegiate athlete and since Tiger would not be attending, the entire banquet had to be cancelled. Needless to say, the supporters of the banquet were quite upset and so was Earl.

Earl felt that Tiger made a huge mistake by not attending the banquet, especially since it was for him. Then Earl told me that if he had not been ill, he would have been able to attend the tournament and be there to support Tiger. Of course, Earl knew things would have turned out entirely different since he would have been there to discuss the matter with Tiger and would have advised him on his choices. Earl would have understood Tiger not wanting to play, but he would have insisted that Tiger attend the banquet.

Once again, in Earl-like fashion, Earl took it upon himself to take care of the situation and try to pacify the very unhappy committee officials. Earl asked them to make other arrangements for Tiger to receive his award. The choices Tiger made during this situation showed that he was not quite ready to make decisions on his own without his father's advice and direction. This was a time when Tiger was trying to live his life his way, and without any interference from his father. Tiger's choice may not have been the best, but it was, after all, his choice to make. Earl should have supported Tiger in his decision instead of coming to his defense and feeling he had to clean up after his son's error in judgment.

Since Earl was always a constant in Tiger's life, Tiger found that he was relying on Earl for simply everything, especially when it came to helping him make decisions. Tiger depended on Earl's supposedly keen and astute advice on every matter involving his life and if he made a wrong decision, Earl was always there to correct it.

For as long as Tiger could remember, Earl had always been there for him. Earl had taken it upon himself to make all of the decisions and handle any and all problems that ever occurred. Over time, it had reached a point where Tiger was relying on his father for everything, not just in life, but definitely in his golf. Tiger was just so accustomed to having Earl around, and as an only child, Tiger had eventually become extremely dependent on the only person who had always been there for him; his father.

According to Earl, when Tiger joined the PGA tour, he found it difficult to make friends with the other golfers. Although I did not agree with his theory, Earl tried to convince me that the other golfers were simply jealous of Tiger since he already had so many accomplishments and records under his belt from his amateur career. After all, Tiger had just won his third straight U.S. Amateur at the age of twenty years old. Because of who Tiger was and because of all the media hype and coverage that was being given to him, Earl felt that the other professional golfers were feeling threatened by his eventual presence on the pro tour.

Earl had also told me that superstars such as Tiger do not hang out with regular golfers and this caused a problem for Tiger as a rookie. Tiger apparently did not feel like he fit in with the others and found himself making friends outside of the golfing arena, with such people as Michael Jordan and Ken Griffey, Jr. Again I questioned Tiger's feeling of non-acceptance, wondering if it was Tiger's huge ego and arrogance that was actually the issue with the other players. After all, it appeared that the majority of golf professionals on tour were just normal guys and were very likable, and all basically in the same position of trying to succeed. Tiger went out on the tour with an entirely different and "better than everyone else" attitude and maybe the other players just did not like it.

One has to understand the pressures Tiger was under as a rookie, especially since he was supposed be the next "chosen one"; the new Jack Nicklaus. But Tiger had one other pressure he had to deal with, the one that related to his color. It was Earl's hope that Tiger would eventually be able to change the perception of blacks in a white dominated sport. And Tiger did, in fact, change that perception in the minds of the majority of people. But initially Tiger still felt that he was not being accepted by his fellow golfers. The problem you have in golf is that it is not a team sport, so you do not have the same camaraderie that you would have on a football or baseball team. Golf is an individual sport and everyone is out for themselves. They only have one person to rely on when trying to succeed and win a tournament and that is themselves and no one else.

So, trying to form a friendship with other golfers on tour can prove to be quite challenging. Yes, they are cordial and congenial with one another while on the course, but becoming close friends does not occur very often. Many of them tend to live in different parts of the country and most likely only see each other at an occasional tournament. And when at a tournament, each golfer is so consumed with their own game that there is not much time to be social.

Tiger had to learn the many lessons about being a rookie in a professional environment, many of which were different from the tournaments he was accustomed to participating in, such as the amateurs. Tiger was now playing with the big boys and he soon realized that he had to learn their way and abide by the many unwritten social rules. Eventually Tiger adjusted and over time found himself accepted.

After Tiger became a proven winner, one adjustment Tiger reluctantly agreed to was allowing himself to be transformed from the person he used to be, especially when it came to his signature fist pump. Fans loved Tiger's enthusiastic gesture because that showed who Tiger really was and they always looked forward to each and every time he would use it. The gallery would get so worked up right along with Tiger. According to Earl, Tiger's agents advised him that his fist pump was not good for his image. So in order to portray a new and improved image, and one which was better suited for that of a champion, Tiger stopped using that expression of excitement and accomplishment after a great shot. It was obvious that none of Tiger's "image makers" cared what the fans wanted, proving that Tiger's newly created image was more important. However, Tiger would soon learn that some of the changes he made and the way he acted were not always for the best.

After settling into the professional golf world, Tiger found there was more to being a golfer than simply playing golf and winning tournaments. Tiger now had sponsors. These were very large companies who were paying him a tremendous amount of money to promote their products, and not just by wearing a label on his shirt or hat for the world to see. Each of these sponsors wanted a full time commitment from Tiger and in return they would pay him handsomely.

What did this mean to Tiger? It meant that in between his already busy golf schedule, he would now have to squeeze in photo shoots, commercials and make personal appearances in order to represent the various sponsor's products or their name. Making a commercial can be quite time consuming and when you have a schedule such as Tiger's, it becomes difficult to find the necessary time to honor those sponsor commitments. Then Tiger had the Tiger Woods Foundation, which also required a great deal of his time. This included many personal appearances, special golf tournaments, various functions and golf clinics that could occur anywhere in the United States.

Being a young man, Tiger found that his life was now being dictated and controlled by everyone else but him. Everyone was telling him what to do and when to do it, and over time, Tiger would find that having a few moments to himself would become a true luxury and many times it was simply impossible. The lessons Tiger learned in the world of golf would be numerous, but for the next several years, it appeared that he was successful in adapting to his new environment and the life that surrounded it. However, one might wonder how long he would be able to survive all of these pressures and having so many aspects of his life controlled by others.

Earl was the one person who was instrumental in helping Tiger to learn the many lessons in life and in golf. Although his lessons started as a small child, Earl continued teaching Tiger as he grew into adulthood, including after he had become a professional golfer. Earl's philosophy was that you never stop teaching because there is always something new to learn.

When it came to Tiger's game, Earl always believed that he was the driving force behind Tiger. He had always been Tiger's active teacher and coach for most of Tiger's life and it was Earl's sole focus to make Tiger into a professional golfer.

However, after Tiger joined the pro circuit, those positions dwindled for Earl, as he had now been replaced with professional coaches. Tiger once again had to adjust as he began to learn new things from new people in his life. There was now an agent from IMG. There were publicists, sponsors, a new swing coach and at one point, even a new caddy. All of these people were giving their own input into how Tiger should act, what he should do and how he should play his game. Tiger's realm of teachers had expanded as he grew into manhood and excelled as a professional golfer.

During this time, Earl's focus turned to Tiger's legacy, which included the foundation, creating tournaments in Tiger's name and ones to benefit the foundation, and making a shrine of the house he lived in, which was where Tiger had been raised. Although Earl's attention was given to other endeavors involving Tiger, Earl still maintained control of Tiger's life and career by handling the business side of Tiger's fortune and remaining his mentor and confidant. Most of all, Earl would always retain the title of father.

One thing I always admired about Earl and Tiger was the special connection they shared. In all the years, I never knew one time when Earl and Tiger were angry with one another. However, if one of them just happened to be upset over a particular matter, either one of them felt comfortable enough to bring the issue to the table for discussion. Earl and Tiger were very open with one another and anger just did not fit into their makeup as father and son. I do remember a couple of times, however, when Earl would tell me, "Yep, Tiger's mad at me again." Of course, I knew that Earl was kidding, as it was a running joke between the two of us whenever we discussed Tiger or my daughter. Earl would say the same thing about his other three children, and usually in jest.

I would jokingly ask Earl, "What did you do this time? Do you want me to call Tiger and set him straight?"

Earl would always respond with, "No, no, it's okay. He's just being a knucklehead again." We would just laugh because none of it was ever taken seriously. Although Tiger may not have actually been angry with Earl, there were times when Tiger did not agree with Earl's thinking or advice, and even times when he wasn't happy with some of the comments Earl had made publicly. But out of respect for his father, Tiger would not get angry with Earl. Besides, Tiger had been raised with Earl's strict military mentality, which meant you do not argue or disagree with your superior.

There were times when I believed Tiger was forced to conceal his true feelings since he was never comfortable in contradicting anything his father said or did. In later years, Tiger even found himself actually defending some of his father's actions. I knew Tiger loved his father so much that he felt a tremendous obligation to always abide by his father's wishes, demands, advice and recommendations, almost as though he was trying to placate his father. Over the years, there were times when Tiger attempted to rebel against his father's constant involvement, but obviously it was also Tiger who still had the need to keep his father close in all respects of his life.

Although Earl knew he would always remain an important part of Tiger's life and career as his father, he also knew his son had grown up. Tiger was no longer the little boy who had spent so much time with him, playing golf, sharing in talks, and enjoying their time together. The two of them had always been inseparable, especially when it came to golf, but now Earl knew a distance would exist between them and their time together would never be the same. Even though his position had changed dramatically, Earl was still able to stay strong and never let Tiger know how lost he truly felt. Earl would only show his love and pride for a son who had become a man.

The most difficult lesson in life which Tiger had to learn was during Earl's illness and again after his death. Tiger was forced to live his life without his father, the one single person who he had always trusted and relied on for almost everything, including guidance and direction. Tiger was now on his own, only trusting business associates who were once strangers to him. Tiger would find himself once again in a position where he would have to make choices, and unfortunately, he made some very bad ones, ignoring how it would affect his professional career and his personal life.

At that point in Tiger's life, he had reached a state of mind where he now believed that he was invincible and above it all and never felt his decisions, no matter how wrong they might be, would have any effect on him. After all, he is Tiger Woods. Sadly, these were the traits that had been instilled in Tiger by his father ever since he was a kid. Earl never realized that Tiger might have been affected emotionally by creating such a dependency and controlling so much of his life. Earl and Tiger thought it was love, but in reality, was it actually an obsession on Earl's part that possibly hampered a child's growth into adulthood?

Many of his life lessons were tough for Tiger to go through, but they were simply part of the learning and growing process. We all have to learn from our own experiences in life, by handling the problems that are presented to us and suffering through the consequences that were created by our choices. Then we just have to move on.

Unfortunately, this is just part of life.

9
BIG CHANGES FOR TIGER

IN THE EARLY YEARS before Tiger turned professional and experienced an extraordinary life and status change, Tiger and Earl were just regular middle class people who lived very normal and average lives. When Tiger was young, he was a smart yet shy kid who had an incredible talent for golf, but who also possessed tremendous determination and drive along with the ability to truly focus on his long range goals and dreams. In his private life, Tiger was a great student, usually being on the honor roll, thus proving that he could excel in just about anything he would attempt. He excelled in other sports, such as baseball and track, but golf was always his first passion. Tiger could be smug and even cocky at times, showing signs of an arrogant and self-righteous attitude, often displaying his ongoing moodiness. Unfortunately, Tiger was not a normal everyday kid, especially when it came to his golf.

Tiger's goal was to become a professional golfer, however, it was understood that his dream would not become a reality until he graduated from college. Earl and Tida expected their son to be fully educated before entering the professional world of golf. Since he was an incredible student throughout his school years, four years of college would be a breeze for him. However, making the choice to attend college was a difficult one for Tiger. Since he was a multiple Junior U.S. Amateur champion while still in high school, scholarship offers were pouring in from all over the United States. Still, Tiger was anxious to play pro golf and truly wondered if it was his time to take the risk and turn professional and play on the PGA tour.

Although Earl was Tiger's constant advisor throughout his life, Earl also controlled and made all of the decisions pertaining to Tiger. And there was one decision Earl was quite adamant about. Tiger had to go to college. Although Tiger had already accepted the fact that college would come first, he still wanted to do something on his own and make his own decisions when it came to selecting the college he would attend. Even though Tiger was somewhat young and still in high school, he soon realized choosing the right college would probably be one of the most difficult decisions he would have to make on his own and he wanted to make sure that he made the right choice.

Due to his exceptional golfing talents and his amateur record, Tiger had been recruited by several colleges offering him a full athletic scholarship, but after much thought and taking into consideration what each college had to offer, he, along with his father's help, was able to narrow down his choices to Stanford University in Northern California and the University of Nevada at Las Vegas.

Since Earl had always been involved in any decision making concerning Tiger, I was extremely surprised when Earl told me he chose not to accompany Tiger on his recruiting trips and he was allowing Tiger to travel to each college by himself. This was totally out of character for Earl since he had always tried to control everything in Tiger's life.

Understanding my skepticism with regard to his actions, Earl then explained that although Tiger was allowed to check out each college and determine which one he preferred to attend, it would most definitely be dad and mom who would eventually have the final say about Tiger's choice.

As an excuse for letting him go alone, Earl tried to use Tiger's age and the fact that he felt it was important for Tiger to start making some decisions on his own. But the problem was that I knew Earl was such a control freak when it came to anything pertaining to Tiger's life that it would be almost impossible for Earl to ever let go and completely step back and allow Tiger the freedom to do what he wanted without his father's involvement. It was almost as though Earl feared Tiger would make the wrong choices, even though he knew his son was intelligent. After all, he raised Tiger and knew his capabilities. Besides, most every choice Tiger made was usually based on the advice and recommendation given to him by his father.

Simply put, Earl needed to be a constant and integral part of Tiger's life, and as his father, he would be the one to decide what was best for his son. After discussing his choices with his father and mother, and after listening to their opinions, objections and recommendations, Tiger ultimately chose Stanford University. However, after a couple years of attending Stanford and due to several incidents and hassles involving the NCAA, Tiger would eventually realize that the choice he had made would become somewhat questionable.

Of course, I often wondered why Tiger chose Stanford, especially since there were several well-known universities with distinguished golf programs in Southern California, all being in very close proximity to his home in Cypress. In addition, the weather in Southern California was more conducive to playing golf compared to the cold and rainy Northern California area. Then I thought that just maybe Tiger may have wanted to move away from his family to finally be on his own and allow himself some much needed freedom. If that was the case, then I honestly could not blame Tiger for making the decision to attend Stanford.

Although Tiger did not fulfill his parent's wishes by finishing college and earning his college degree, Tiger did attain his goal by becoming a professional golfer. In doing so, Tiger reached all new levels in the sport, causing him to become extremely popular among the fans. Even though Tiger had become the richest golfer in the history of the sport, there was a part of the old Tiger who still existed, a side of himself that he rarely showed in public. Unlike the way he grew up and his years at Stanford, due to his new wealth, Tiger was now a big high profile celebrity who was living a lavish lifestyle, with huge mansions, private jets, a one hundred and fifty-five foot multi-million dollar mega yacht, and traveling all over the world. Tiger was still young, so having fun and hanging out, partying and gambling in Las Vegas and the Bahamas, among other places, was just the norm for a single rich guy.

However, in private there was still a part of the old Tiger who still enjoyed his video games, cave diving and just hanging with his friends. But when it came to his video games, Tiger had become so hooked that he would play every chance he got. To him, playing his video games was a tremendous source of relaxation and a form of competition.

I remember when Tiger was living in his Florida corporate condo and he realized that he needed more space to house his video games. It wasn't long before Tiger decided to purchase his first house. After discussing it with Earl, Tiger chose a very large house, but he just didn't feel it was big enough for his gaming area. So Tiger decided to have the house totally renovated, even tearing out the walls in a couple of the rooms to make one large game room that was strictly for his video games. This new area in Tiger's home became his sanctuary; his own private place for solitude.

Another big change for Tiger was adapting a persona for the public. Since the private side of Tiger and Earl were completely different than the personas they seemed to always be portraying for the public, not many people, other than his family and a few close friends, actually knew the real Tiger and Earl. The problem was that they were always cautious as to whom they chose to be close to and most people were simply not part of that chosen group.

Although I knew that some of their old values and behaviors still existed in their private lives, I just assumed Tiger and Earl were simply showing a new and different side to themselves in order to look more important and to impress the public and the media with their new wealth and fame. For example, Tiger, like his father, would portray one side of himself when in the public's eye or when the camera was on, and present a totally different side when he could relax and be himself.

When interviewed after a tournament or giving a press conference, Tiger would come across as confident, stoic and reserved, carefully choosing his words. Yet when I listened to the way he talked with his father about the same tournament, Tiger would be more relaxed, judgmental and self-criticizing. When in private, the arrogance that Tiger usually demonstrated on the course gave way to his frustrations and insecurities at never being able to achieve the perfection he required of himself. Tiger knew when to be his real self and when to switch gears into superstar mode for the benefit of the camera or media. After all, thanks to his father, Tiger had unwillingly been subjected to the media all of his life and was trained accordingly.

Unfortunately, the person who Tiger portrays in public is one that had been created for him shortly after he became a professional golfer and would soon be described as his "image". Of course, it was supposedly the new and improved version, created just for Tiger and his new role in life. The fun loving, outspoken, and fearless competitor who came out as a rookie with his signature fist pump would soon be molded into a completely different person, one who was supposedly better suited for that new image. Tiger was now doing and saying what everyone else expected of him. In public, Tiger had a role that he was forced to play, whether on or off the course, however, in private, he could simply be himself and many times craved those precious moments where he could find solace away from the public eye.

After seeing Tiger's new transformation, I questioned why he just couldn't be the same person in public that he was in private. Why does he have to be somebody he's not? Why does Tiger have to act so differently just because he is in front of the camera?

I even went so far as to ask Earl these same questions, and he responded by explaining that Tiger was the one who never really wanted all the hype and publicity as he just wanted to go out on tour and play golf and, of course, win tournaments. However, because of Tiger's ambitions to simply play golf, it was necessary for someone else to take charge and change his direction in order to create long term popularity and prosperity for Tiger's future. Earl said he knew the day would come when Tiger would become a champion, and he also knew that a champion must be different than the other players. According to Earl, he and Tiger's agents redirected Tiger's thinking and created a persona and direction that would be more fitting for a champion.

I finally understood that it was Earl and Tiger's agents, who were instrumental in shaping this new path for Tiger's future. They all believed they knew what was best and they had insisted that Tiger abide by their recommendations and changes. Since the new agents were experts in the field of establishing and promoting images, Earl convinced Tiger that in order for him to accomplish everything that had been planned out for him by his agents, it would be necessary for him to make the recommended changes. Earl also assured Tiger the eventual outcome would be profitable and most definitely be well worth it.

According to Earl, Tiger reluctantly concurred and decided to go along with their plans, but in his heart, Tiger objected. Earl insisted that down the road Tiger would learn to appreciate their decisions and the ultimate results. When all was said and done, I often wondered if Tiger ever truly accepted the prescribed changes and could that be the reason why we see so much frustration, almost like a form of resistance, coming from him.

Unfortunately, when away from the cameras, Tiger was still extremely dependent on Earl's support and advice, much of which came from their close bond and their father and son talks. As Tiger grew up, their special talks were constant, giving opinions and advice or simply sharing their feelings and thoughts. I knew how important these talks were to his son and how Tiger grew up always trusting and relying on the contents and memories of their many conversations.

From these many discussions between father and son, Tiger not only gained tremendous trust in his father, but he was also taught the many values that he would eventually carry through life. These were the times in which Earl would teach Tiger about making choices in his life and how to ultimately make his decisions correctly. Earl knew where Tiger's career might be heading and he also knew Tiger's life would be a road full of many twists and turns, so Earl was concerned about preparing Tiger for all of the crossroads he might eventually encounter.

Because of the many guidelines that were set by his parents throughout his life, Tiger always tried his best to never disappoint them, and especially his father. I remember on several occasions when Earl would remind Tiger that no matter what he did in life, his parents would never be disappointed in him. It was important to Earl that Tiger grow up to be secure in the knowledge that whatever he did, they would always support him.

However, not long after Tiger turned professional and his career and popularity had escalated to unforeseen levels, Earl revised his statement by strongly asserting that if Tiger ever did anything wrong, the entire Woods' family would be negatively affected and the results would ultimately cause Earl and Tida to be extremely disappointed in him. Tiger's parents actually believed that they were now very important people because the rich and famous Tiger Woods was their son. They did not want to be embarrassed by anything Tiger did or said as though everything was now about them.

I guess it's a good thing that Tiger's affairs happened after Earl died. Now that would have been disappointing to Earl. But, of course, Tida was there front and center to voice her own disappointment in her son, although publicly giving the illusion that she was showing her staunch support.

10
YOU OWE ME

TIGER WAS VERY BLESSED because never once in his entire life did he ever have to experience any financial problems. Tiger was a millionaire at the age of twenty years old. Prior to attaining his tremendous fortune, he had always been supported by his parents and he even attended college on a full athletic scholarship. In a way, Tiger was fortunate he never had to encounter a normal life of pinching pennies.

However, when Tiger was growing up and before he turned professional and instantly becoming a multi-millionaire, Earl did encounter a few minor financial difficulties. Raising a child to excel in a particular sport and eventually become a sports figure can be financially challenging at times. During the early years when Tiger participated in junior and amateur tournaments, Earl found there were times that his modest income would barely stretch to cover the extra incidentals created by Tiger's golf. Many of the extra expenses included tournament fees, green fees, equipment, the hiring of instructors, and travel expenses. Since Earl and Tiger would have to drive to some of the out of town tournaments, they were forced to stay in inexpensive motels and keep on a tight budget. However, the costs increased greatly when Tiger chose to play in the tournaments that were farther from home as this now required the additional costs of both airfare and rental cars.

Earl and Tida had made a commitment to Tiger and to each other to do whatever was necessary to finance Tiger's golf, even if this meant they would have to budget their money differently in order to accommodate Tiger's expenses. They chose to put Tiger's golf needs and outlays ahead of their own needs and wants in life and they were satisfied with their decision, never once doubting the choices they had made. According to Earl, they were doing it for Tiger, as well as for themselves, knowing that some day they would benefit financially from their efforts and sacrifices.

Over the years, Earl made sure Tiger was aware of the fact that once he turned professional, he would take care of his debt to them by taking care of his parents financially. In Earl's mind, Tiger owed them for what they had sacrificed for their son. Of course, while doing so much for Tiger and his golf, Earl was once again putting himself in the spotlight and living vicariously through his son's talent, knowing full well that someday he, too, would become important and wealthy.

While attending all of Tiger's tournaments, it had become a ritual between Earl and Tiger to always take the time each night to have one of their father and son talks. What was unique about Tiger and Earl was they could talk about anything and everything, and not necessarily always talking about golf. This father and son were so extremely close they were very comfortable in sharing absolutely any topic with each other. Of course, many of their talks included the outcome of that day's round and the upcoming round, with Earl voicing his concerns and formulating a plan for Tiger's next day's play.

Earl would always share everything with Tiger during their talks, especially things about his and Tida's financial situation. Frankly, I think this topic should not be shared with children, but Earl thought otherwise. But, of course, Earl had a future agenda, so he wanted to make sure Tiger was aware of the circumstances surrounding the cost of his golf. It was almost like Earl was placing a guilt trip on Tiger, and at times even exaggerating the actual facts of their situation.

Knowing this information, Tiger was aware that his playing golf was causing a financial burden for his parents and many times Tiger just wanted to know if his golf was always going to be a financial struggle. Tiger was also feeling somewhat guilty that his parents were willing to sacrifice so much for him, although he had been made aware that someday he would have to take care of his debt.

I remember the time Earl told me about one of their earlier father and son talks. Earl explained how Tiger was so concerned about the fact they would always have to stay in the budget motels and drive to each tournament. Tiger had asked Earl if it was always going to be like this.

Earl explained to Tiger that someday everything would get better, but for now they just had to make the best of it. Earl confided in me as to just how much Tiger's questions really bothered him. He was doing the best he could for Tiger although he always wished he could have done so much more for him. Unfortunately, Earl was never able to get in a position to do it differently.

When Tiger was growing up, Earl was not a rich man, but he did have sufficient income, a military pension and savings to cover all their bills including Tiger's necessities in golf. Earl just did not have very much left over to enjoy family vacations and other extras.

Earl shared his feelings with me and I assured him that Tiger understood the situation and appreciated everything he was doing and many times Earl agreed. Earl had reminded me how, in the long run, he would not have to worry because he knew his efforts would someday pay off for him, especially when Tiger finally turned professional and played on the PGA tour. Thinking back to our many conversations, I often wondered if Earl was doing all this for Tiger or to benefit himself.

Earl continued to carry the additional financial obligations of Tiger's golf into the years of his playing in Junior Amateur and the U.S. Amateur tournaments. The costs Earl incurred increased as Tiger progressed into more demanding tournaments, including his participation in several of the PGA tour events as an amateur, such as the Los Angeles Open, which was held at the Riviera

Country Club. There were other tournaments that Tiger played in, but this was the first one that would require that he have a professional caddy.

Unfortunately, Earl discovered it would be quite expensive to hire a caddy and it was money Earl just did not have at the time. Earl knew this opportunity to play in a PGA tour event was very important to Tiger and since he never wanted to disappoint his son, Earl called me and asked if he could borrow one thousand dollars to pay for Tiger's caddy.

Trust me when I say back then Earl was a proud man and it was extremely difficult for him to ask me for the money, especially since it was such a large amount. But Earl was comfortable in knowing I would never think less of him simply because he was asking for my help. Without any hesitation, I loaned Earl the money, especially since I knew it was for Tiger. Earl also took great pride in making sure the loan was repaid in a very short period of time.

Tiger was always aware of his family's financial situation, as Earl was never shy about sharing everything with his son. Luckily for Earl, the problems with money were never really severe as he always had enough money to cover everything. However, Earl did his best to convince Tiger not to worry about the financial matters and that it was Tiger's job to simply play golf, thus trying to create a worry free environment for his son. But Earl told me that Tiger still felt the stress and suffered some guilt from the family's sacrifices. I think the financial information Earl shared with Tiger growing up eventually caused Tiger's feeling of obligation as he got older.

Personally knowing what Earl and Tida went through for him in order to excel in golf, I feel Tiger felt responsible, and from that, he gained even more determination to become the best. It was now his goal to eventually be in a position where he could repay his parents for everything they had done for him throughout his life. As it turned out, Earl helped himself to Tiger's money, guaranteeing his own financial security.

Tiger always knew when he turned pro it would be his responsibility to support his mother. Earl had primed Tiger for this mission for many years. What Earl did not tell Tiger was that he would also be supporting his father, but in a less direct way than his mother.

Earl's need for fame and recognition was always apparent. However, over the years prior to Tiger turning pro, Earl disguised his true desires for wealth from his unsuspecting son, which was to elevate his own wealth, status and personal lifestyle. As Tiger got older and the prospect of his professional golf career grew closer, Earl eventually made his expectations known to his son. This was another form of pressure Earl chose to place on Tiger's young shoulders, not to mention his calculated manipulation of his son.

After Tiger turned professional and began to share his wealth with his parents, Earl once told me the money he received from Tiger was actually put into the form of a salary from Tiger's corporation to the tune of a couple million dollars. After all, at the time, he had the title of president and he was controlling Tiger's career and Tiger's earnings. In reality, Earl was simply a figurehead with very little responsible, especially since Tiger's corporation was originally set up for the sole purpose of taxes and shielding all of Tiger's personal assets. Earl also received a substantial amount of money from the Tiger Woods Foundation and from the sale of his books, although much of the royalties went directly to the foundation. In actuality, Tiger was Earl's main source of income, because Tiger was giving Earl the money, just as he was giving money to his mother.

But, of course, Tiger was only doing was he had been told to do early on in his life.

Earl explained how he wanted to feel like he was earning the money himself, so he took a position and was given a title in the corporation that he had the attorneys set up for Tiger. At this point, Earl had become a multi-millionaire, thanks to Tiger, but Earl was still convinced he was earning his share of the money. This entitled Earl to feel it was his own money and he could do or act however he pleased, including causing others to be impressed with his new wealth.

I remember when Earl told me about the time he had played a round of golf at the Navy Golf Course and afterwards he met with some of the old golfing regulars in the clubhouse. They were asking him how it felt to be a millionaire and Earl cockily snapped back at them and bragged that he was not just a millionaire, as he was now a millionaire several times over. None of the men said a word, but their expressions said it all. Earl was not pleased with their reactions to his statement and told me the guys obviously did not appreciate his candor. Gee, Earl, ya think? Apparently, they, too, did not feel he was the same old Earl they used to know and liked years before.

One of the many times when Earl and I were in Las Vegas, I remember this one night after Earl had lost all of his money at the blackjack tables and he and I were walking down the hallway to his suite at the Mandalay Bay Hotel and Casino. Out of the blue, Earl asked me, in a very arrogant and superior tone, "Don't you just love being here with a millionaire?"

I just turned and stared at him in complete shock, thinking why in the world Earl would ask such a question, especially to me. The problem I had was I just never thought of Earl in that way. After all, I was there to be with Earl, not a millionaire, especially since I had known and accepted him for so many years and long before his wealth. So, I just snapped back at him and said, "I guess it's better than when you didn't have a pot to piss in." Then he just stared at me in astonishment. Touché!

However, the part about the money that I could not understand was the way Earl personally treated it and how he acted regarding it. The old Earl I knew was somewhat conservative and was very careful with his spending. The "new" Earl seemed to flaunt it a lot more and use it to appear important. Sometimes I believed that since Earl came from a modest background, he just did not know how to act appropriately with his new wealth.

Obviously, Earl was also conflicted, not knowing at times how he should really use his money or even how he should act because of it. When he was in Las Vegas, I noticed how Earl had a tendency to get into his "role playing" as the public image of Earl who now had wealth and status. It was almost as though his losing a large amount of money at the gaming tables was simply for show, and a part of the role he felt he had to play. After all, Tiger was very wealthy and gambled quite often. So according to Earl, he, too, had the right to be just as important as Tiger and flaunt his money accordingly. Sadly, Earl acted this way in most every aspect of his life.

Then again, it wasn't really his money, now was it?

11

SEDUCED BY WEALTH AND FAME

SINCE I HAD KNOWN Tiger and Earl for many years, I knew the people they were before and after Tiger's acquired fame and wealth. Back then, Tiger and Earl used to be just ordinary people. Earl was a hardworking, middle class man who supported his family and lived in a modest tract home in an average, yet respectable, area of town. Tida, Tiger's mother, was a housewife and a devoted Thai mother, dedicating her life to raising her son. Prior to his civilian life, Earl had spent twenty years in the military as an officer with a couple of tours of duty overseas. This was a normal family who had typical financial struggles as they made the necessary sacrifices in order to finance Tiger's sport. The Woods' family was your average middle class Americans.

Not long after Tiger joined the PGA tour, his popularity grew throughout the world, and he had not only become a golfing sensation, but Tiger also became an international celebrity. Along with his many golfing achievements, Tiger also acquired extremely lucrative endorsements from several new sponsors, all of which was in addition to the money he earned for his tournament wins on tour.

Technically, Tiger already had contracts lined up for millions of dollars the moment he held his press conference in 1996 and stated the words, "Hello World", at which time he announced that he was turning pro.

The money that Tiger's new sponsors were offering was not an amount that would simply provide Tiger and his family with a financially secure lifestyle. We are talking about an extraordinarily large sum of money, to the tune of well over forty million dollars. And it would be this money that would instantly change Tiger, Earl and Tida's lives forever.

Unfortunately, this money would not only change their lives, but it would also affect almost every aspect of who they used to be and who they would become as they allowed the money and fame to alter their lives. Tiger, Earl, and even Tida, would no longer be the average middle class Americans, formerly known as just the Woods' family who lived down the street.

Once Tiger had money, his life changed dramatically, literally overnight. As for Earl and Tida, their instant wealth simply came from their son's success and fortune. However, over a short period of time, I noticed some serious changes in their personalities and attitudes and most definitely in the way they lived their lives.

At one point, I began to wonder where these changes were coming from and why they were allowing themselves to be transformed so completely by the money Tiger was earning. After all, the Tiger and Earl I knew would never allow such changes to occur. At least that's what I thought.

I am sorry to say that I was wrong and these people who I thought I knew so well began changing right before my very eyes. Their actions made me think about all their money and how was it possible that someone suddenly learns to handle such immediate wealth. I mean one day they were struggling to make ends meet and the next day they literally had an amount of money that was beyond their wildest dreams. Then I wondered if it was too much too soon. Tiger, Earl and Tida just did not know how to handle all that money and make a smoother transition to their new position in life.

Yes, it was wonderful this incredible opportunity presented itself to Tiger, especially after the many years of hard work and dedication he spent toward achieving his goal as a professional golfer. He was very fortunate there were sponsors out there who chose to take a chance on him and offered him such lucrative contracts, considering his lack of presence in the professional arena. After all, not all athletes who have gone through the same struggles in their lives as Tiger did are offered such an amazing opportunity.

After seeing the changes in Tiger, and even in Earl, I was hoping things would be different with them and they would remain the same people they had always been prior to Tiger's new success and wealth. I guess that was just too much to ask for since apparently anybody and everybody can and will be swayed and seduced by what money has to offer and Tiger, Earl and Tida were no different.

Why do I include Earl's name in this discussion, especially since it was Tiger who was the super star and the person who earned the money? Mainly, because Earl also gained tremendous wealth simply by being the father of Tiger Woods, just the same as Tiger's mother. Tiger gave his father money which elevated Earl's own financial status, taking him from a struggling ex-military man turned civilian to an extremely wealthy and financially secure multi-millionaire. Earl had a position within Tiger's corporation, but it was still Tiger's money from that corporation that was given to Earl. It came down to the fact that if Tiger had not been as successful, Earl would not have had the wealth which had been provided to him.

Not only did Tiger allow his wealth and his new status in the celebrity world to drastically change him, but Earl, too, felt it was necessary to change himself and his life accordingly. After all, he was the father of Tiger Woods and he not only believed he had earned it, but that he also deserved it. Just imagine how Tiger felt. Not only was he supporting himself, but now he was put in a position where he had to support both of his parents and, sadly, they expected it from their son.

I remember a conversation I had with Earl regarding Tiger supporting him financially. Earl bluntly stated, "Hell, yes, Tiger owes me. He wouldn't be where he is today if it weren't for me. Look, Linda, I raised him, taught him how to play golf and sacrificed a lot of time and money to make him the best. So, do I feel I deserve his money? Damn straight I do. And Tiger feels the same way on the subject. We have always had an understanding. He makes it big and he takes care of us. Call it back pay or just loving your parents, but Tiger felt obligated." But the question is, who exactly made Tiger feel obligated?

With Tiger's tremendous new wealth and fame came Earl and Tiger's thinking that their money and status would give them the right to change and to elevate themselves above the other regular people in this world. All of a sudden they believed they could act superior to everyone. It didn't matter where Tiger and Earl came from or what their background was. Just because they now had money, they were now instantly better than everyone else. One day they were normal, everyday, average people, being part of the regular society and the next day they were no longer a part of that class, simply because their new found money had upgraded them to a new and higher social level.

And because of their money, Tiger, Earl and Tida believed they were better than their former class of friends. Since Tiger was now rich and he was now famous, the Woods' family was no longer just "ordinary" or "average". They were above it all. All of a sudden they had power and felt entitled, and they could now demand a higher level of respect from everyone. All this occurred in a very short period of time and all because Tiger was suddenly famous and had money.

Considering Tiger and Earl's background and upbringing, an interesting question is how did they learn to be who they are now? Did they simply wake up one morning and their personalities and attitudes were automatically changed to coincide with their new wealth and status? Did they take a quick online course on how to prepare themselves for the new lifestyle in which they would be living? How did they know what to expect from their new wealth?

Some of the answers to these questions could be that maybe they went around and solicited advice and suggestions from their friends and family, except for the fact that many of those individuals were not wealthy either. So perhaps they chose to read a "How To" book. Everyone knows about the "Dummies" series of books, such as Yoga for Dummies and Knitting for Dummies, so maybe they read a book on "How to Act Wealthy for Dummies"? Simply put, you just do not go from being a simple, average, middle class person to knowing how to act rich and superior in just one day, especially without making some mistakes along the way. But Tiger did just that and it wasn't long before Tiger and his parents were living their lives in conjunction with their new and vastly upgraded "status".

In a very short period of time, Tiger had acquired a private jet, mansions, security guards and even a mega yacht. Tiger was living the high life and maintaining the image that the money had created for him. He had even purchased a large expensive home for his mother and even bought her a new Mercedes and provided her with an ongoing income. Earl, of course, was receiving "his own money" from Tiger and from the Tiger Woods Corporation. There was nothing wrong with Tiger sharing his money with his parents, nor was it wrong for him to make his own large and extravagant purchases. But it was wrong in the way they had allowed themselves to feel as though they were now superior to others only because of their wealth.

Of course, these changes would be indicative as to the reason why Tiger has become the person he is today, and also why he made some unfortunate errors in his life. Maybe these situations happened because Tiger did, in fact, come from a humble life and was unable to handle his sudden fame and wealth. Maybe he was overwhelmed and seduced with his new status in life, eventually succumbing to everything that the fame and wealth had to offer. Obviously, Tiger made the choice to ignore his earlier lifestyle and its values and standards. Tiger gave in to his new way of life and decided to live according to the lax value system that goes along with a wealthy lifestyle.

Although Tiger was only a golfer, it wasn't long before he gained the distinction of a famous high profile celebrity, a title that has never been bestowed on a professional golfer before. Other golfers on tour are not necessarily recognized as celebrities; however, they are still extremely popular in the golfing world.

And it seems that Tiger and Earl were only accepted in that new celebrity world because they were now both rich and famous. Remember, it was Earl who did everything he could to promote Tiger to the world in order to elevate his status.

It is sad that prior to Tiger's wealth, the people in high society would never have looked at him or his family twice or even acknowledged the fact that they existed. But because they now had money and because of Tiger's fame and popularity, they have now been accepted. Basically, I could win the lottery and the next day I would be rich. Does that mean that I can now rub elbows with the rich and famous and be one of them? Am I now accepted only because I have money? Of course, it does.

Because of his fame and wealth, Tiger truly believed he had become invincible. Tiger was now above it all and above everyone else. Instead of being friendly and approachable and one who mingled with his "regular" friends and acquaintances and the average people in society, he was now less sincere, unapproachable and overly confident almost to the point of being cold and arrogant in his demeanor and toward others, except for his new found celebrity friends.

I remember when Tiger was quoted as saying, "In order to get my own space and time to be alone, I need to be ruthless and cold to everyone." Couldn't he have achieved the same thing by simply being a little nicer to people? I mean, what harm would it have done if he had just put forth an effort to be kinder and a little more sincere toward others, especially his fans.

On several occasions, Earl and I had discussed the fact that Tiger had become so outwardly arrogant toward others, and personally, I felt Earl should have been more concerned with the changes that were occurring in Tiger. However, Earl refused to acknowledge that he was the actual instigator in Tiger's attitude because Earl was the person who had taught and encouraged Tiger to be ruthless and superior to others. After all, Earl believed that since Tiger was a champion he deserved to be treated like a king and to have the power to rule his kingdom any way he chose. Earl truly believed that Tiger's position and status within the golfing world made him royalty and Earl and Tida were part of that royal family. Sadly, to Tiger, Earl and Tida, everyone else in their new and old world were simply peasants.

Tiger chose to become a golfer. He chose to be good at his sport. And yes, Tiger was talented, and yes, Tiger knew he had to protect himself from certain areas of society, especially the media. But it was Tiger who "chose" to remove himself from the world in which he once came from and place himself among the high and the mighty, which included the rich and famous. He went from a regular guy who just played golf to an arrogant, unapproachable famous guy, flaunting his wealth and fame with his new status and position in life. After all, according to his father, Tiger was a champion and champions are superior to everyone else.

Let's be honest. If he had not been rich and famous, Tiger would never have been in the same position to cheat on his wife with those women. Simply put, if Tiger did not have his current status and wealth, those women would never have given Tiger a second glance. Without money and fame, Tiger would have been just a regular guy and those women were not interested in being with just a regular guy.

Regretting the final outcome of his actions, only Tiger knows why he felt it was necessary to be with other women, leaving his wife and children at home. However, it was quite obvious that Tiger truly believed that because of who he was and the status he had earned, he could get away with it, especially since he felt he was above it all. Tiger was being selfish and thinking only of himself. But in a way, you can't blame Tiger for all of his actions. Tiger was only being the person Earl had raised him to be. Remember, Earl had spent years teaching Tiger to be selfish, believing it was a quality necessary to be a true champion.

Since his fame, Tiger has forgotten about all of the "little" people who were there for him in the early years before he became someone so famous. It appears he only remembers his current arena of friends and surroundings, thus forgetting about his humble beginnings and the many values he was raised with.

Tiger seems to have also forgotten about some of the many people who helped get him to his current stage in life. It seems as though Tiger's new and improved life has caused him to lose sight of the more important aspects of his past and current life and the people who exist in it. These are the people he has disappointed because of his feeling that he is literally superior to everyone, including them, all due to his wealth and his fame.

A perfect example of this would be when Tiger received his first sponsor exemptions to play golf when he first came out as a rookie on the PGA tour, such as the Greater Milwaukee Open and the Las Vegas Invitational. Although these sponsors made it possible for him to play in his first tour tournaments, Tiger has never again played in those tournaments, even though Las Vegas was his first PGA tour win. He should have been more grateful to those people who took a chance and gave him sponsor exemptions in order for him to be able to play in his first tournaments. He should have shown his loyalty by returning the next year as the defending champion, but unfortunately, Tiger chose to ignore them and not show his appreciation. Obviously, after winning the Masters and suddenly being on top, these tournaments were no longer prestigious enough for Tiger's new status. Therefore, they were removed from his future tournament schedule even though they marked the beginning of Tiger's career.

Like Tiger, Earl had also forgotten his own roots and chose to let the money and status dictate his life. He chose to remove himself from his prior life and family and live a life of wealth and fame and, for some reason, allow other people to believe that he had also become someone famous. The only problem with Earl was that the money and fame was not his. It was his son's. Even so, Earl still capitalized on that fact. Tiger was the person making incredible sums of money through winning tournaments and endorsements, however, Earl lived off of Tiger's money and fame. Earl chose to take advantage of Tiger's fame by writing books and appearing on television shows. Earl even believed he was entitled to join the golf commentators in their booth and give his insights during the tournaments in which Tiger was playing.

Earl truly believed he had become an important "somebody" simply because he now had money. And just because he raised Tiger Woods, famous golfer, for some reason, Earl also thought he was now an authority on the game of golf. But sadly, Earl was just Tiger's father and the real fame belonged only to his son.

Tiger had become a true golfing sensation and everyone wanted to be around him and say they knew him. He was always invited to all the right parties by all of the various esteemed groups of people. His status within the golfing world had proved that he had truly arrived. The paths Tiger started to travel took him into arenas that were new and foreign to him and his family, and found they were now welcomed into entirely new social circles. Since Tiger's roots and his upbringing were completely different from the caliber of his new social circle, Tiger found he had to adjust accordingly in order to travel the new road that had been mapped out for him by society. But how did Tiger learn to travel in those circles?

Most of the time, Tiger was somewhat apprehensive about venturing out on these new avenues, even doubting the sincerity of his acceptance. After all, no one had ever attempted to invite him prior to his wealth and position in the golfing world. Also, Tiger was still somewhat shy when exposed to certain groups of people, even though you would not know it from the way he played golf. Tiger was smart, so conversation with this new group of people was never a problem. However, knowing how to act rich and feel accepted, now that took a little more work. So, hanging with the rich and famous was a slow learning process for both Tiger and Earl; knowing what to say and when to say it and feeling comfortable when doing it.

Of course, it didn't take Tiger long to make friends with Michael Jordan, Mark O'Meara and Ken Griffey, Jr., but while doing so, he left many of his friends from the past behind.

Tiger and Earl were well educated, but they had never actually been exposed to that particular level of society, which included the President of the United States and the Duchess of York, among many others. There were times when they would have conversations with Jack Nicklaus, Arnold Palmer and other sporting greats, but that was different. They were different. These athletes were stars in the golfing world, but they were never actually considered to be true "celebrities". And because of the calmer, less flashy lives they lived, these stars still had great respect for all others. They acted like regular people just like Tiger and Earl used to. However, Tiger and Earl lost that part of themselves somewhere along the way. With Earl, he was no longer just a father of a young son with a talent for golf who was simply talking to a famous professional golfer. In his own mind, Earl was now the father of Tiger Woods, which elevated him to a higher plateau than the average person he used to be, and to a position equal to or better than these proven stars.

Another characteristic about both Tiger and Earl was their attitude toward the money. Everyone knows Tiger has become the highest paid golfer in the history of the sport. But when Earl told me about the times when Tiger had gone to the Bahamas and Las Vegas and would gamble in the private areas of the casino reserved strictly for the high rollers and celebrities, the rich and famous, I was extremely surprised at the amount of money he played with. Earl told me how Tiger would bet stacks of ten thousand dollar chips on one hand and think absolutely nothing about it.

One night while I was at Earl's house, Tiger had called from Atlantis in the Bahamas just to say hello to his dad. While on speaker phone, I heard Tiger brag to his father that he was not having a great run at the tables and he was down one hundred and eighty thousand dollars. He then commented that as soon as he got back on a roll, he would try to win some of it back. Tiger and Earl were laughing and joking about the amount of money he had lost and Earl even reminded Tiger he shouldn't worry since he had lost more than that many times before.

Earl then told Tiger to remember back to all the times when he was down over three hundred thousand dollars and sometimes even more, so he stressed to Tiger to have fun and not to worry. Earl then said, "Hey, it's really no big deal, right? What are a few bucks?" Earl looked over at me and just smiled truly believing what he was telling his son was okay.

After he got off the phone with Tiger, I expressed my shock at the amount of money Tiger had just lost while gambling. Earl told me it was only money and it won't be the last time Tiger loses that much. This was a comment I would never have expected Earl to make, especially considering the financial struggles he and Tiger had endured over the past years prior to Tiger turning pro. In his usual manner, Earl defended Tiger's actions by saying, "Tiger earned that money and can do whatever he wants with it. What Tiger spends on his gambling will never even come close to putting a dent into what he has already earned. Besides, to Tiger, it's simply pocket change."

I just thought to myself that even if I did have that kind of money, I would never be able to simply "throw" that much money away, no matter what the reason. In my opinion, that's considered really foolish and expensive fun! But I guess if you have it, you can afford to flaunt it.

This made me think about all the other golfers who have millions of dollars from playing golf and from their endorsements, such as Palmer, Nicklaus, Trevino, Couples and the list goes on. You never hear about them acting the same way as Tiger, like super rich people, nor do you hear about them flaunting their wealth or their position. So why does Tiger, or especially Earl and Tida?

Even though I had known Earl for many years, I never knew that he also liked to gamble. One time when we were in Las Vegas, I remember asking Earl about his gambling and he explained that since he now had money, he could finally splurge and have some real fun. He told me that playing blackjack is what rich people do, so since he was now rich and he could gamble just like Tiger does, he decided to take up blackjack. He also made sure he always received the royal treatment from each hotel and casino he visited. After all, he was Earl Woods and should receive no less than his famous son.

Considering Earl's roots and former lifestyle, I was truly surprised to discover that he would even consider just tossing money away for no good reason. This occurred many times while in Las Vegas when Earl would simply throw out six hundred dollars, twelve hundred dollars or more at one time as his bet at the Blackjack tables and all I could do was just sit back and cringe as I watched Earl continue to lose.

Earl was so inconsistent and reckless with his betting at the tables and he would just laugh and state, "What's the big deal? It's only money."

No wonder Tiger has the same attitude toward money and gambling. Like father, like son! It also made me wonder if Tiger played blackjack as bad as his father and that was the reason he was always losing so much money.

As he continued to play, and, of course, continued to lose, I recalled the time when Earl arrogantly mentioned to me that he had another ten thousand dollars in his room if he blows through the fifteen thousand dollars he had on him. *Fifteen thousand dollars!!* What was he thinking? I knew both he and Tiger could definitely afford their gambling losses, but it just reminded me again as to how much Earl had changed from the early days. It also bothered me that these comments were coming from a man who years earlier needed to borrow one thousand dollars from me to pay for Tiger's caddy. Now he was just throwing it away!

Since Earl was now rich, and in order the act the part, he felt it was necessary that he have a full time staff that would always be there for him and could constantly cater to his needs. Now remember, Earl had a very small fourteen hundred square foot house and he was the only person who lived there. But Earl had a staff of three girls which consisted of one housekeeper, an assistant housekeeper and his personal assistant. In addition, Earl had a limousine service on call at all times with his regular driver, Les. And I guess I shouldn't forget about his masseuse who came to his house on a weekly basis. Earl once commented that it was one of his favorite perks about being wealthy.

Must be nice to have such a wealthy son!

Tiger's mother, Tida, also allowed herself to be affected by Tiger's wealth and fame. In fact, at times it appeared she actually took advantage of the fact that her son's popularity and status had increased to an all new level. Not only had she acquired a new house and cars from Tiger, but her son was also supplying her with enough money to support her new and vastly improved lifestyle, which was considerably different than when she was living with Earl. She, too, was acting like she was rich and famous, forgetting that it was her son who had all the money and had earned his own fame. I mean, just being Tiger Woods' mother does not make her famous, too!

Not long into Tiger's career and as Tiger's self-appointed business manager, Earl decided it was necessary for Tiger to lease a jet on a permanent basis. In Earl's mind, and in justifying his decision, Tiger had become such a huge celebrity that the jet would allow him to fly in private and would prevent Tiger from having to deal with the fans and crowds who supposedly mobbed him at the airports. Apparently, it had become difficult for Tiger to avoid all of the people and the media each time he attempted to travel on a commercial airline. Of course, when I think back, I cannot recall hearing about Tiger ever being mobbed by people at any airport, nor do I remember ever seeing any pictures of any incidents in the media.

What did make sense to me was when Earl admitted the jet was really for Tiger's convenience, which would eliminate him from having to go through the time consuming airport lines and waiting at the gates. Then the real truth came out. Earl stated that Tiger is a celebrity and has tremendous wealth and, therefore, he should travel in style just like all celebrities and rich people. Besides, Earl knew he and Tida, Tiger's mother, would also benefit greatly from the jet as they would have access to it whenever they wanted. For them, this would be just another perk from having a rich son.

Since Tiger had his own private jet, Tida made sure it was accessible to her whenever she needed it, whether it was to attend one of Tiger's tournaments, visit her son in Florida or to simply go on one of her many "Tiger paid" vacations. According to Earl, Tida would call Tiger and expect him to send the jet for her at her beckoned call so she could go wherever she wanted. Tida always attended all of Tiger's tournaments and functions and whenever Tiger was flying to one of these events, whether nationally or internationally, he would simply land in California to pick up his mother, and, of course, fly her home afterwards.

Many years earlier, when Tida left Thailand to be with Earl, no one in her country even knew who Tida was. However, due to Tiger's success and his new celebrity status, Tida has become quite popular in the eyes of her former countrymen. After all, she is the mother of Tiger Woods and when he would go to Bangkok, she was able to bask in the glow of her son's stardom.

So the question is still unanswered as to why Tiger, Earl and Tida truly believed it was necessary for them to act as though they were superior to all others on this planet. Just because a person is good at something does not necessarily give them the right to expect others to cow down and kiss the ground they walk on. They are not royalty. Famous, yes, but Tiger is just a golfer and a superior athlete. Simply because of his wealth and the status that he has received in the world of golf should not warrant Tiger's sense of arrogance and his "better than everyone else" attitude he has been demonstrating. Tiger and Earl were just regular people before, so why were they not able to continue to be just regular people who just happened to have a lot of money?

I never could understand why people feel money does, in fact, change them and all of a sudden, elevates them into society? What people forget is that money is an inanimate object and is incapable of changing a person. It is the person who allows the money to change them. What Tiger and Earl forgot was true success is not measured by fame or wealth.

12
TAKING CHARGE OF TIGER'S LIFE

EACH YEAR, THERE ARE SEVERAL young and upcoming golfers who have spent many years working long and hard to perfect every aspect of their game. They hope one day they will finally achieve the ultimate goal of becoming a professional golfer and playing on the PGA tour. At one point in their lives, the game of golf became their passion and each one of them made the decision that someday they would turn professional. All of their dreams would then become a reality. These individuals just want to go out and earn a living playing the sport they love.

With Tiger, I knew his goals were a little different. Yes, Tiger had a passion for the sport of golf, and yes, he spent years working hard to attain his eventual goals. But Tiger had a father who had his own personal agenda regarding his son. Earl and Tiger's agents decided to take advantage of Tiger's talent and passion and turn his love for golf into something else. They turned his career into a business; and, more importantly, a brand. And, of course, it was a business with Earl at the helm and in control of everything. After all, Earl had always seen Tiger as a commodity instead of a person, and decided to capitalize on that fact.

We all know playing golf, like any professional sport, is a profession, therefore, golf becomes their business. However, with Tiger, as soon as he turned pro, I watched as he was immediately transformed from a player into a big corporation, almost to the point of being a multi-faceted conglomerate. It was never Tiger's choice to go so big so quickly, especially since he was still young and all he really wanted to do was just play on the PGA tour as a professional golfer.

To be perfectly honest, I knew when Tiger was very young that it was not Earl's original vision to create such a widespread business for Tiger. However, when Tiger was a teenager and Earl contacted the worldwide management agency IMG, he soon discovered his son could make a tremendous amount of money through various sponsor endorsements. From this, a new and more profitable path for Tiger's future was immediately established. Earl explained to me how the meetings were set up with Nike and other interested sponsors who were all willing to take a chance on a relatively unknown Tiger Woods as soon as he decided to turn professional. This was when Earl realized the new possibilities for making Tiger's career more lucrative would also be beneficial to himself. Not long after several conversations and negotiations with the agents at IMG, plans were made, contracts were prepared and Tiger's future was carefully and strategically mapped out.

Over the years, I watched as Earl successfully implemented his plans for Tiger as he continued to market and promote his son, ultimately trying to create a celebrity status for Tiger, although somewhat unnecessary. However, it was not until Tiger started having thoughts of turning pro that the experts had become involved and a more formal approach for Tiger's career was devised. Once Tiger made his official announcement to the world that he had decided to become a professional golfer, all plans to market and promote him on a much larger and grander scale were immediately put into motion.

Thanks to IMG and their marketing strategy, and along with Tiger's eventual tournament wins, it didn't take long before Tiger became a household name. With this fame also came tremendous popularity and name recognition both on and off the course. The fact that Tiger also became a media sensation right off the bat didn't hurt either. And then, of course, his popularity increased and his superstar status gained even more momentum once he won his first major tournament at the Masters in 1997.

This major win transformed Tiger from a dangerous rookie to a dominant force to be reckoned with and the fans just loved him. The problem was that once Tiger started winning, it was no longer just about golf as it was now all about image and money.

Early in Tiger's life, not only was Earl the one person who coached and trained Tiger, but he was also the instigator when it came to trying to bring Tiger's name to the forefront when he was just a child. Earl had always been Tiger's most avid fan and he had appointed himself to be his son's personal publicist. Tiger was very successful in the junior and amateur golf tournaments, but these events were never considered to be newsworthy, so basically, no one really knew who Tiger was. Earl decided to take it upon himself to promote his son to the media and to hopefully create an interest in Tiger.

Unlike other fathers, Earl's fixation on Tiger's talent led him to believe his son should be known by everyone and was going to do whatever was necessary to ensure Tiger would become well known and be viewed as a golfing sensation, almost to star status. He truly believed Tiger was one of kind and Earl wanted everyone to see how special and perfect his son was.

Even after all of Earl's hard work and dedication toward creating publicity for Tiger, it still ended up where only a handful of people had ever heard about Tiger. Basically, anyone outside of Southern California had no clue as to who he was. Sadly, back then, nobody really kept up with amateur golf so most people could care less who the young players were and that is still true even in today's amateur golfing arena.

I remember when Earl was working to promote Tiger and his tremendous talent as a Junior World and Junior U.S. Amateur golfer and I was surprised to learn Earl actually thought it was only right that he, too, should be a part of Tiger's success. Earl believed he was also special and worthy to be as important as his son. After all, in Earl's mind, he was the one who created Tiger Woods. To hear Earl tell it, he was the father who worked so hard and sacrificed so much to get Tiger to this point in his life. It was almost like Earl felt like he was the only parent in the entire world who ever did anything for his child. So, because of Earl's strange power of logic, Earl once again ended up taking charge of and directing Tiger's career.

In reality, Earl was literally controlling all aspects of Tiger's personal and professional life. Since Earl and Tiger had always been a "team" and because they always did everything together, it was only right that Earl be the one person to guide, oversee and take charge of his son's professional career. Earl's theory behind this control was he would take care of all of the business, the money and the decision making, thus freeing Tiger up to simply focus on his golf and to continue working to be the best. Sadly, Earl did not see it as control or running Tiger's life. He only saw it as a "team" effort, feeling Tiger needed his constant and astute advice and guidance. However, you have to keep in mind that Earl spent twenty years in the military and had no business knowledge at all. But according to Earl, he knew everything about everything.

Tiger's professional career as a golfer began, starting with his televised news conference announcing to the entire world that he had made the decision to turn pro. Prior to Tiger's proclamation, Earl and IMG were involved in the negotiations with both Nike and Titleist and preplanned contracts had been constructed. Once Tiger turned pro, the very lucrative contracts were signed and it was now time for the experts to begin their work on creating a new future for Tiger. Once again, Earl was at the heart of it all. No matter what was going on in Tiger's life and career, it was always Earl's compulsive need to get involved, no matter what the circumstances.

Originally, it was Earl who took it upon himself to be the one who contacted and then made future arrangement to retain the services of IMG, the management agency who would eventually represent Tiger and assist in taking his career to all new levels. It was Earl who dealt directly with IMG and told them exactly what he wanted for Tiger. It was also Earl who decided what sponsor endorsements Tiger would initially sign with and which offers would be considered at a later date.

Earl also oversaw and directed Tiger's tournament schedule, tactically planning the appropriate tournaments that would best benefit his son. According to Earl, the purpose of this strategy was to provide Tiger with sufficient down time and to allow Tiger to concentrate on the tournaments with the highest visibility, namely the major tournaments, and also those which would be the most financially beneficial.

And, of course, when it came to Tiger's earnings, Earl would also personally take charge of each investment as he worked alongside of their chosen money management team of advisors. Earl once told me he was the only person who made all the decisions regarding Tiger's money and investments. He just did not feel comfortable trusting anyone else with Tiger's earnings and no one could do anything without going through him first. Of course, Earl truly believed he knew more than anyone else, especially the financial advisors.

Yes, Earl did great things for Tiger's future, especially getting him set up with IMG. Of course, Tiger was an amateur and was not allowed to participate in any of the planning or negotiations. Therefore, Earl handled all of it for Tiger. But Earl didn't do it just for Tiger, as Earl, like always, had his own personal agenda and it wouldn't be long before Earl showed his true colors.

Even after Earl formed the Tiger Woods Foundation, it was Earl who was instrumental in deciding what percentage of Tiger's earnings would be donated to their charity, making sure it was always an amount to help keep the foundation financially stable. I remember when Tiger won the one million dollar first place at his World Challenge Tournament in Thousand Oaks, California, and Earl told Tiger he had to give one half of it to his foundation. And, of course, Tiger always did what his father expected and donated the five hundred thousand dollars.

In order to continue his control, Earl had decided he would appoint himself to the position of President in Tiger's new corporation. Earl also appointed himself President of the Tiger Woods Foundation. In Earl's mind, by taking these positions, he now had even more justification when it came to making any and all decisions for Tiger. Although Earl indicated that the decision making was a joint effort between himself, Tiger, and his agents, the end result was always based on Earl's strong and adamant advice and suggestions. Ultimately, Earl would always have the final say. Due to his position as President, and that of Tiger's father, Earl took it upon himself to handle all of Tiger's business, including dealing with Tiger's agents, the management teams and being involved in all sponsor negotiations.

It bothered me that instead of stepping aside and letting Tiger grow on his own and handle his own business and affairs, Earl chose to once again insinuate himself into Tiger's life and career. Earl confided in me that he truly believed Tiger was not capable of handling such important details at this stage of his life. Sadly, it appeared that Earl was not giving Tiger the credit he truly deserved. Earl had a tendency to always take charge and thought he was the only one who knew exactly what was best for Tiger, almost as though his way was the only way. Of course, Earl's own ego and over the top obsession with his son prevented him from allowing Tiger the freedom to take charge of his own life.

Earl was convinced that, since they were so close, Tiger truly wanted and needed him around. In one way or another, Earl was always able to justify his smothering and dictating presence. Of course, Tiger really had no choice when it came to Earl's power over him. Earl had always manipulated Tiger's life and his golf, so Tiger was basically forced to accept his father's continued presence.

Earl was so fanatical when it came to his son that in Earl's mind Tiger had to always be showcased as the star. Earl needed to show how special and perfect his son was. Earl felt this would not be done without his own expert advice and input when it came to the media, agents, sponsors and general public. Unfortunately, Earl truly believed that not only had he created Tiger Woods, superstar, but he was also the one single person who made everything happen for Tiger throughout his life and career, including building Tiger's empire. Earl was convinced that without him, Tiger would never have achieved his current status and fame, nor would he have attained his tremendous wealth. It was a proven fact that Earl always took the credit for everything, especially when it pertained to Tiger. What Earl never understood was that Tiger would have earned his empire on his own merit and talent even without Earl. The truth is, IMG wanted Tiger; Nike and other sponsors wanted Tiger. They wanted Tiger, not Earl.

When it came to his career, Tiger was no longer just a young man playing golf. From the way I saw it, Earl had turned Tiger's love for golf into a business where bits and pieces of Tiger were being sold off to the highest bidder and he was now selling his soul in order to pacify his father's own personal desires for fame and wealth.

Tiger's career was now considered to be a highly profitable business. Tiger's name had now been branded and he was now making one hell of a lot of money from it alone. Although this business was basically a separate entity, much of it was still driven by Tiger's success and popularity on the course, but the income had nothing to do with his tournament play or the money he was earning on tour. Earl made sure that when it came to the bottom line, it was all about the money. The money Tiger would produce for his sponsors; the money he would earn from his own clothing line; the money from all of the video games; and, of course, the money generated simply from the use of his name.

I remember the time when Earl was trying really hard to convince me that he and Tiger were never in it for the money. I just looked at him and knew he was full of crap. I even went so far as to ask him if that was really true, then why were so many contracts for all of the money already in place before Tiger ever took his first swing of the club as a professional? Earl just smiled back at me knowing I already knew the real answer. He basically confirmed what I already knew. Of course, it was for the money, especially on Earl's part. For years prior to Tiger turning pro, Earl had always talked about how much money Tiger could make on tour. Why do you think Tiger had to be the best? Simply put, the best is always the most successful and the most successful always makes the most money.

I then thought about the hundreds of other golf professionals who have only dreamed of such an opportunity with sponsors and agents, leaving them to be satisfied with just playing golf and earning their living doing what they love most in life. But why was Tiger so different, especially since he had not even proved himself yet as a professional on the PGA tour?

For Tiger, the future was obvious. Earl explained how IMG was going to brand Tiger and make him and his name their main selling point. They would focus extensively on brand marketing, similar to that of Michael Jordan and Donald Trump. Earl's theory was they needed to keep Tiger's name and face in the forefront and always fresh in the minds of his fans and the public in order to maintain his popularity. Earl strongly believed that over time, names and faces of sports figures and celebrities have a tendency to fade away and once they are out of the limelight, people will forget. However, if you keep someone popular and constantly in the public eye, the end result can be quite lucrative. Earl also wanted to have longevity in Tiger's fame which would result in Tiger's name being worth a whole lot of money. It was no longer just about Tiger being a golfer. Tiger was now a brand, and brands make a lot of money. Of course, this monetary value was based solely on his success on the golf course. No success, no stardom, no money!

As part of the marketing ploy, Earl and IMG had to establish a new and appropriate image for Tiger. This was the image Tiger had to live with at all times, the one he had to present to the public. According to Earl, Tiger never understood why it was necessary to have an image and change who he was, especially since all he ever wanted was to just go out and play golf like all of the other golfers on tour. Yes, Tiger wanted to be the best, but he still could not understand why they had to create all the hype and marketing and promote him to the public and media, unlike other golfers? Was it simply for the money that everyone could make off of Tiger? Of course, it was! And you know this was the case with Nike. They may have paid Tiger millions of dollars, but they made it back a thousand fold. Nike took a chance on Tiger just like they had taken a chance on Michael Jordan years earlier. And look how that turned out!

Ever since Tiger signed with Nike, a Nike representative or his IMG agent, Mark Steinberg, would be with Tiger at all times. Whether it was at one of his tournaments, the Tiger Jam concert in Las Vegas, or any other event, function or party that Tiger was attending, these business people were always around Tiger. Even before Mark Steinberg, Tiger's first IMG agent, Norton Hughes, was also constantly around and even hung out with Tiger in his early days as a rookie. But why?

According to Earl, Tiger's importance and superstar status warranted having the Nike reps and his agents around to support Tiger. It was Earl who expected and even demanded that these reps and agents stay around Tiger in order make him look and feel even more important. But when I thought about Earl's reasoning,

I started to wonder if these people were only around Tiger in order to protect and guard their own investment from other sponsors and marketing agencies.

I recall meeting many of these people on several occasions, including a few times in Las Vegas while Earl and I were at the blackjack tables or after a Tiger Jam concert and even in Hawaii at the Mercedes Championship tournament. Why was there such a need for their constant presence around Tiger? Were they there just to keep him happy or was it for their own personal glorification to be around such a superstar? Makes you wonder where they were when Tiger was having all of his so-called affairs, especially the ones in Las Vegas. I'll bet Nike and IMG were not happy campers when they discovered what Tiger had been doing in secret. They did, however, choose to stand behind Tiger and support their client throughout it all, unlike many of Tiger's other sponsors who ended their relationship quickly.

Simply because of all the lucrative endorsements and special attention Tiger received, many people thought he was setting himself apart from the other golfers. Tiger was, in fact, a superstar and had broken many records, but his substantial endorsements and his new celebrity status and enormous popularity is what made him different. Earl once told me that some people alleged that the attention Tiger received was extreme and was considered to be detrimental to the sport of golf. Earl explained that the people who made these comments were simply jealous and envious of the many opportunities that were presented to Tiger in addition to what he had already accomplished in his life. This included his three straight U.S. Junior Amateur wins and his three straight U.S. Amateur wins. Tiger was the one who set himself apart from the others because of his skill level and ability to always be the best.

Additionally, the attendance of spectators at every PGA golfing event and tournament had increased to all new levels, also contributing to higher prize money. As far as being detrimental to the sport, most of the golfers on tour would deny this assumption when it pertained to the prize money, especially since the tournament winnings they shared had increased tremendously since Tiger's arrival on the pro circuit.

As far as the general golfing fan is concerned, Americans love a winner and Tiger is definitely a winner. Tiger, therefore, cannot be detrimental to the sport and, in fact, having a dominant player on the PGA tour was the best thing to affect golf since Arnold Palmer. Sadly, since Tiger's fall from the top, the PGA has not seen any one individual who has replaced Tiger's position of dominance or his popularity.

As part of their long term business plans, many times Earl shared with me how he wanted to form a charitable foundation to benefit children, using Tiger as the main resource and prominent figurehead. However, this was a project that was originally Earl's dream and conceptual vision and he hoped it would eventually become a joint effort between himself and Tiger. Of course, Earl's so called dream only entered his mind when he realized Tiger could eventually be rich enough to fund such an endeavor. Initially, according to Earl, Tiger was not even involved in the creation of the foundation, nor was he ever interested. Earl's decision to have the foundation associated with Tiger's name was mainly due to the influence it would have in regard to obtaining donations and sponsorships.

Although several prominent sports figures and celebrities have established or worked with recognized foundations, Earl wanted Tiger to be the first black athlete to establish a charitable foundation in his own name as soon as he turned professional. Earl explained how the foundation would also present Tiger to the public and to the children around the world as an incredible role model figure adding to his already growing reputation and popularity.

One stage of the marketing strategy that had already been planned for Tiger was how he was expected to accept the position and responsibility of being a role model. This new role model image was shaped by Earl in order to increase Tiger's popularity and name recognition and to also coincide with the new image Earl wanted Tiger to portray, not only for the Tiger Woods Foundation, but to the entire world.

Of course, Earl just naturally assumed Tiger would be receptive and accept this new position, not taking into consideration the additional pressures and responsibilities it would place on Tiger's already heavily loaded shoulders. I was afraid keeping up this new image would also create even more stress for Tiger as his reputation would now be judged on his personal life as well as his ability and performance on the course as a golfer. However, Earl truly believed his son could handle each and every responsibility that was given to him. Once again, Tiger was pushed into a position by Earl, forcing Tiger to abide by his father's wishes and expectations.

There is a big difference between reputation and image. Tiger's reputation is that he is possibly the best golfer of all time. This is based on fact and his ability. The image of Tiger as a role model and a perfect human being was simply a creation by not only his father and the Tiger Woods Foundation, but also by the media.

I remember an advertisement with Charles Barkley, Tiger's friend, who was also promoted to be a role model in the eyes of children. He once stated in one of the Nike television commercials that he is considered to be a role model simply because of his ability and popularity as an all-star basketball player. He further explained he does not consider himself to be a role model because that position should be reserved only for the parents of a child. Charles was aware that not all children are able to grow up and become a star athlete, so he strongly believed an athlete should not be singled out as a role model. He added that children should be encouraged to seek out and excel in all areas of life, not just in sports.

After hearing those insightful words, I thought maybe Earl should have listened more closely to Charles Barkley's philosophy and then maybe some of the pressures Tiger was under would have been alleviated in his personal life. But then I thought about the way Tiger was raised and the kind of role model Earl had been for Tiger and realized Earl fell a little short in that department.

There was one area of business where Earl had absolutely no control over and that was the escalating prize money awarded to each player on the tour. Larger television contracts, which were primarily attributed to Tiger's popularity, resulted in the PGA increasing the total purse amounts available at each tournament to levels that were inconceivable prior to Tiger's appearance on the PGA tour. This was reminiscent of an earlier time when Arnold Palmer caused a new and sudden interest in the sport of golf. Unfortunately, due to the era in which he played, Palmer was not able to garner as much money for the players as Tiger did.

I remember a few years after Tiger turned pro and Earl and I were sitting in his living room talking about how the tournament winnings and sponsor endorsements had increased.

I asked Earl, "When Tiger was growing up, did you ever think he would make this kind of money or affect the world of golf the way he has?"

Earl responded with an arrogant tone in his voice, "Of course, I did."

I then questioned Earl as to his response, "Ah, come on Earl, I'm just not buying that. There is no way you or anyone else in this entire world could have ever fathomed that Tiger would ever change golf so significantly. You would need a crystal ball to predict the future and I know you don't have one."

At that very moment, Earl truthfully admitted, "You know, Linda, when Tiger was growing up and playing great golf, I always knew he would one day be great and break many records, but when it came to the money, no, I never did foresee the money increasing to these levels. But it makes me proud to know that it was my son who made it happen and changed the sport of golf so radically."

Earl knew the money was beyond what anyone could have ever imagined, especially since up until then, there had not been that much money being paid to the winners, and the few sponsor endorsement contracts that were offered to golfers were far from being lucrative. The top golfers on the tour made an extremely good living, however, the new television contracts and increased public and media interest in the game had resulted in making it possible for professional golfers to earn millions without even winning one single tournament. Earl explained how Tiger's lucrative contracts with his own sponsors benefited the other players, not only in their negotiations, but in the number of available contracts being offered.

When you think about it, was it actually Tiger's presence on the tour that brought more people to the game of golf or was it simply all the hype and marketing that had surrounded him. In Tiger's case, people constantly heard about Tiger Woods. These people were curious about Tiger Woods and they wanted to see Tiger Woods in action. More and more people started going to tournaments and showing more interest in golf, thus increasing the attendance to all new levels.

The marketing of Tiger most definitely worked. Yes, it was Tiger's performance that made him great, but it was the marketing and advertising ploys that made him popular. I could not believe the end result created such a phenomenon.

Due to Tiger's tremendous popularity around the world, he was fortunate enough to have the opportunity to play in several foreign tournaments. I mean, who would turn down the chance to be paid a couple of million dollars just to play golf, even if you never win. These are appearance fees and what is so incredible about the foreign tournaments is that no matter how Tiger does, win or lose, he keeps the multi-million dollar fee in addition to any money he wins. Besides, Tiger makes more money playing in these tournaments than he does playing in any tournament on the PGA tour.

After Tiger had established himself on the PGA tour, Earl explained how Tiger's schedule needed to be rearranged in order to work around his sponsor commitments, foreign tournament appearances and most importantly, the major tournaments on the PGA tour, but still always fulfilling Tiger's minimum play requirements set by the PGA. As Tiger established himself on the tour, he did not play as many tournaments as the other professionals because his father wanted him to put more emphasis on winning the majors. I remember the time when Earl just laughed and quipped, "It's not like he needs the money, especially from the smaller, insignificant tournaments!"

If times had not changed and the money on tour had remained the same as when he first came out as a rookie, Tiger would probably be more motivated to go out and win all the tournaments he could instead of a selected few and just the majors. I remember there was a time when Tiger wanted to play as many tournaments as he could simply because he wanted the opportunity to play golf and to win.

I guess you kind of lose your motivation to struggle and try to win when you already have several hundred million dollars in the bank.

It reached a point where it was no longer about Tiger's golf. Everything was now all about the money, the image, his personal life, his mansions, his yachts, and his many sponsor endorsements.

If Tiger came out as a rookie without all of those endorsements and the money, he still would have been just as successful and dominant on the course, maybe even more so. He may have had more wins because he would have played in more tournaments. Tiger probably would have broken just as many records, if not more.

Tiger would have been able to concentrate more on his golf game and winning without all of the interference from the media, his sponsor commitments, appearances and his other obligations including his charity foundation. He may not have been such a huge media sensation nor would he have had the same celebrity status he now possesses, but I know he would have been just as popular simply because of the way he played golf. His fans loved Tiger the golfer, not necessarily, Tiger the big celebrity.

Also, Tiger's personal life would never have been an issue and he would not have been as affected by the media hounds. Tiger's arrogant and unapproachable attitude and sense of superiority may not have increased to their current levels and he might have simply remained the brash, outspoken and motivated young man who first came on tour as a rookie. And even if Tiger did have an affair, people would not have cared as much and it would not have escalated into a scandal or a media circus. He would have simply been a great golfer who screwed up.

It was Earl, the business, and the management team who created the new "image" for Tiger, causing him to lose his privacy and his ability to function as a normal athlete in his sport. It was Earl's constant control, involvement and overbearing influence over Tiger's life that placed him in the position where he was forced to live up to an image instead of letting Tiger just be himself, which would have been enough for most people.

13

IT'S ALL ABOUT THE IMAGE

TIGER FIRST ANNOUNCED HIS DECISION to become a professional golfer in his carefully planned out television news conference that became known as the "Hello World" speech. This announcement was made soon after Tiger had won his third U.S. Amateur Championship and his agents and Earl were hoping this news flash would be a great marketing maneuver and introduction to the public and the media for Tiger. However, most everyone was surprised by the announcement as no other golfer, or any other athlete in any sport for that matter, has ever held a press conference, especially on television, to declare their entry into a professional sport. But, of course, this was just another example of Earl continuing the "media monster" effect and making sure his son got noticed and received the recognition that Earl thought Tiger deserved.

It is a known fact that Tiger had won a record three straight U.S. Amateur championships, but he had only made the cut in seven of the seventeen professional tournaments he participated in as an amateur, never winning any of them. He was, therefore, known by the other golfers, but he was a relative unknown to the general public because he had not received any type of coverage for his play against the professional golfers. But when you think about it, can anyone actually name, or do they even care, who are and were the previous U.S. Amateur champions?

Some of the other amateur winners who came out on tour with strong amateur records did not receive the same media hype and recognition that Tiger did, nor did they feel it was necessary. This esteemed group included Arnold Palmer, Jack Nicklaus, Mark O'Meara, John Cook, Scott Verplank, and Phil Mickelson. The question is why was it so important for Tiger to let the public know that he was turning professional? What set Tiger apart from everyone else who ever came out on tour? Simply put, the answer is "image", which translates into money. Unfortunately, many thought Tiger's press conference was nothing more than a self-indulgent and over the top spectacle.

When Andre Agassi first burst out onto the tennis scene, the catch phrase for his many commercials was "image is everything". Obviously Tiger's agents took this to heart when dealing with their new client. Earl told me how the agents were carefully molding an image for Tiger and had multi-million dollar contracts in place before he ever joined the PGA tour. Nike and Titleist were only some of the sponsors who had signed Tiger with early contracts for amounts of money which were unheard of in the sport of professional golf.

Earl told me about the Nike advertisements featuring Tiger that were ready to air by the time he played in his first tournament. No other golfer in the history of the sport came out with so much hype and so many preplanned contracts as Tiger did and, of course, the media had been alerted to this information so they would be prepared to report it all to the public. Although the money from the sponsors was extremely lucrative, Earl knew it would also cause an extensive amount of additional pressure for Tiger. After all, Tiger now had an image to protect and sponsors to satisfy, so he had even more reason to try to always win. But it was because of that new image and all of the pressures stemming from the tremendous expectations of the sponsors, media and public, that made Tiger feel that he could not let anyone down by losing. It was all about the image, and if you have a perfect image, you are not allowed to fail. If you fail, then your image will be tarnished. This not only pertains to Tiger's ongoing performance as a professional golfer, but also to all aspects of his life.

When Tiger first came out on the PGA tour as a rookie, he acted like he was actually having fun, expressing emotions with his signature fist pump and speaking his mind. It was his unique brashness coupled with his ability to play golf that initially attracted his huge following. The fans, many of whom had never even been interested in golf, now flocked to see this new superstar.

I remember after Tiger's initial wins on the tour, he did a televised interview with former U.S. Open champion turned golf analyst Curtis Strange. This is when Tiger stated that he enters every tournament expecting to win and he personally feels "second sucks". After their short interview, Curtis Strange reacted to Tiger's statement by commenting that Tiger would eventually learn that this kind of attitude would not work on the professional tour. However, after Tiger won the 1997 Masters in Augusta by a record margin of twelve strokes, Curtis Strange was forced to do a second interview with Tiger where Strange retracted his previous statement and admitted that the professionals really did not know just how good Tiger was. It appeared Tiger's brashness with the media was working for him.

However, Earl explained to me that because of Tiger's brash comments, it had been determined by himself and Tiger's agents that part of Tiger's current attitude needed to be toned down. This is when they decided to help groom Tiger's image so that he acted more like a professional instead of a fun loving rookie. After they had mapped out the direction they wanted to go, they began to work with Tiger on his outspoken nature, trying to get him to become more cautious in his statements, thus forcing him to choose his words more carefully. Basically Tiger was now having to watch his P's and Q's while in front of the camera or doing interviews.

Unfortunately, as a result of these required changes, Tiger became more conservative and was appearing to be more reserved, sometimes even stoic. Eventually, Tiger's signature fist pump began to disappear. The rookie who appeared to be having so much fun on the course now had given way to a newly created image of a mature professional.

It appeared that Tiger's advisors were trying to create an image more like that of Jack Nicklaus, who was reserved and confident, but was sometimes bland, instead of one similar to the hard charging and outgoing Arnold Palmer. When you think about it and the way golf is now played, I am thankful that Chi Chi Rodriguez, who had fun with his sword playing putter, and Lee Trevino and Fuzzy Zoeller, along with all of their great humor and their silly antics, never came in contact with an agent who wanted to change their images. Simply put, they were fun to watch and the fans loved them, and they made the game of golf what it is today. I often wonder if he were playing today, would Arnold Palmer's agents tell him to quit hitching up his pants or stop smoking because it did not present a good image. Today you have to do everything for the media, which includes being politically correct.

Although Tiger's agents created a special image for him, one that would garner huge contracts and would have him marketed as a superstar and accepted as a celebrity, there were other images Tiger would need to portray. There was his own self-image, the real person Tiger wanted to be, both on and off the course, but couldn't. Then there was the image the media created and the one the public always expected to see whether he was playing golf or was in the public's viewing. The image his sponsors had created for Tiger was one that was to be presented at all times, an image that would transform Tiger into what they believed the world wanted and would be relayed by the media.

Then there was his father, the one person who knew Tiger better than anyone else, and he had created his own special image for his son. This was an image of the person Earl thought he wanted his son to be. Earl wanted Tiger to be this perfect and honorable person with solid values and one who could become a role model throughout the world. This was Earl's fantasy image for his son, one that he simply created in his own mind.

Everyone had their own expectations of what they wanted or needed Tiger to be. But with all of this, I often wondered if Tiger truly knows who he is anymore or has he become conflicted with himself and with the many demands and expectations that have been placed on him over time.

I remember asking Earl about why did Tiger have to have an image and be molded into someone that everyone else wanted him to be. Why couldn't he come out and just play golf and simply be himself? Earl explained how his sponsors needed to create an image in order to better sell their products and to increase Tiger's popularity. It did not matter how many tournaments Tiger was winning, he still needed to maintain his level of popularity. For business purposes, these images and marketing strategies were imperative in order to keep Tiger's name fresh in the minds of the fans. Basically, it was now all about keeping sponsors interested. No popularity, no contracts.

With this new image, Tiger and Earl's egos and feelings of self-importance became so inflated they actually believed it was now necessary to shield their private lives and their real selves from the public and the media. But I could never understand why? I mean, Tiger was only a golfer, not a high ranking figure or anyone else of great importance for that matter. And what about Earl? He was only Tiger's father.

So, why was it necessary to go to such great lengths to protect themselves from the media and the public? Simply put, it was Earl who had convinced Tiger that because of his new status within the golfing world and because of his new wealth, they were now important enough to warrant the media's continued interest and their need to get a story on someone famous. Therefore, Tiger and Earl felt it was necessary to maintain their privacy and keep that part of their lives secret from everyone.

I believe Tiger and Earl's continued need of secrecy created an allure about them which I think caused people to be even more intrigued and left the media and public wanting to know more. It appeared to me that Earl and Tiger created this interest by only giving the public and the media small doses of themselves which made them appear to be mysterious and illusive, thus creating much curiosity because of the unknown. Earl believed that it is only human nature for people to want to know more.

If Tiger and Earl had been more open about themselves and their lives, and if Tiger had acted like other golfers on tour or like any other athlete, there would not have been as much interest in him. Besides, how many other golfers on tour are considered to be a celebrity, much less to the extent of Tiger?

Not one single golfer!

Keeping secrets had become a way of life for Earl and Tiger, so my protecting their secrets was just part of the norm. It was simply part of the loyalty one had with Earl and especially with Tiger and you just never felt the need to reveal anything. But to be completely honest, there was really nothing to reveal. Nothing was really out of the ordinary. However, Earl still did not want anyone giving information to the wrong people or mentioning anything that could be misconstrued and be negatively directed at Tiger. They expected complete loyalty, not just from me, but from everyone who surrounded them, just as Tiger did within his own "camp". Trust and loyalty means absolutely everything to Tiger.

The ongoing secrecy that surrounded Earl and Tiger was always deemed necessary in order to protect Tiger's career and image. Although it was the media that created the image that made Tiger so famous, it was Earl and Tiger who felt there was a need to live a life of secrecy for the sake of that image. However, it was also Earl who chose to create a particular image for Tiger which put him into a different light with the media and with the public. The role model image that Tiger had to live up to forced Tiger into a position of always having to be perfect in everyone's eyes. Because of this role model image and the image that the media had created, no matter what Tiger did, whether good or bad, it was going to be of media interest, thus causing Tiger to guard himself from any unnecessary or inaccurate reporting.

Earl got so carried away with his fear of the media and his own self-importance that he felt anything Tiger might do, right or wrong, would not only affect Tiger, but this would have great consequences on Tida and himself. Since Tiger was the celebrity and the one with an image to protect, I could never understand what gave Earl a valid reason to feel this way. I could understand this position if a son of the President of the United States did something wrong as it would definitely affect his father and his position, but how could Tiger's actions ever affect Earl and Tida and who would really care?

The necessity of keeping up Tiger's image and the secrets that went along with that image, forced Earl to maintain a certain lifestyle, a perfect example of which was misleading the public and media to believe that he and Tida were still together as a couple, when in actuality, they had been separated since Tiger had turned pro in 1996. If it had not been for Tiger's new image and Earl's need for his own importance, the public would have been aware of their separation. But they didn't want anyone to know Tiger's parents were no longer together as this might tarnish Tiger's so called perfect image. After all, how would it look to everyone if they knew Tiger did not come from that perfect family life and from perfect role models?

Again, I truly believe that because of Earl's fixation on his son, this too was only imagined in his mind.

In reality, was it the media that caused Tiger and Earl to be so secretive and feel they had to hide or was it part of the strategy created by Tiger's agents and Earl to build up and take advantage of Tiger's tremendous talent, thus creating a celebrity status and world fame? They simply used the media as a vehicle to promote Tiger for their own benefit. Tiger became a household name all over the world, but was it because of his golf or was it because of the marketing and promoting that had been established for him? Let us not forget that the more popular a person is the more products will be sold by his sponsors.

14
DEFENDING TIGER

IT HAD BECOME QUITE obvious Earl was indeed consumed with Tiger and his career, especially since Earl truly believed that Tiger was beyond special and could never do anything wrong. Earl was convinced that Tiger was different than anyone else in the entire world, never truly seeing his son as just a normal human being or even capable of making normal mistakes. For years I saw how Earl's obsessive and overly protective nature increased and eventually Earl's outlandish actions and statements went off the charts, almost to the point of paranoia.

Over the years I realized Earl had taken it upon himself to be Tiger's lifelong caretaker and protector. For some strange reason, Earl needed to be the one single person who would shield his son from all of the many adversities in life. Earl decided that since he was Tiger's father, he was the only person who would be able to always protect his son from this "big, bad world" and from all of the injustices and wrongdoings that could be and would be directed toward Tiger. No matter what occurred in Tiger's life, I knew Earl would always be there to defend Tiger, making sure to always clean any slate that had been marred.

Earl's unexplained need for protecting Tiger began from the time his son was just a small child and continued throughout his life. Earl's protection mode escalated tremendously when Tiger joined the PGA tour and Tiger's marketing agents and the media had created his new image. Since Tiger's popularity had risen to all new heights when he became the most famous golfer in the world and the athletic hero of the media, Earl had become even more fanatical when it came to protecting Tiger's career and his new image. Earl was like a big papa bear protecting his little cub and if anyone approached his perfect son or even attacked, Earl would immediately pounce and come to Tiger's defense.

One of Earl's many protection processes was his constant defense by portraying Tiger as a victim, causing him to continually make excuses for his son. These excuses would usually be aimed at the media, especially after one of their attacks were made and, in Earl's mind, were directed unjustly toward Tiger. Earl honestly believed that it was his duty to protect Tiger from the media's scrutiny and their unwarranted harassment. Many times over the years, it was standard practice for Earl to portray Tiger in a more perfect light in order to ward off any further attacks from the media. Earl just assumed that if he painted a certain picture of

Tiger, the media would follow his lead and project the same about his son. Unfortunately, this did not always happen the way Earl had expected and it was not long before Earl learned the media and the public will do as they please, not really concerning themselves with how Earl wanted Tiger represented to the world.

Earl had a tendency to get upset, and at times, I witnessed his anger when he felt Tiger was being treated unfairly, whether it was in his personal life or in regard to his golf. To be honest, I was surprised to see Earl get so upset and outraged over comments made in a magazine article or from commentators on television. Earl truly believed no one had the right to talk negatively about his very talented son. After all, Tiger was perfect and Earl could not understand why everyone else could not see that same perfection. From the time Tiger was just a small child and showed off his talent in golf, Earl knew his son was special. And because of his amazing talent, Earl felt that everyone should also see Tiger as being special and better than anyone else. There were many who did not agree with Earl's assessment of Tiger, leaving Earl to lash out at anyone who disagreed with his opinions. Earl could never understand why so many people wanted to strike out at Tiger's ability and talent and why they wanted to disprove the fact that he was an exceptional golfer, especially during the first few years Tiger was on tour and was not playing as well as he should have.

Each time Earl and I discussed this topic, I realized even more how Earl was not able to fully understand what his past actions had actually done to Tiger. It was Earl who had built Tiger up to the media in the first place and had set the media and public's expectations so high that it would, of course, create a considerable amount of doubt about his ability if Tiger was not able to live up to their standards.

Earl initially started with the hype when Tiger was young, and unfortunately, it simply snowballed from that point on. Earl could not see the damage that had been created from his own actions and now he was blaming everyone else for the subsequent results. He also never took into consideration what affect all of this would have on Tiger.

Tiger had an incredible talent early on and because of that talent, Earl believed his child should have special and exclusive treatment. Whenever Earl assumed that Tiger was mistreated or suffered an injustice by others, I watched as Earl would become an overly protective father, doing what was necessary to fight for his child by defending him. Earl honestly believed his child deserved more because Tiger was unique and very different from all of the other children.

One time when we were in the clubhouse after playing a round of golf at the Navy Golf Course in Cypress, California, I remember Earl telling me the story about the time when Tiger was not allowed to play that same course. Earl explained that when Tiger was around four years old and playing with him at the Navy Course, an incident occurred leaving Earl to believe the course was discriminating against his son because of his age. The management at the course had a rule that no child under the age of ten years old was allowed to play at their course, even if they were accompanied by an adult.

Although Tiger had a talent for golf, at four years old he still did not have the same distance or playing ability as an older child, much less an adult. Basically, Tiger should not have been on a full size course. He was just a little kid playing with his daddy, but to hear Earl tell it, Tiger was excellent at the game and could beat most adults. I knew Tiger was good, but he definitely was not that good. Most of the adult players and members were voicing their complaints about Tiger being allowed special privileges to play on the course and after hearing all of the negative comments about his son, Earl decided to talk to the head pro in order to obtain special permission so that Tiger could be allowed to play with him. After watching Tiger demonstrate his golfing abilities, the head pro thought it would be okay for Tiger to play on the course and gave his permission to allow the under aged Tiger to continue playing with his father.

However, other members of the golf course did not quite see it that way and they vehemently objected to the special privileges that were being given to Tiger, especially since their own young children, who were under the age of ten years old, were not allowed to play under any circumstances. They balked at the head pro's decision to make special arrangements just for Tiger, stating that his decision was showing unwarranted favoritism. All of the members could not understand why Tiger, a four year old child, was allowed to play golf on their course when everyone knew it was against the written rules. Besides, he was still too small and just did not have the ability or played a good enough game to keep up the pace with the adults, thus causing unwanted slower play. So, the members caused enough of a ruckus with the management and forced the issue, resulting in Tiger being banned from playing at the course until he was ten years of age.

Earl was ex-military and could play the course any time he wanted, but now he would not be able to play there with Tiger. Earl told me how completely outraged he was with their decision because he knew Tiger was a good enough player, unlike most children his age, and he adamantly believed an exception should have been made for him.

Earl just could not understand what all the fuss was about from the other members; after all, it was Tiger we were talking about. Of course, since Earl was the only person at the time who thought his son was exceptional in golf, he naturally assumed everyone else should feel the same way. But rules are rules, and in this case, special allowances could not be made, even for Tiger.

Tiger was an okay golfer at four, but he was not great. Earl took total offense to the rejection from the Navy Course and felt a prejudice had been made toward his child, and with his anger, Earl stopped playing at the Navy course for the next few years, until Tiger became of age. It wasn't long before Earl soon discovered, and to his dismay, that age limit rules existed at almost all of the courses, including military courses. So Earl was now forced to have Tiger play at Hartwell, which was a local small par three course. At Tiger's age, everyone thought Hartwell was more appropriate for him. In fact, the course even had its own golf instructor, Rudy Duran, who began to work with Tiger as his new swing coach, and of course, along with Earl.

I even told Earl that he should have seen the entire incident as a blessing since the new instructor was able to take Tiger and his game to the next level. When Earl looked back on it, he agreed with me and was thankful for the direction it went. However, Earl was still angry at the management of the Navy Course for the "injustice" he believed they inflicted on Tiger. In Earl's mind, he honestly believed he was right and everyone else was wrong, simply because it was not fair to Tiger. Frankly, at four years old, I don't believe Tiger could have cared less where he played golf or that he even understood about any rules, much less that an "injustice" had occurred. It was Earl who wanted his son to play with him and it was Earl who did not get his way.

Earl ended the story by telling us that he had told the course management he would never again return because of the embarrassment they had caused his son and himself. Since we were all sitting in the clubhouse at the Navy Course after our round of golf, Earl felt he needed explain why he and Tiger were now playing this course again after the story he had just shared with us. Earl said that times had changed and when Tiger became of age, it only made sense that they return. Besides, he said it was the only course that was so close to their home and it cost less to play. I just thought, so much for holding out for what you believe in! Earl had caved in and convenience and price soon took precedence.

I remember the time when Earl and I were discussing Tiger's first appearance at the Ryder Cup Matches. Since Earl had always accompanied Tiger to all of his tournaments, Earl was, of course, planning to go with his son to the Ryder Cup in Spain. However, there was a rule that prevented Earl from traveling with the Ryder Cup team members, since the players were only allowed to bring their wives or girlfriends. Earl was so upset that he could not go with Tiger. At the time, I just could not understand why Earl was so furious with a rule he knew existed and had always been in place, and why he was feeling it was a direct and personal attack on himself and Tiger.

I even asked Earl why he didn't just fly over by himself to be with Tiger. Earl felt he should not have to go alone because he was Tiger's father and he should not be singled out and excluded from the team. Earl also had the gall to believe that because of who he was, he should have been invited as part of the official entourage. Earl was only the father of one of the golfers on the team, so what made him feel he was different from everyone else? This made me wonder about all of the other fathers of the members of the Ryder Cup team who were restricted from flying over with their sons and if they were also throwing hissy fits. For some strange reason I just didn't think the other fathers were having the same reaction as Earl.

Earl also told me that since it was Tiger's first Ryder Cup and he was in a foreign country, alone with no one to talk to and help him with his game, it was necessary that he be there for his son. Again, Earl did not have enough faith in his own son's ability to survive without his presence. I tried to make him understand that Tiger was there with all of the other players and it should have been an exciting time for him. No matter what I said, Earl still felt it was imperative that he was there for Tiger.

Earl actually believed there were times during the tournament when Tiger needed him and his advice. So Earl spent countless hours trying to phone Tiger in Spain, many times unable to talk to him due to the time change. Earl, and even Tida, were both so upset that they were not able to maintain constant contact with Tiger.

And then to make matters worse, Tiger did not play well during the entire event and Earl angrily stated that if he had been allowed to attend, he could have prevented Tiger's poor play.

Earl had honestly convinced himself that he was the one single person who could have corrected Tiger's poor performance. Many times, Earl had told me that he could prevent eighty-five to ninety per cent of the problems Tiger usually encountered on the course. Because of the fact that he was not allowed to go with the team, Earl actually ended up blaming the PGA for Tiger's poor play performance. To me, and I am sure to others, Earl's thinking was far from rational, but whenever it came to Tiger's golf, Earl was always over the top and quite self-serving.

However, after hearing Earl's explanation of the entire incident, I started to wonder if Earl was simply embarrassed by Tiger's performance, never imagining the fact his son might not be perfect and from that he needed to blame someone else for Tiger's inconsistent play. Knowing Earl, I think this scenario was most definitely plausible.

After the Ryder Cup incident, Earl's anger caused him to contact the PGA and voice his disapproval regarding the situation. He did everything in his power to have the traveling companion rules changed, even requesting that special exceptions should be made in order to accommodate only him. Earl truly believed that rules should not apply to Tiger, or even himself, since after all he was the father of Tiger Woods.

Although he was unsuccessful in his efforts with the PGA, Earl still maintained these rules needed changing to benefit all of the players, not just Tiger. But if Tiger had not been involved, Earl would never have put forth any effort to change any rule on behalf of any other player. Only when things pertain to Tiger will Earl react and strongly apply his input and his demands.

Doesn't this remind you of the incident at the Navy Course when Tiger was only four years old and was not allowed to play because of his young age? They, too, did not accommodate Earl's demands by changing the rules. In fact, whenever he felt there was an injustice being imposed on his son, Earl was consistent in his efforts by repeatedly writing letters, calling and contacting the people in charge, always on Tiger's behalf. Although Tiger may not have shared the same feelings as his father in regard to the so-called "injustices", Tiger was placed in a position where he had no alternative except to allow his father to continue his ongoing campaign to protect him.

Although Earl's irrational actions continued throughout the years, I remember when Tiger was in his mid-twenties and once again, Earl reacted and took action on Tiger's behalf regarding a comment written in a golf magazine. Tiger asked his father to just back off and not do anything, but Earl proceeded against Tiger's wishes. Earl's meddling had become a common practice for Earl despite Tiger's requests.

Not long after the Ryder Cup and Tiger's poor exhibition of play, Greg Norman, who was the European team captain at the time, made an innocent comment about Tiger. He had made his own assessment about how Tiger was not currently playing well and definitely not up to all of the hype that had come out about him. He also stated that this was quite normal during the course of a career and, after all, Tiger had only been a professional golfer for a year and was not playing well at the end of 1997. Simply put, Greg was only stating the facts and his motive was not to make Tiger look bad.

However, as was typical of Earl, he saw this as an outlandish statement and immediately took offense to the comment. Earl felt what Greg Norman said was a direct and personal attack on Tiger and his ability and how the comment was totally uncalled for. Earl retaliated by saying that he would take Tiger's rookie record over Norman's any day and then proceeded to make his standard excuse for Tiger, stating that Tiger's current poor play was due to his being overly exhausted. Tiger was a young and healthy twenty-one year old. How tired could he get? Of course, this was a perfect example of Earl's over-the-top protective and defensive nature, thus demonstrating his constant control of his son and protecting his son's newly created image.

There were numerous other times when Earl had become angry or outraged by someone else's actions, especially when he thought the outcome might adversely affect Tiger and his precious image.

Another incident was about the NCAA and all of the problems he and Tiger had incurred when Tiger was in college at Stanford. Earl hated the control that the NCAA had over Tiger and absolutely everything he did, whether it was pertaining to the school's golf team or off campus and in private. Earl felt the rules and regulations that Tiger had to abide by were getting totally out of hand. Of course, Earl believed that because of who Tiger was and that he had many accomplishments already under his belt in the golfing world, his son should not be compared with the other members of his team and should not have to abide by the same rules. Earl's thinking was Tiger should receive special treatment and be allowed to do whatever he or Earl wanted.

Simply put, Earl wanted a special set of rules put into place just for Tiger and he also wanted to change those rules whenever he saw fit. Earl got so tired of having to continually battle with the NCAA that it eventually reached a point where Tiger decided to make some new choices in his life. Of course, this was when the NCAA became the contributing factor in regard to Tiger quitting college and becoming a professional golfer.

Whenever Tiger did anything that caused criticism from the media, or anyone for that matter, Earl was quick to respond with one of his typical defenses or excuses. It's strange how you never hear about other fathers of athletes making comments in defense of their sons. These fathers may advise their sons on how to handle their problems or a particular situation, but Earl was the type of father who would immediately jump in and take control of it himself. Earl seldom allowed Tiger the opportunity to defend himself and for some unknown reason, Earl strongly believed he needed to shield Tiger. Yes, Earl was overly protective of his son, but at what cost to Tiger?

When Tiger was growing up, Earl made excuses each and every time Tiger made a mistake on or off the golf course. Even when Tiger displayed his anger, threw a tantrum or showed his arrogant attitude, Earl was right there to endorse them. Earl would defend Tiger's poor play and even justify Tiger's childish reasons for wanting to quit in the middle of a round. Once again, Earl was simply turning a blind eye to any of Tiger's shortcomings. If Tiger did not show complete perfection in anything he did, Earl quickly defended Tiger's actions before anyone could criticize or verbally attack him. Earl was always right there with the perfect excuse. In Earl's mind, Tiger could do no wrong. The problem was Earl had a difficult time backing away from anything Tiger was involved in, as he feared he would not be able to defend and protect his son if he was not there.

Once he was on the PGA tour, Tiger became a media darling, so there was less criticism toward Tiger. Although there were more expectations placed on Tiger, the people were less quick to judge. However, Earl still remained vocal whenever he believed it was necessary. If articles were not to Earl's liking, Earl would speak out and make sure that Tiger's reputation and image was not affected and was still being held up to the highest standards. If there was a particular reporter who Earl did not like or believed a journalist would not be favorable toward Tiger, then Earl would refuse to allow him an interview with Tiger or himself. This was even true before Tiger was on the professional tour. No matter the situation or the circumstances, Earl was always there with the necessary words that would defend his son, even if he had to slant the truth to his own liking. Earl did what he had to in order to make everything benefit his son.

When all was said and done, was Earl protecting Tiger or was he only protecting the image that he wanted to maintain for his son? Then again, in Earl's mind, he was also protecting himself by making sure Tiger's actions were not an embarrassment to him. After all, he created Tiger Woods and Earl could never look like he had failed with his creation.

Earl actually believed he was always rightfully justified in protecting his son, especially as an adult. Not only did Earl make excuses for Tiger, but he continually believed in the merits of his own actions. I found Earl usually defended his actions by stating that he was only doing what he thought was right for Tiger or by claiming it was because of his love for Tiger that he did this or that. Unfortunately, however, one cannot place all the blame on Earl as it was both Earl and Tida who shared this inexplicable need to smother Tiger, both as a child and then as an adult, many times feeling Tiger was incapable of functioning without them. They actually believed they were a valuable asset in Tiger's life, thus rationalizing their constant interference and presence.

Although Tiger had grown into a man, I knew it was both of his parents who were unwilling to ever let go and allow Tiger to become the person he needed to be in life. Instead of encouraging Tiger to learn from his own mistakes, I feel it was always Earl who prevented Tiger from such lessons, thus trying to insulate him from the world and from eventually discovering who he really was. However, both Earl and Tida just naturally assumed it was their place and responsibility to do everything for Tiger and to be with him at all times. Even if Tiger was not nearby, they would continually call and check up on him. According to Earl, Tiger needed to know that his parents were always there for him. If Earl was, in fact, correct in his beliefs, it proves Tiger was definitely dependent on them and continually relied on their constant protection, guidance and presence.

The frustration Tiger felt must have been overpowering for him at times because I am sure Tiger found himself being pulled between the incredible love he had for his mother and father and the overwhelming need to break away and stand on his own.

15

STEALING THE SPOTLIGHT

TIGER'S FAME AND WEALTH came by virtue of his own ability and his hard work, however, with Earl, it was a conscious choice to take advantage of the publicity and the fame of his son. Earl truly believed that because he was Tiger's father, he should also participate in all of Tiger's fame and success by sharing the spotlight. Earl actually thought he was deserving of the same fame that was achieved by his son. And since Earl was the person who raised Tiger and coached him from the time he was just a little boy, Earl decided he was entitled to create his own persona as a celebrity, stemming only from that of Tiger.

Tiger is just another human being with an incredible talent in a particular sport. There have been many like him over the decades in every walk of life, not just in sports. But Earl never considered his son to be like anyone else. Earl believed Tiger's talent was far superior and could never compare with the performance or talent of any other individual who had ever made a mark in the world. And because of Tiger's amazing golf talent, I watched once again as Earl selfishly chose to insinuate himself into Tiger's popularity and fame. Of course, Earl had been doing this since Tiger was three years old, but ever since Tiger turned pro and became wealthy, Earl was now in the big league. Most of the time, when Earl was in public or on television, he always appeared to portray that he, himself, was better than everyone else, just because of who his son was. I was surprised to see how Earl put on airs and acted as though he was someone special and was worthy of the same popularity as Tiger.

Yes, Earl raised and trained Tiger, but the way I saw it, he was only his father, not the person out there having to deal with all the trials and tribulations that life was dealing him or all the pressures and scrutiny that had now become his life. This was now Tiger's life. It was understandable how Earl was beyond proud of his son, but it was his son's success, not his.

And, yes, Earl wrote several books about raising and training Tiger. He had interviews and speaking engagements and had also become known as "the father of Tiger Woods". And it was Earl's dream, not Tiger's, to start the Tiger Woods Foundation and the Learning Center to help children. However, if he had not had Tiger as a son, Earl would not have had the acclaim, popularity or the wealth he had received from Tiger and from the foundation.

Therefore, if Tiger had not become a famous golfer, Earl would have remained just Earl Woods, regular person.

In Earl's mind, he assumed that he deserved the distinction and recognition simply for being the father of a famous person. Earl believed the athlete Tiger had become was a direct result of all of Earl's hard work and training, not allowing for the fact Tiger, himself, was the actual driving force. In a way, Earl never really gave Tiger any of the credit he deserved for his accomplishments, many times taking all of the credit for who Tiger had become. Whenever Tiger would do something great, this was when Earl would state, "I taught him well," or "Tiger became who he is because of me," or "I trained him to be the best," or "I taught him everything he knows". He went so far as to state, "I'm the one who made him a champion". Earl was always of the opinion that he made Tiger great. It was always I, I, I, I. It was always about Earl. He actually felt that he deserved his own accolades for what he had done for his son.

The public did not give Earl that fame as it did with Tiger. Earl just created it for his own self ego, possibly to satisfy the status and ranking he once had in the military, or maybe the status he would have had if he had been able to play professional baseball, but was denied because of his color. Earl honestly felt that years earlier he had been deprived of the opportunity to establish a name for himself and create his own legacy. However, now Earl had an opportunity to achieve his own status and legacy, one that was shaped only by him, but was based solely on his son's reputation and ability.

Thinking about what Earl did made me wonder how Tiger felt about being forced to constantly share his own well deserved spotlight with his father. Not only did Tiger have to strive to maintain his own status within the world of golf, but because of Earl's self-created fame, Tiger was now forced to also maintain a status for his father. The way Earl saw it was if Tiger failed, then Earl had failed and Earl would never have allowed anything to jeopardize what he, himself, had created. In Earl's mind, anything Tiger did would reflect on Earl, good or bad.

Many have questioned Earl's continued control and constant presence in Tiger's life, in his business affairs and in his golf, just as I have. It is true Earl and Tiger had always considered themselves to be a solid team and did everything together. However, Earl could have chosen to stay in the background, establish the Tiger Woods Foundation, counsel and assist Tiger and basically remain anonymous like so many other fathers of famous athletes and celebrities. But that was never in Earl's plans. In my opinion, Earl should have stepped back and let Tiger bask in his own glory and success. After all, Tiger was an adult and was perfectly capable of functioning on his own without his father, but of course, Earl thought otherwise.

How does one who never had a reason to become famous create fame for himself? Earl did it by insinuating himself into Tiger's life and career and taking part of what belonged to Tiger for himself.

As Tiger was growing up, Earl had created situations which caused Tiger to be subjected to the media and television, ensuring the necessary publicity to help pave the way for his eventual career in golf. Since Tiger was not well known in the early years, Earl tried to make sure his son became a so-called celebrity at an early age, thinking it would increase Tiger's chances for recognition, popularity and fame later on. And who was with Tiger during each and every interview or appearance? It was Earl who made sure he was always present, always making sure that he, too, was interviewed and sharing in the glory right alongside of Tiger.

Prior to Tiger's stardom, Earl was completely unknown and his views and opinions were never solicited by anyone, much less the commentators at a professional golf tournament. Although he had appeared briefly with Tiger during a few television programs where Tiger, as a child, showed off his talent for golf, never once was Earl asked to be interviewed or to have a long discussion on any subject with any of the hosts. Tiger was their main attraction, not Earl. Appearing with his son gave Earl a taste of fame, small as it was, but in Earl's mind, he was still on television and being noticed. This was Earl's fifteen minutes of fame, however, as Tiger continued to excel, Earl ended up craving even more of the spotlight.

After Tiger turned professional, Earl chose to attend each and every interview and appearance with Tiger. Earl also made sure he attended each and every Tiger Jam concert and after party held in Las Vegas, every function or award banquet Tiger attended, and all of the golf clinics Tiger participated in, including the ones that were sponsored by the Tiger Woods Foundation. Anything public or newsworthy, Earl would always be present. At times, I became curious as to whether or not Tiger had asked his father to be there or did Earl just take it upon himself to share the billing with Tiger.

But why did Earl feel it was necessary for him to tag along with Tiger wherever he went? Since Earl had become Tiger's crutch, Tiger most likely felt like he needed his father there. I guess there was no reason for Tiger to stop doing what he had always done. Earl created this dependency early on making sure Tiger would always need him.

But according to Earl, he was only there to support Tiger. Support is one thing, but Earl's obsessive and controlling behavior was an entirely different situation. Unfortunately, whenever Tiger made an appearance or just went anywhere, for that matter, Tiger knew he would never be alone since Earl or Tida, or both of them, would always be with him. Sadly, as their son, Tiger was never in a position where he could push his parents away and tell them no. I wondered if Tiger was just being an obedient son and simply felt obligated to accept his father's claim to the spotlight and he was forced to once again abide by his father's wants and demands.

I even imagined if Tiger had ever been in the Olympics and won a gold medal, I am quite sure Earl, or both of his parents, would be standing next to Tiger on the podium when he received his medal. No other parent or coach has ever accompanied an athlete in that respect, but I just know Earl would be there, sharing in Tiger's spotlight and probably demanding a gold medal of his own.

It reached a point where Tiger could not shine by himself without his father right beside him, almost like it was the "Earl and Tiger Show". It was obvious Earl got carried away with his "Team Tiger" concept as it appeared he was trying to live his life through Tiger's success and fame. However, when I look back at

Earl's actions, I wonder if it could have simply been jealously on Earl's part. Possibly! Was it Earl's tremendous pride he had for his son? Absolutely! Were Earl's self-serving actions over the top? Most definitely! Were Earl's actions necessary? Not at all!

Most fathers do not feel it is necessary to take some of their child's success for themselves. When I think about it, not even the relatives of royalty or celebrities or even relatives of the president of the United States take advantage of their family connections in to order to seek fame or recognition for themselves. Off the top of my head, I can't think of one relative who has stood out in public because of their child's or sibling's popularity. When you think of Joe Montana, Apollo Ono, Andre Agassi, Derek Jetter, Wayne Gretsky, Phil Mickelson or anyone else for that matter, not one of their fathers have ever taken advantage of their son's success to promote themselves in any way, shape or form. Generally speaking, no one has heard about any of their fathers, much less know them by name. Strangers would probably never even recognize them at the local grocery store.

But when it came to Earl it was different. He had an overpowering hunger for his own fame. Simply by being Tiger's father, Earl used society for his own vehicle to establish personal success and accomplishment, as though he had become someone of great importance. Earl's self-promotion included sharing the hosting responsibilities with Tiger at the Sherwood Country Club in Thousand Oaks where Tiger's World Challenge tournament was held every December. Earl would strut around like he owned the place and his arrogance especially showed when he would award the trophy to the winner, a position he gave himself and was responsible for each year. And, of course, the trophy was a statue of a "Tiger", which according to Earl, was his own idea in order to further promote his son. I'm surprised Earl didn't have a bronze bust of himself presented as the trophy since he claimed that establishing the tournament was all his idea.

When he was attending the golf tournaments Tiger would be playing in, Earl made sure he was always invited into the television commentator's booth to be interviewed and share in a discussion about Tiger. Since Earl believed he had become an authority on the sport of golf simply because of who his son was, his presence allowed him to give his own commentary and analysis of the games of other professional golfers. After all, Earl trained Tiger Woods, so who would know more about golf than Earl?

In addition, Earl was also asked to give speeches to various groups around the country, including Robert Schuller's Crystal Cathedral in Garden Grove, California. This church has one of the largest televised congregations around and Earl felt very much at home standing behind the pulpit as he made his speech. Even when he appeared with Tiger on the Oprah Winfrey show, Earl believed he had finally made it to the top and he was now in his own element. But why did Earl feel it was necessary for him to share an appearance with Tiger on the Oprah show or anywhere else, for that matter? Tiger was an adult and it was Tiger who was the professional golfer being interviewed. This should have been Tiger's moment to shine, not Earl's. But, as usual, Earl was always there.

I knew Tiger had been affected by Earl's actions and Earl had even indicated how dissatisfied Tiger had been on many occasions.

Why do you think Tiger chose to attend a college that was over four hundred miles away from his parents when there were several great universities in close proximity to their home? Also, why did Tiger leave the sunny state of California and move to Florida, three thousand miles away from his parents, as soon as he joined the PGA tour? Answer? His freedom! Unfortunately, even the distance never stopped Earl.

Earl's constant need to be noticed and accepted continued over the years, never really stopping at any given point in Tiger's career, or at least until Earl's illness started to progress and he was forced out of the public eye. It's sad to think that the only way for Earl to back away from intruding on Tiger's life was to have his illness stop him.

Although Earl could never acknowledge that his participation and constant obsession to be with Tiger was overly excessive, I was worried what the eventual outcome of that obsession would be when Tiger no longer had Earl in his life. Frankly, toward the end, Earl, too, was concerned about what Tiger would do without him in his life, but for all the wrong reasons.

I had become familiar with Earl's obsession not only for recognition, but also for his own fame. Over the years, I came to accept Earl's arrogant behavior, even though I had a difficult time understanding it. Personally, I felt his need to be as important as his son seemed totally unwarranted, but I eventually gave in to his actions and comments.

However, there was one thing I never could understand. Why did Earl feel it was necessary to wear a hat with his name on the back of it? This hat was quite important to Earl and it was Earl's arrogance and new status that contributed to his wanting to be noticed in public. Earl truly believed he deserved the recognition and had earned the special distinction the hat gave him because he was "the father of Tiger Woods". Earl thought the hat was an important part of who he was, but if Earl was not wearing his golf hat that had *EARL WOODS* embroidered on the back of it, people hardly ever recognized him as Tiger's father, much less as Earl Woods.

I can't stress enough how important being noticed was to Earl. This hat was Earl's method of making sure everyone would recognize exactly who he was, almost like a walking billboard. He knew when to wear it and when not to wear it, depending on whether or not he felt like advertising the fact he was Earl Woods and the father of Tiger Woods. Earl truly believed that he deserved the same recognition and admiration as his son and wearing his signature gave that to him.

When Earl wore his signature golf hat that cleverly depicted who he was, strangers would just walk up to him and simply start talking about Tiger or ask for his autograph. However, when Earl was at a more formal function with Tiger, it was not necessary to wear his hat as he knew everyone would just naturally assume he was Tiger's dad. However, since his special hat had become a part of his normal golf attire, Earl always wore it to all of Tiger's golf tournaments and even when he, himself, was playing a round of golf.

When Earl wore his hat, he felt extremely important and he believed it was necessary for him to broadcast his identity in public by wearing it. I think he truly thought "the hat" was a way of being acknowledged and allowed him to share in Tiger's success. Most importantly, the hat let it be known that he, too, had attained prominence, even though it was only through his son's fame and success.

It was not until after Tiger turned professional and gained sponsorships when Earl started wearing his signature hat. The first hat Earl started wearing was from Tiger's first sponsor, Titleist. The next hat was from Nike and carried the standard Nike logo. The last set of hats were also from Nike, but had Tiger's "TW" logo on the front. No matter what the logo was, or the sponsor, Earl always demanded they provide him with several cases of hats, all with his name embroidered on the back. With Earl, his hats were similar to that of a business card, making sure people knew who he was.

What always seemed odd to me was in all my years of golf, I had never seen anyone wear a hat with their name on it, not even the pros, but especially not the father of a professional golfer. But Earl wanted everyone to know who he was, especially when he attended all of the tournaments Tiger was playing in. His hat always solved the problem if the camera only caught the back of Earl's head while it was scanning shots of the spectators. That way if the camera failed to show Earl's face or if the announcer failed to mention Earl's name, at least everyone knew it was Earl from the back. People watching television could get excited and say, "Oh, look, there's Tiger's dad. Can't see his face, but the back of his hat shows it's him." Even the famous hug between Earl and Tiger at his first Master's win only showed the back of Earl's head and Tiger's face. No one ever had any doubt Tiger was hugging his father. Earl had shown the millions of viewers it was really him since everyone could see the name "EARL WOODS" on the back of his hat.

Exactly what was the real purpose of these hats? Was Earl afraid people would not recognize him as the father of the most famous golfer in the world? So what if he wasn't recognized. I'm sure very few people in the world could identify Phil Mickelson's father or any other pro golfer's father, for that matter. But if they were wearing a hat with their name on it, then everyone would know who they were. And these fathers probably could care less one way or the other about being identified in public. Each of these fathers know it is their son who is famous, not them, and the father also knows just being a professional athlete's father does not necessarily make him famous or entitled to share in their son's spotlight. These fathers unselfishly and proudly respect their son's glory and their self-attained success.

But Earl was different. He ignored the fact that it was his son who worked so hard to make a name for himself and all of Tiger's successes were based on his ability as a golfer. The fame and accolades Tiger earned were not Earl's. Just because Earl and Tiger shared the same last name, Earl should not have capitalized on that fact and made himself known just because of who his son was. Many times I wondered how Earl's behavior made Tiger feel, knowing his father was taking advantage of him and everything he had accomplished in life as a professional golfer.

During public interviews and appearances, Earl would always give the impression to the audience he was someone undeniably special and famous. But each time he appeared like this in public, he seldom needed to wear his signature hat. The hat was not necessary because he had already been introduced as Earl Woods, Tiger Woods father, by a host, a commentator, or an announcer telling the viewers exactly who this man was. When circumstances occurred and there were no formal or verbal introductions, "the hat" would do the trick and make the introduction for him.

Of course, when you think about it, you never see any of the professional golfers have their mom and dad go to every single tournament either, unlike Tiger's. His mother, Tida, has always made sure that she attended every single tournament Tiger played in, usually wearing Tiger's Sunday red, but never wearing a hat with her name on it.

16
BACKGROUND CHECK

THE PUBLIC NEVER HAD the opportunity to meet the private Tiger and Earl as they never portrayed that particular identity in public or to the media. There was so much more to know about them, much of which they never wanted the public to know. I discovered many years earlier the purpose behind their acting differently in public was because they wanted to make sure the public never found out about who they really were in private, the side of themselves that involved their secrets and their frailties. This was the side of their personal lives they wanted to hide, a side of themselves I was very familiar with. This carefully protected private life included such defects as broken marriages, hidden relationships, paranoia, ignored and cast aside children, racial prejudices and kinky sex habits. Since these characteristics would not normally be considered image making qualities and knowing that they would deflate the perfect family perception, one could see the importance of their hiding the truth.

Whenever they were in public, Tiger and Earl truly felt it was necessary to play a role which was designed to mislead the public and media. They came across as though they were the perfect father, the perfect son, the perfect golfer, the perfect family, perfect in every way, as though they could do no wrong. Although Earl had tried to convince me otherwise, I still believed their role playing was designed to simply slant the truth in a way to make everything more favorable toward them. Besides, it was Tiger who had an image to maintain.

Throughout the years, there were many times when Earl would open up to me about the difficulties he experienced throughout his life. Not only was he trying to survive in another loveless marriage and learning to cope with the adjustments of civilian life after many years in the military, but he was also raising a potentially gifted son and worked endlessly to help coach him to be a great golfer. Earl was basically grooming Tiger to become a professional golfer and was hoping and expecting that Tiger could accomplish things in life that he himself was never allowed to do in his own life which included changing the perception of blacks in a white dominated sport.

Earl's father and mother died when he was in his early teens and he was raised by his oldest sister. According to Earl, during the years when his parents were alive, he was fortunate enough to be taught strong and solid family values and learned many vital and impressionable lessons about their race. Although Earl learned these lessons well, Earl's life was still affected by many of the racial problems that occurred throughout the next several years.

Not many people knew about Earl's difficulties with race and how he felt about being black. Earl had to endure discrimination not only in his private life, but also in the military. Over the years, I saw how Earl continued to allow discrimination and race to have a tremendous effect on him and held inside a lifetime of bigotry, which continued to eat at him and eventually have a negative influence on his overall view of life.

Many times Earl was quite outspoken about his feelings and I thought he sometimes went a little overboard with his viewpoints, as though he was still living in the past. I mean, there were times when Earl would literally come unglued, ranting loudly about various topics, voicing his objections and opinions about the many injustices that occurred, or even might occur, in his or Tiger's life. Eventually it reached a point where Earl began using his son's fame and status for his own personal platform to subtly let people know how he felt about the many injustices he experienced and used his past as a current reason for anger. Unfortunately, Earl was unable to accept the fact that times had changed, and in turn, people have also changed. No matter what was said or how it was said, Earl, on occasion, still had a tendency to connect many comments or actions as being racial.

Over the years we had several conversations on this subject, but during one particular discussion involving the hate mail and death threats that had been directed at Tiger, Earl was quite emphatic when he told me how much he truly hated the way so many people still treated black people. He just felt it was so cruel, especially in this day and age. But Earl's problem was he didn't know what he hated more, the way people treated blacks or his being black. Earl confided that he basically thought that he hated being black because of the way he had been treated by whites in the past.

Even after all these years, Earl still held a grudge which stemmed back to his college years in regard to his playing baseball. Earl truly believed that because of his color, he was denied the ability to have a promising professional career in a sport he loved. Earl told me about the time when he had been accepted to play for the Monarchs, a team in the Negro professional baseball league. Earl turned it down because he felt that with his great talent he should have been given the opportunity to play in the real major leagues, along with the white players.

Publicly, Earl has stated that he chose the military over a career in baseball, but he told me that he ended up going into the military because he had been rejected by the majors and he felt insulted that his only alternative would be to play in the Negro league. Earl was truly convinced that he would have had an extremely successful career in baseball and may have even become famous had he been given an equal opportunity. He strongly resented the fact he was never allowed to have the chance to get his name in the record books, have a baseball card with his picture on it or be acknowledged as a famous sports figure and role model.

Basically, Earl felt cheated out of his dream and the possibility of fame and recognition, all because of his color. When it came to Tiger, Earl once told me, "They stopped me from a great career in sports. By God, they are not going to stop my son." He further proclaimed, "I will do everything in my power to make sure my son will be the first black champion in golf."

Earl could not understand that he was not being singled out because he was black. Although unfair, it was simply that he was raised in an era where most blacks were treated the same way he was. Sadly, Earl grew up thinking that it was only against him and he truly believed it was an individual injustice and attack on him personally.

Throughout the years, Earl shared his thoughts and feelings on the subject with Tiger, thinking he was protecting his son, when in fact he was teaching Tiger to grow up with the same resentments and prejudices. Instead of just believing his son would make it in golf based on his own talent, Earl felt he had to take it upon himself to push and showcase Tiger simply because of color. Tiger was raised with his father's biased mentality which created a continuous negative influence throughout his life. Sadly, Tiger had to grow up always knowing his own talent and success had to compensate for the opportunity that Earl had always believed he was denied.

Unfortunately, because of his own personal perspective regarding race, Earl was going to use Tiger to create a cure for all of the wrongdoings that he himself had endured in the past. He had held a grudge against society his entire life, holding so much resentment inside. Earl knew he needed to let it go, and tried many times, but the rage dominated too much of his thinking. Earl had to live with his memories and was unable to ever forgive or even forget.

Many times when Earl talked about his feelings, he would become extremely vocal and would demonstrate tremendous anger and frustration toward the racial problems, whether it was the past or the present, and especially when we discussed the discrimination that still existed on many of the golf courses. Of course, I understood his frustration because Earl was raised in an era when segregation and discrimination was very real for him and was a very sad and unfortunate fact of life.

I remember Earl telling me a story about the time when he and Tiger were at a country club in the South. This was when Tiger was still in his teens and playing in an amateur tournament. He and Tiger were having lunch in the restaurant at the golf course, and Earl was convinced that everyone was staring at them because they were black. In Earl's mind, he felt they all believed that Tiger and he had no business in the restaurant and should be in the back washing dishes. I was simply shocked to hear Earl's paranoia. I asked Earl if it was possible that they had recognized Tiger as one of the top Junior Amateurs. However, Earl was convinced that it was a racial thing and to him there was no other explanation.

After all these years, Earl still harbored many negative feelings, especially since he was raising a son who he believed would have to deal with similar issues in golf and in his life in general. This is not to say Earl was not proud of his heritage, because he was very proud, but Earl just wanted his son to be accepted and he had hoped that one day Tiger could break through the social color barrier and be recognized simply for who he was and the talent he possessed. Although there had never been any racial incidents or anything that would indicate there would ever be a problem, Earl still believed because of his own past issues, Tiger might be treated differently once he became a professional golfer.

It was because of their color that Earl was convinced they had a harder road to travel and had more to prove than most people. Desperately fearing non-acceptance, Earl set out to show everyone that Tiger should be accepted in the golfing world. And to achieve this, Earl felt he had to push his son to perfection in order to be the absolute best or else he would never get the recognition that Earl believed Tiger was entitled to.

Earl also told me that most people feel there are no black role models in the world today.

He said, "People have a perception that all black athletes are nothing more than bums and criminals." I just looked at him and questioned his comment as it seemed completely inaccurate and I could not believe these words were coming out of his mouth.

I responded with, "What about Michael Jordan, Willie Mays, Jackie Robinson," and the list went on and on. Earl responded with, "They were not real role models. If they had been considered a role model, then they were only viewed as such by black people." Earl honestly believed that white people do not have black people as role models.

All I could think about was Tiger and the warped viewpoint on life he had to grow up with because of Earl's narrow minded and self-absorbed thinking.

In another conversation, Earl had commented that blacks are basically excluded from playing golf and there have never been very many black players on the professional tour, much less any black champions. I agreed with Earl when he stated that over the years, many golf courses would not allow blacks to play golf and it was not fair, but times have definitely changed and there are now more equal opportunities for people. I mentioned to Earl that maybe the reason blacks don't play golf is because they simply do not like the game. After all, golf is not for everyone. He agreed with my statement, but he continued to believe there was still a prejudice toward blacks, referring once again to the golf course restrictions. Then I commented that another factor could be they just never saw any money in the sport compared to the money offered in other sports such as basketball, baseball and football.

Everyone knows that over the years and before Tiger turned pro and golf became so popular, golf winnings were quite low. So unless you were consistently good, it would be difficult to earn a significant amount of money. When you think about it, just because blacks don't play golf does not necessarily mean they are being discriminated against. I also reminded him you don't see many black Olympic skiers or swimmers either. So does that mean those sports discriminate? In a way, Earl had somewhat agreed with my thinking and my point of view, but he still believed he was correct in his own opinion and stood firm on his position.

After a lengthy discussion on this topic, I gave in to Earl, fully understanding he was adamant in his thinking and beliefs. Earl was making color an issue which only substantiated the fact that he was still holding a grudge and simply would not let it go. No one could ever blame Earl for the way he felt, and it was sad that he, or anyone else for that matter, had to ever endure such prejudices throughout their lives.

After Tiger turned pro, Earl began to assume that money could buy you everything and provide you with a great life. He used his money to fit into a world that he never felt he belonged in before, simply because of color. What is so disheartening is even with the wealth and status Earl had eventually attained through Tiger, the money still could not help him overcome his feelings of the past. Sadly, money can never heal scars.

Although Earl felt strongly about the racial issues, he still chose to have several white friends, me included. I think it made Earl feel like he was more accepted. He used to tease me that I must be color blind because I only saw Tiger and Earl as just Tiger and Earl. Nothing more, nothing less.

17

TIGER'S OUT OF CONTROL FATHER

EVEN THOUGH HE WAS ONLY the father of Tiger Woods, Earl still believed it was imperative that he put on airs and present a more impressive and regal image to the public. His newly created persona was somewhat different than who Earl really was, especially when he was in the privacy of his own domain. It was the public side of Earl that sometimes embarrassed Tiger with his off the wall comments and over the top actions pertaining to Tiger's greatness or Earl's arrogant attitude of self-importance.

There were many occasions when Earl, and even Tida, would do or say things that would annoy Tiger. The problem was that because of the love Tiger had for his parents, he was unable to stress his feelings to them about their actions. All of his life, Tiger had been told that his father knew best and everything Earl did for Tiger was done for a good reason, so it was difficult for Tiger to ever question his father's motives or actions. In addition, Tiger always felt obligated to his parents for the time and sacrifices they contributed to his golfing career.

Although Tiger had become the bread winner in this family and was supporting both of his parents, Tiger found that he still had absolutely no control over them. Tiger was forced to live with the way Earl and Tida were choosing to act. In effect, Tiger's sense of obligation to his parents overrode any of the embarrassment or discomfort they might cause him.

In private, Earl always had a demeanor about him that was very easy going and relaxed. Although the arrogant, know it all attitude part of Tiger and Earl stood out in the public's eye, and especially when they were in front of the camera, they were both totally different in private. Earl was intelligent and always had his words of wisdom which were convincing and soothing, no matter the topic. He was very self-assured and confident, yet gentle and kind. Earl could really be quite charming most of the time. His humor was mellow, yet sometimes impish. In fact, you really did not want to tangle with Earl's wit, as you would most likely lose every time.

Tiger was so much like his father, sharing many of those traits and at times they were almost like two peas in a pod. Their close and special bond was a constant in their private lives, seldom showing that side of themselves to the public.

However, due to Tiger's success and wealth, Earl eventually changed his behavior, especially whenever in public. Once Tiger turned professional and made it possible for his father to live a better life, Earl decided he had now earned the special bragging rights as Tiger Woods' father. Well, really it was as Tiger Woods' wealthy father.

Many people, especially people in the media, thought Earl's many comments about his son were sometimes outlandish and over the top. Trust me when I tell you they were not far from the truth. Earl's actions toward Tiger were like no other and his comments were sometimes bordering on bizarre. Most of Earl's statements came from his know it all, better than God complex that began to surface over the years as Tiger's performance in golf gained prominence.

One of the problems Earl had was that he loved to mentor. And I do mean it was a problem. Although Earl did, at times, give some sound advice, I felt he could get carried away with his own self-proclaimed philosophical ability. However, frankly, I think Earl just loved hearing the sound of his own voice. Knowing the way Earl was in regard to his mentoring, I actually sympathize with Tiger because his upbringing constantly revolved around Earl's mentoring and his many, many, many words of wisdom. Or at least Earl thought they were wise words.

Earl was really good at manipulating people and situations. His words were always convincing and extremely believable and even at times, seemed sincere. However, Earl had a way about him that was similar to that of a cult leader, leading his flock and expecting everyone around him to be his faithful followers. I, too, was a part of his group of followers, and unbeknownst to me, I was coerced into believing and trusting the things Earl said. I was a grown adult, so just imagine what Earl's words and actions did continuously to Tiger from his childhood into adulthood.

For some reason, Earl thought he knew everything about everything and he wanted to share this with his son, and anyone else who would listen. Earl always had an answer to every question and a solution to every problem. He believed he knew how to turn every negative into a positive. Throughout the years he shared his knowledge and his own life experiences with Tiger in hopes that Tiger would take his words and his astute advice with him as he grew into adulthood and hopefully see the world through Earl's eyes.

When you think about the way Tiger was raised, it is a shame Earl relied on his mentoring skills to raise Tiger rather than setting a better example of values for his son.

Earl's words were, at times, quite mesmerizing and I, too, would tend to believe most of what he said to me. I always trusted that Earl knew best, just as Tiger trusted him all of his life. After all, Earl had taken an "EST" seminar in the early 1980's, so he had convinced himself, and others, that he knew what he was talking about. In fact, because of the EST course, Earl now thought he knew everything.

EST was known officially as The Erhard Seminar Training for personal development. From their website, EST states that their purpose was "to transform one's ability to experience living so that the situations one had been trying to change or had been putting up with, clear up just in the process of life itself. The seminar was aimed to enable participants to shift their contextual state of mind around which their life was organized from the attempt to get satisfaction or to survive, to an experience of actually being satisfied and experiencing oneself as whole and complete in the present moment."

I have no idea what in the hell this statement means, but all I know was Earl was totally sold on the knowledge he gained at the "two week" seminar and claimed he applied much of what he learned in many parts of his life. This definitely explains why Earl made so many strange comments, especially the ones about Tiger

Earl thought he had something to say and he was convinced that people wanted to listen. He even demonstrated that fact when he would call me in the middle of the night to share his thoughts or feelings, not ever caring if I had been asleep or not. He always assumed if he was awake, then I should be awake, too, since Earl never believed talking or simply having something to say should be ruled by the clock.

Earl led people to think he single handedly made Tiger into the golfer he is today and, as a result, Earl then fed off of that recognition. Earl had convinced himself he had become a world renowned golf guru and thought all people were clamoring to hear his words of wisdom by inviting him to lectures and speaking engagements. Earl thirsted on these gatherings as the lectern would become his pulpit and the audience would become his congregation and as he began to "preach" to the people, he knew they would be spellbound by his every word. This was from a man who used to be just a military officer and just a husband with children, but who now had a life that had reached an entirely new level. This meant he had become the man who "created" Tiger Woods.

A perfect example of his actions would be the time when Earl was invited to speak at the Crystal Cathedral in Garden Grove, California, for Reverend Robert Schuller's televised evangelical program called Hour of Power. This program aired every Sunday morning. Earl had the gall to request an invitation to speak at the church and Earl made his appearance on television in front of millions of viewers and church goers. He stood behind the pulpit and preached to the congregation and the television audience about how he raised Tiger Woods and single handedly brought him to fame. It was because of Tiger that Earl had now become an "authority" on raising children from all walks of life. Since Earl truly believed he had this special ability to inspire everyone in the world, he shared with everyone his thoughts and feelings about life, hoping all would follow his lead.

Earl also spoke about how his son, Tiger Woods, would be a role model for the entire world and because of his multi-ethnic heritage, Tiger had the ability and popularity to bring the East to meet the West and he would bring the world together in a way that no one could ever imagine. He told the congregation how Tiger would one day be as great as Gandhi and Mandela and his role in golf and in life would have political ramifications and give Tiger a power which would be like that of a minority president.

Over the years, Earl really believed that Tiger had changed the world and in his heart and mind, Earl was convinced that Tiger had done so much and had already changed millions of lives.

However, when you think about it, outside of golf, what has Tiger actually done to change the world? Tiger is only a golfer, not the next messiah.

And, no, Tiger does not walk on water!

Earl was quite serious about his comments and discussed his feelings with me many times over the years. Earl was actually convinced that people from all walks of life wanted to hear his words of wisdom and he just naturally assumed they trusted and believed every word he had to say. I honestly believe if Earl was alive today, he would give Tiger all of the credit for the United States having elected its first black President.

Every single word that Earl ever spoke, whether it was in public or in private with Tiger, eventually had some effect on Tiger and the way he lived his life. With each word and with each and every speaking appearance, Earl continually demonstrated his over the top addicted obsession with Tiger and with his golf.

When you think about Tiger, it must have been difficult for him to hear his father constantly take credit for something he had accomplished on his own and with his own hard work, talent and ability. Also, think about how hard it must have been for Tiger, who was trying to launch a career in sports, to hear his father keep uttering comments that his performance will transcend the sport of golf and have effects on the entire world. Now this is what I call pressure!

It's sad to say, but Tiger just wanted to come out and play golf and everything was supposed be just about Tiger. Unfortunately, Earl took so much of that away from Tiger, in order to claim it for himself. Tiger did not want the world that Earl created. Tiger just wanted to be the next Nicklaus, not the next Gandhi.

18
PLAYING THE FAME GAME

SINCE TIGER WOULD BE COMPETING in the Mercedes Tournament of Champions in Hawaii, Earl thought it would be fun if we also attended the tournament. Earl and I had been in pubic together many, many times, but this particular trip would turn out to be different because the public setting would be more focused on Tiger. Much of what occurred over the next seven days would once again reaffirm my belief that Tiger's own haughty attitude and his outlook toward others most definitely came from his upbringing and his father's teachings.

The day I was to fly out of Las Vegas, the weather was so bad that my flight was delayed a couple of hours and I was worried I would miss my trip to Hawaii all together. Eventually my flight took off, barely giving me enough time to meet Earl at LAX and make our flight to Maui.

After landing, I spotted Earl standing nearby at one of the airline counters talking on the phone. Since I had just arrived, I had no idea who he was talking to, but the more I listened, I noticed Earl was showing quite a bit of anger and aggression toward the person on the other end of the phone. I soon realized Earl was talking to someone from Delta Airlines and he was trying to get them to hold our flight to Maui until I had arrived. As Earl turned around and noticed me standing there, he immediately told the person that I had finally arrived. This is when Earl demanded they send a courtesy cart to our terminal to pick us up.

I could not believe the airline would even consider holding the plane for us, but as Earl explained, he simply told them he was "Earl Woods, Tiger Woods' father" and he had demanded their cooperation. Although, I am sure the person on the other end of the phone could care less who Earl was and who he was the father of, they still reluctantly obliged with Earl's request and actually held the plane for us. I was not the least bit surprised to hear that Earl was again using the "I am the father of someone famous" card to demand what he wanted.

After our arrival at the Kahului Airport on Maui, I noticed my luggage was nowhere to be found. After checking with an airline official, I was informed that my luggage and my golf clubs were still back in Los Angeles and might arrive sometime that night on their next flight.

Suddenly, Earl raised his voice and barked at the employee, claiming how this was a huge inconvenience for us and demanded they deliver my luggage directly to our hotel immediately upon its arrival.

I tried to make Earl understand that it was not the airlines fault as they were unable to get my bags off my plane from Las Vegas and onto our flight to Hawaii because I was so late due to the weather. I mean, hell, I barely made it myself, so how could my bags?

Surprised by Earl's actions and feeling somewhat sorry for the young employee, I just thought to myself, "Well, once again Earl gets his way!"

This was when Earl told me we could have avoided all these hassles if we had just flown here on Tiger's jet. He said Tiger could have picked me up in Las Vegas, then picked him up in Los Angeles and then we all could have flown straight to Maui. Unfortunately, that didn't happen because we decided to leave a couple of days before Tiger needed to be at the tournament. But at least we knew there would be no problems going home because we were, in fact, flying home with Tiger.

Since we were staying at the Kapalua Bay Hotel, Earl had made arrangements for us to play golf the next day at the nearby Kapalua Bay Course which was next to the Plantation Course where Tiger would be playing in the Mercedes Championship Tournament.

Upon our arrival at the golf course, the starter immediately informed us that, per Earl's request and for our privacy, he would make sure the group in front of us was at least twenty minutes ahead, and he would not be sending out another group behind us for at least another twenty minutes. He wanted us to take our time and enjoy our round. Wow, was I surprised. In all my years of playing golf, I had never seen that happen before.

Then after an attendant brought us our cart, all of a sudden three more attendants appeared out of nowhere, each one trying to assist us. They were all scurrying around us, falling over each other trying to do more, such as getting us plenty of towels, water, balls, tees, and even extra ice. Everything was "Mr. Woods this" and "Mr. Woods that". In the end, we had amassed eight Kapalua monogrammed golf towels, two dozen logo balls and enough water to sink a ship.

Earl was just eating up all of the attention, actually feeling he was deserving of their treatment. The attendants repeatedly asked if there was anything else they could do for us and I honestly thought they would have each given us their first born if we had asked. After everyone finished sucking up to "Tiger's father", we were finally ready to head off to the first tee. Since everyone at the golf course had acted this way for Tiger's father, can you just imagine what would have happened if Tiger had joined us?

On the first tee, I took my stance and I nervously waggled my club. Then I waggled it again and again, something I seldom do. All of a sudden Earl yells out at me, "Just hit the damn ball!" I looked over at him, flipped him the bird, then I proceeded to take my swing. As we drove down the fairway, Earl and I could not stop laughing at what just occurred.

After our round of golf and when we returned to our hotel, we ran into Jim Furyk and his wife, Tabitha, in the lobby. Not long after that, Nota Bogay approached us to say hello. Since Nota had been Tiger's teammate at Stanford, the three of us talked for quite a while. Afterwards, Earl turned to me and actually had the gall to ask me how it felt to be around a celebrity such as himself and in the mix with everyone.

What? Where in the hell did this question come from? Earl actually made it seem like I was a complete nobody and this should all be a big deal for me, obviously thinking I had never been around any "real celebrities" before. I just did not feel it was necessary for me to give him a response nor was it the time or the place for me to share my own many celebrity experiences. Thus, I just politely smiled at him and said nothing.

The problem was, I frankly never considered athletes to be celebrities and I certainly did not consider Earl to be anything more than who he had always been in the past. So, to Earl's dismay, he saw that I was not really all that impressed. Being around Earl for as long as I had, I should be accustomed to Earl's attitude and comments, but he never failed to surprise me with something new.

A couple of days later, we decided to attend the Mercedes Championship Tournament which was being played at the Kapalua Plantation Course. When I drove up to the security check point, the guard asked to see our passes. Since I was not aware of our having any passes, I asked Earl, "Do we have any passes?"

Earl looked over and in a testy tone, sharply snapped back at the man, "We don't need any damn passes. I am Earl Woods!"

The security guard leaned down so he could look inside the car and noticed Earl. The man immediately apologized by stating, "I am so sorry Mr. Woods, I didn't see you in there." The man continued by saying to us, "No, of course you don't need a pass,

Mr. Woods. Please just drive straight ahead to the clubhouse valet and they will take care of you there."

After all these years, you would think I would be used to his over inflated ego, but he never ceased to amaze me. I guess I don't understand why he feels it is necessary to treat people so rudely and with such arrogance and entitlement.

After I parked the car at valet, Earl and I walked over to the first tee box where Tiger was waiting for his time to tee off. As we approached the roped off area, I noticed several TV cameramen and photographers scurry toward us, each positioning themselves just right. Tiger came over, hugged his dad, said hi to me, and then Earl started in with is typical coaching to Tiger. He started to tell Tiger that he needs to focus and concentrate more on his putting if he wants to win. The problem is, Tiger does not like to be told anything when he is in the middle of a tournament and especially standing on the first tee. Earl knows this, but sometimes he just can't help himself. This was when Tiger glared at his father and testily stated, "Yeah, I know Pop, I know. I got it." Fortunately, Earl backed off and then wished his son luck.

After watching Tiger hit a long and perfect drive down the center of the fairway and since Earl never walks the course, he and I decided to go into the clubhouse to get out of the sun and to get a drink at the bar. On our way, and as we were passing by one of the ESPN reporters, Earl decided to stop and talk to the reporter and offer him a short interview about Tiger and himself.

Unfortunately, Tiger was not in the lead nor was he playing all that well, but Earl still spoke about Tiger's perfection and what a great golfer he is. Earl then made his typical excuses for Tiger's poor play. Just before the interview ended, the reporter asked Earl whether or not he thought Tiger would be in the top five for the last day of tournament. Earl was completely honest by stating, "Let's just see how Tiger does today. This will, of course, be the determining factor, won't it?" Frankly, Earl's tone sounded a little bit testy and I could tell from the reporter's expression that he thought so, too.

As we approached the clubhouse, Earl started to complain about how he always dreads going into the public places, especially at Tiger's golf tournaments, because he knows he will get mobbed by all of the people wanting his autograph. Earl also commented on how it ticks him off because the people only want his autograph because he is Tiger's father and not because he is well known in his own right.

As we walked through the clubhouse toward the bar, a couple of people approached him, all strangers to Earl, and either asked for his autograph or talked to him like they had been friends for years, yet only wanting to discuss Tiger. Noticing only a few people were approaching Earl, I wondered if he wasn't wearing his golf hat with the name EARL WOODS monogrammed on the back of it, would anyone have known who he was at all.

After we finished our drinks about forty-five minutes later, I was still looking around for the so called "mob", which obviously never materialized. This was when Earl stated he could not take any more of it and wanted to leave the clubhouse, which we did, leaving the imaginary "mob" behind.

After we left the clubhouse, Earl and I walked over to the area where the other pro golfers were waiting for their tee time. Some of them were at the driving range, but some were standing nearby, so Earl decided to say hello and talk with them for a little while. As Earl and I approached Rocco Mediate, Jasper Parnevik, and some of the other golfers, I was surprised to hear how they all referred to Earl as "Mr. Woods". I thought it was strange, although I was sure they all did it out of respect for an elder. However, it almost appeared their salutations were given because they felt Earl commanded that kind of respect from everyone simply because of who his son was in the world of golf.

I remember there was a time when we first started playing golf together and when Tiger was still young, and Earl would have given anything in the world to simply have any pro golfer acknowledge him and just call him Earl. Boy, how times have changed.

Part way through the tournament, Earl wanted to leave as he was beginning to get tired. After the young man in valet brought us our car, we headed back to the hotel, ordered room service and finished watching the tournament on television. Not long after the tournament was over, the telephone rang and it was Tiger. He told me to tell his dad to turn his damn cell phone on because he had been trying to call him for over an hour. Not wanting to get in the middle of this one, I quickly handed the phone to Earl. To comply with his son's request, Earl fumbled through all of the pockets in his luggage, grumbling the entire time, until he finally retrieved his phone. Earl hated his cell phone and at times just wanted to forget he even had it. But for Tiger, it was his way of staying in constant communication with his father when they were on trips or at tournaments.

Once Earl had reassured Tiger that his cell phone was on, they continued with their talk. As always, Earl and Tiger discussed his round in detail. Earl was telling Tiger, yes, you are behind, but you need to focus more. Then he reassured Tiger that he was not in a slump and that he should stop saying that he was not going to win. Earl firmly told Tiger, "You are my son and you can do this. Remember all the training you have had. You will turn things around and win this tournament. Besides, there is no reason why you can't win." Earl tried to explain that Tiger was not up against anyone who could beat him, so he should just focus on his game and especially his putting. Earl ended with, "Don't worry about what people are saying, you still have two days to pull this off." Earl was firm with his delivery, making sure Tiger understood every word.

Although I had listened to these conversations many times over the years and I knew the contents of these talks were normal for Tiger and Earl, I just started thinking about Tiger growing up and all the times Earl would tell Tiger what to do, how to act and what to say. Once again, I was reminded of just how dependent Tiger was on his father and his constant advice and reinforcement which is why they phoned each other daily. From my perspective, Tiger had become a young adult and Earl simply needed to let go. But due to Earl's controlling nature, letting go of his son was just never going to happen.

After Earl got off the phone with Tiger, he turned on ESPN to catch up on all of the sports. Suddenly, Earl called out to me and said, "Look, you're on TV." And there I was, standing next to Earl and Tiger. Apparently they had filmed the segment at the course earlier when we were at the first tee talking to Tiger. As I sat down and watched the footage on the TV, Earl spoiled the moment by bragging, "See what happens when you are around important people!!" I just turned and looked at him, confused by his comment, and wondered where did that come from, and most importantly, why?

Comments like this one made me realize even more how much Earl and Tiger had changed. Over the years, I noticed many changes in both Earl and Tiger's behavior and I was attributing it to who Tiger had now become.

It seemed as though any time that Earl was at one of Tiger's professional tournaments where the media was present, Earl acted as though he was on "stage" whenever he was around Tiger. Earl truly believed it was his own time to shine and he had the right to share in Tiger's glory. Many times I questioned why Earl needed to be famous, too. After all, he was only a golfer's father.

During our time in Maui, Earl had talked to me on numerous occasions about Tiger playing in the tournament and how he expected more perfection from his son. From the comments Earl made, it appeared that he was truly upset over Tiger's play and eventual loss.

Earl explained how he felt guilty that he was not able to help Tiger play better in this tournament. Although they had their daily talks after each round, Earl still believed he was unable to get through to Tiger enough to produce a win. Earl has always been there for Tiger and has always helped him with his poor play, but this time his advice didn't improve Tiger's performance and this bothered him. Earl always felt responsible for the outcome of

Tiger's play level. After all, according to Earl, he created Tiger Woods. Earl would get upset when Tiger didn't win because he knew his son could have done better.

I told Earl, "You are not so godly, so powerful or so magical that you can *make* Tiger win a tournament. That part of Tiger's game is out of your control." I also told Earl, "No matter how perfect you expect Tiger to be, he is still only human." Earl knew Tiger always does his best when playing in a tournament, but I told him, "If Tiger loses, it's no one's fault. Maybe Tiger played great, but someone else played better. Not even Tiger can win every single tournament." Earl knew I was right and agreed with my thinking as he tried to feel a little better regarding Tiger's loss.

At the end of our seven day stay in Maui, Earl and I headed off to return our car to the rental agency. As we waited outside for the limousine to pick us up and take us to Tiger's private jet, Butch Harmon pulls up in a white Mustang convertible and said he was there to take us to the airport.

Earl looked at Butch and said, "And just how do you expect all of us and our luggage and golf clubs to fit into that tiny car?"

Butch looked at the two of us, then looked over at all the luggage and the two sets of golf clubs, and then looked back at the small car and laughingly said, "Oh, shit! This definitely is not going to work. I guess I had better send the limo for you after all."

Earl quickly laughed, "Gee, Butch, ya think?"

Earl and I just laughed at Butch's reaction as we envisioned ourselves trying to stack everything into that small car. Earl just questioned where Butch's head was at and jokingly stated, "And this is the guy who is Tiger's swing coach. That's scary!"

After the limousine picked us up, we finally arrived at the airport, where Tiger's private jet was waiting. Shortly thereafter, Tiger arrived in his own limousine. As he stepped out, I noticed Tiger was carrying several bags of food from McDonald's. I just stood there and laughed, thinking what is wrong with this picture. To me, Tiger has always been just Tiger, but it was still funny to see "Tiger Woods" get out of a stretched limousine carrying bags of McDonald's Chicken McNuggets, fries and drinks and then walk up the steps to his lavish private jet

Tiger just flashed his typical smile and then, acting as though absolutely nothing was out of the ordinary, he laughingly teased, "What? It's our dinner? It's better than the food on the plane." Everyone just laughed. This reminded me of when he was younger and how mischievous, yet innocent, he could be.

Then I realized some things never really change and that was Tiger's love for McDonald's food. Well, maybe things did change a little, especially since Tiger could now afford to buy out the entire chain of restaurants, if he so desired. However, based on the image that Tiger portrays as a well-trained and extremely wealthy athlete, it's hard for people to believe that Tiger is actually a fast food junky.

Of course, Tiger was gracious enough to bring enough food for all of us and we ended up "enjoying" Chicken McNuggets and fries on our flight home instead of the lavish spread of food that had been provided on the plane.

Once again, this made me realize how the private side of Tiger is a far cry from who he is when in the public eye and when he has to portray that perfect image.

As I looked out the window of the plane, I realized during our trip to Hawaii just how much Earl had changed over the years, mostly when he was in the public eye, but especially when he was around Tiger and the media. But the more I thought about it, Earl was only playing the fame game, simply because his son was Tiger Woods. Sadly, Earl deemed it necessary to resort to such tactics of using his son in order to be noticed and to feel important. Each time I would see Earl's personality change, I wondered how Tiger must have felt, always having his parents around and always watching them act as though they are famous, too.

Then again, Tiger had always been programmed to see his father differently than everyone saw him, so just maybe, Tiger never really saw anything odd about his father's behavior.

And then, of course, Tiger's mother, Tida was also onboard the jet. Remember, she goes everywhere with her son. Tiger never leaves home without her!

Trying to once again protect Tiger, Earl reminded me how Tiger may not be all that talkative after losing the tournament. I knew Tiger needed time to mull over his game and retreat into his "zone". Since he did not win the Mercedes Championship, Tiger would most likely be in a sullen mood. Tiger hadn't changed. He had always been that way.

However, after Earl had fallen asleep, Tiger came to the back of the plane to talk to me. We talked about a lot of things including his bleached blonde hair. Tiger and I joked about the fact that it should be growing out soon and how it was a definite mistake, one he will probably never make again. We also talked a little about the tournament.

I commented, "Sorry you lost the tournament. I know how you hate to lose."

Tiger shrugged his shoulders and replied, "Yeah, but it's all in the mindset. All week, my putting sucked and I just couldn't pull it together."

I tried to be consoling as I carefully responded, "Well, at least there are more tournaments coming up that you will be playing in and as usual, I know you will give it your best."

Tiger simply smiled and once again shrugged his shoulders, as though he agreed with me.

We talked for a while longer and then Tiger decided to watch a movie with Butch. It appeared he was still wound up from the tournament and couldn't get to sleep yet. A little while later, I looked over and saw Tiger preparing his bed. I think Tiger was more tired than he would admit because it wasn't long before he hit the sack and fell asleep.

After Tiger had fallen asleep, I looked over at him and I was reminded of when he was just a small innocent boy with braces on his teeth, playing with his mother's clubs and only dreaming about days like this one.

19
WHERE IT ALL STARTED

TIGER WAS RAISED in a modest fourteen hundred square foot tract house in Cypress, California, and lived there with his parents until he left to attend Stanford University in Northern California. Once Tiger joined the PGA tour in 1996 and received his first sponsor money, Tiger immediately purchased a home for his mother, at which time she moved out of the family home and away from Earl. Basically, they separated and ended their marriage.

Earl, on the other hand, chose not to move from the family home simply because it was where Tiger grew up. Since Tiger was now living in Florida and traveled on the PGA tour, Earl believed that remaining in his house where all the memories with Tiger took place would make him feel closer to Tiger. Of course, since

Earl had been in the military for twenty years and moved around quite a bit, Earl had no desire to move again.

Earl's small house was unlike the expensive and much grander house that Tiger bought for his mother, Tida, in Tustin Ranch, California, or the large pricy house Earl's daughter bought with the money Tiger gave her.

This was the house Earl had purchased back in the mid 1970's and the one he had spent years of hard work earning the money to pay for. He took such pride in the fact that he alone bought this house, with no assistance from anyone else, and it was only his sweat and his earnest money that went into making this house his home.

Earl vowed that he would never move as this house held many years of fond memories, especially the ones with Tiger and his golf. For some reason, Earl was extremely steadfast about preserving his house, so much so, that if anything should ever happen to him, the house was to be made into a museum and become a public shrine to honor Tiger. Earl wanted people to have the opportunity to visit the house and see where Tiger had grown up, thus leaving behind a legacy for both him and for Tiger. To keep the house as a shrine was so important to Earl that he had transferred the title of the house into a trust in 1998, making sure that it was never to be sold.

To update his home, Earl had a designer renovate basically everything throughout the entire house. And even though Earl tried to convince me that he had spent over five hundred thousand dollars refurbishing the house, including new furniture, I personally thought that he had over exaggerated that amount by at least four hundred and fifty thousand dollars or else he was grossly overcharged.

Earl realized that five hundred thousand dollars was an extravagant amount to spend on a fourteen hundred square foot tract home that was built in the early 1970's, but to him it was not an investment that he was hoping to recover in a future sale. In Earl's mind, he was creating an eventual museum commemorating Tiger, thus justifying the excessive expenses. I remember one time when he told me how this house should become a national monument because it was the house where Tiger grew up. I just smiled at Earl and thought to myself, "Now that is way over the top in the ego department, even for Earl. I mean, since when do they dedicate national monuments to golfers?"

Earl's home was an ordinary, yet well-manicured, house that sat on the corner in an older, unassuming neighborhood. When it came to his obsession for Tiger and his golf, Earl went a little overboard when it came to his decor. As soon as you enter the front door, you suddenly notice the inside looked more like a museum dedicated to Tiger than just a regular home. On the right side of the foyer as you entered through the front door, there was a long wall that had been named Tiger's "wall of fame" and was completely covered in large pictures, awards and memorabilia chronicling many years of Tiger's amateur and professional career. Some of the framed pictures showed Tiger with Sam Snead, Arnold Palmer, Jack Nicklaus, and others depicting Tiger's major tournament wins, including the now famous picture of his first Master's win where he was hugging his father. The house was not about Tiger the person, or Tiger, the little kid who grew up there.

The house was about Tiger, the golfer. Sadly, Tiger, the person, had no individual personality there.

Throughout the house, you would notice an added theme, one that just happened to be Tigers, as in the actual animal; however, the majority of it was dedicated to Tiger, the golfer. Even in his patio, Earl had a large Tiger engraved into the glass of the dining table. Over the fireplace was a very large, incredibly well painted portrait of Tiger which, according to Earl, was painted and presented to him as a gift by an inmate who was serving a long term sentence in the prison system. In front of the fireplace was a large rack holding several of Tiger's old putters, all of which had been gold plated by Earl.

Many times these putters reminded me of how Earl had always insisted on remaining Tiger's putting coach, even after Tiger joined the PGA tour. Earl told me that he even had it written into Tiger's contracts with his swing coach Butch Harmon and then Hank Haney that no one, except for Earl, would ever work with Tiger on his putting. Simply put, Earl felt he was the only person who could continually perfect Tiger's putting.

I also remember a time when Earl and I were watching Tiger play in a tournament on television. Tiger had been having a real problem with his putting and Earl was very concerned, but just could not figure out what he was doing wrong, much less how to correct it. As I watched, I noticed how Tiger was standing too far away from the ball, as he usually stood more directly over the ball. After telling Earl what I had noticed, he watched more closely and then agreed with me. He just could not understand how he had missed such an important part of Tiger's stance and set up.

After Tiger had finished his round, Earl called to alert him as to what he was doing wrong and how he should correct the problem. Tiger's putting improved during the next round, and, of course, Earl would never let Tiger know that someone else noticed the problem and brought it to Earl's attention.

If Earl was not at one of Tiger's tournaments, then Earl would always watch his son on television. Whenever I was at the house with Earl and we were watching a tournament together, Earl would always lean forward in his big leather chair and make comments, such as, "That's my boy!!" But if Tiger wasn't playing well, Earl would sternly say, "Tiger, what in the hell are you thinking" or calmly say, "Tiger, think it through" or "Come on, Tiger, shake it off." Of course, Earl was talking to the television, but there were times, because of the bond Earl and Tiger shared, I honestly felt Tiger could actually hear what Earl was saying.

Earl's house had three bedrooms, one of which used to be Tiger's while he was growing up. During my visits to Earl's house, I would sometimes envision Tiger playing his video games on his computer or doing his homework as a teenager or simply sitting back on his bed dreaming of the future that he might one day have in golf. Maybe he had just come home from one of his amateur tournaments and was frustrated with the way he had played. Knowing Tiger, I am sure he spent endless hours concentrating on what he had done wrong and what he could do to play better during his next tournament. After all, Tiger had been taught to be a perfectionist and he had to be the best. His bedroom was his sanctuary where he allowed himself his private times, away from the world of golf and a place where he could focus only on himself. I knew many of Earl and Tiger's father and son talks took place in Tiger's room over the years, after which Tiger was left to ponder his own feelings about each conversation within his own space and privacy.

During Earl's renovations, Tiger's room had been totally redecorated, leaving no evidence of a young boy or teenager. The baseball cards had been removed. There was no computer to play video games. Nothing was left in the room to indicate that it had once been the bedroom of the world's greatest golfer. The room was tiny so all that now remained was a small bed and a nightstand and one simple frame hung on the wall with a collage of pictures of Tiger.

This bedroom no longer had the markings of ever being that of a young man's room. It seemed strange that, considering how obsessed Earl was about his son, he would allow the room to be changed at all. Nothing of Tiger's was left behind.

Earl's obsession with Tiger continued when he had a replica made of each trophy Tiger had won at a major tournament; one for the Masters, the British Open, the U.S .Open and the PGA. According to Earl, each trophy cost approximately twenty-five thousand dollars to have replicated and they all sat on display in the foyer.

The house had a two car garage, but in all the years Earl lived there, he had never parked a car in it. Shortly after moving in, and in order to pacify his love for golf, Earl immediately turned his garage into a miniature indoor driving range where he could practice his golf swing and perfect his game, complete with mat and golf net. Although Earl had only been playing golf for two years prior to Tiger's birth, he had become completely hooked on the game.

Earl spent many hours in his garage working on his swing and it would be during these practice sessions when Tiger would get his first glimpse into golf. This was where Tiger learned how to swing a golf club as he watched his father practice while he was still in his high chair. Tiger was only eighteen months old when he took his first golf swing after spending endless hours mindfully watching his father's every stroke of the club.

Earl had explained to me how Tiger's first swing was left handed because he was literally mirroring the swing that he had seen Earl take. Needless to say, Earl immediately changed Tiger's left handed swing to a right handed swing, and, of course, the rest is history.

Over the years, the garage had become crowded with several large piles of magazines and newspapers, each one containing an article that had been written about Tiger. Also crammed into the garage were cases of Earl's signature hats, boxes of extra books Earl had written, all of the memorabilia and awards Tiger had received over the years, plus many large framed pictures of Tiger. There were also several sets of golf clubs and golf bags that had been given to Tiger and Earl by Titleist and Nike, who were just two of Tiger's many sponsors.

There was so much golf equipment and so many boxes of balls and supplies that Earl could have opened up his own golf shop. Even though the garage was chocked full of many other items, Earl made sure that he and Tiger always had enough room for their practice net and large mat.

I remember the time when Earl took me out to the garage and gave me a copy of his book, *Playing Through*. He was thinking about writing another book, but he wasn't sure if he had written everything he wanted in this book, so he asked me to give him my opinion and some ideas. After reading it, I personally thought it was slanted, over the top, self-serving and an arrogant display of ego and falsities. But, of course, I wasn't about to tell Earl exactly what I thought.

When Earl asked me how I liked it, I told him, "Good book. But you and I both know that a lot of what you wrote is not true, right?"

Earl said, "Yeah, but no one will ever know. They will believe whatever I write and whatever I want them to believe."

Yep, that was Earl's thinking, alright!

After leaving for college, Tiger would return to his childhood home only as a visitor, as it was no longer his home. Earl once told me that it took Tiger quite a while to adjust to the new décor and especially the parts that were dedicated to Tiger. He felt it was nice that his father loved him enough to create the "museum", but indicated that it was a little over the top. This made me wonder if Tiger simply turned a blind eye to his father's obvious obsession with him.

This house was where it all started for Tiger. From the time he picked up his first golf club and until he left home, this was the place where many hopes were created and countless dreams were envisioned. Many of these dreams would be fulfilled, eventually leading Tiger toward the next phase of his life; one that was even beyond his own imagination.

Tiger lived in this house until he went off to college, leaving behind his television, video games and computer, but taking with him a lifetime of lessons. This was the home in which Tiger would never again live, as a new journey for him was just beginning; the journey that would lead him into manhood and a future career as a professional golfer.

Earl's home created a lifetime of wonderful memories for Tiger, but sadly, Earl's own life journey ended in this house on May 3, 2006.

20
SELF-SERVING AGENDA

ONE THING EARL HAD ALWAYS wanted to do as soon as Tiger turned pro was start a foundation to help and inspire children and to learn the game of golf. Earl had always talked to me about his ideas in creating such a foundation ever since I first met him. As time went on and as Tiger became more successful in the Junior Amateur and the U.S. Amateur, Earl realized that his son had become even more special and he could now broaden his ideas for his charity.

This was when Earl's main focus changed and his goal was to now help promote Tiger as an inspiration and role model to all children. As Tiger grew and as he became more successful, Earl decided that he himself should also be considered a role model to all children worldwide. After all, he had raised, trained and created

"Tiger Woods" and, according to Earl, there was no child in the world better than Tiger. And in his own mind, Earl was convinced there was no father in the entire world better than himself.

Earl decided that he wanted to take the many solid values he had been raised with and share them with the world through his foundation. Since he was Tiger's father, Earl believed that he had gained such infinite wisdom and vast knowledge and was convinced that the entire world wanted to learn from him. And then with Tiger's success and increased popularity, Earl's own ego had led him to believe that he was the oracle of everything that was right. Earl honestly considered himself to be an expert on raising children, on the sport of golf and on life in general. Earl actually thought that what he knew could change the world and his own charity would be the basis for his teachings to be passed down to future generations. Unfortunately, he needed to use Tiger's success in golf as his platform to attain those goals.

Earl saw himself as the perfect father who raised the perfect son. Of course, Earl forgot about his other three children from his first marriage and totally disregarded the kind of father he was to them. Putting those thoughts aside, Earl still believed he and Tiger were the perfect duo who would satisfy the needs and fill the voids that existed in many children's lives throughout our country. Earl was going to teach parents how to be better parents and raise absolutely wonderful and perfect kids just like Tiger. Over the years, Earl even wrote books on those various subjects. As time went on, Earl's long term thinking led him to believe that his and Tiger's benevolent work would eventually become worldwide. Earl genuinely thought that simply because of Tiger's success in golf, they could change the entire world. Earl's thinking was that since his teachings would enable Tiger to be accepted by the world, Tiger's fame would go far beyond the realm of golf.

Once Tiger made the decision to turn professional and Earl discovered Tiger would be making a great deal of money from some major sponsors, Earl decided to consult with various experts about creating the Earl Woods Foundation to benefit children. Earl believed that the foundation would honor himself and carry his name.

Unfortunately, the experts in this field did not agree with him and advised him that the foundation would most likely not succeed unless it was educational based and was put in Tiger's name. Since Earl was the father of Tiger Woods, Earl was under the impression that he, alone, was an important enough person to create such a foundation.

However, it turned out to be a huge blow to Earl's ego when he discovered that a foundation in his own name would not draw the necessary sponsors and donations required to insure its success and longevity.

This is when Earl made the decision to have the experts create the Tiger Woods Foundation feeling that, even though it was in Tiger's name, it would still be his own legacy through his son. Earl finally accepted the fact that if the foundation carried Tiger's name, it would have a better possibility of succeeding. Although very disappointed, Earl knew that carrying the name of the Tiger Woods Foundation, the charity would also have the ability to gain more sponsorships and donations, and the real point was to make the foundation flourish and become long lasting.

As soon as Tiger turned professional and started playing on the PGA tour, his sponsorship money and tournament winnings enabled Earl to form the Tiger Woods Foundation and years later build the Tiger Woods Learning Center. Earl told me that the charity was his own idea and not Tiger's. Tiger never really cared about wanting to create a charity even though Earl had discussed the possibility of it and his ideas with Tiger over the years. Tiger was like, "Sure, Pop, whatever you want to do is fine with me. I just want to play golf." After all, a fourteen year old does not think or care about saving the world. He only cares about how far his two iron will go.

It was strange how Earl formed the foundation so early in Tiger's career, especially since Tiger was still relatively unknown. Sadly, Earl never took into consideration how his new endeavor would place many additional pressures on Tiger and on his new career. Earl selfishly chose to use the foundation to create a new image and position for Tiger as a role model, one that Tiger would be expected to live up to.

In addition, Tiger's responsibilities for the foundation would add many more commitments such as golf clinics, appearances and speaking engagements, not to mention his presence at the Tiger Jam concert in Las Vegas, the foundation's annual fundraiser. Tiger would be expected to perform all of his duties for the foundation, which would be in addition to his already very busy tournament schedule and the contractual obligations he had with his existing sponsors.

In addition, all of these functions allowed Earl to bask in the limelight along with his son. Obviously, however, Earl forgot that it was Tiger's own hard earned fame and glory and Tiger should not have to share that with anyone, even with his father.

The additional pressures that were placed on Tiger because of Earl's concept concerned me at times. This made me wonder if these positions were forced on Tiger or did he knowingly agree to them. According to Earl, Tiger was not all that receptive to his plans, but Earl was eventually able to convince Tiger. Earl had promised Tiger that the foundation would benefit from his success and in turn, Tiger would benefit from the foundation, giving Tiger more popularity and continued name recognition. And because of the use of his name, his participation in clinics and appearances, and his own personal donations, Tiger did assist with the foundation's success.

Since this was his initial concept, Earl felt he should maintain total control of the Tiger Woods Foundation, but he was advised against it especially since he had no experience in running a nonprofit organization. Sadly, in order to pacify his own ego, Earl led people to believe that he was more involved in the foundation than he really was.

When the foundation's Board of Directors came up with the idea to build the Tiger Woods Learning Center at the Dad Miller Golf Course in Anaheim, California, this became an extremely emotional time for Earl as he was beyond proud of this particular project that carried his son's name. This Learning Center was going to benefit local children and assist in their education and could possibly give them a new direction in their young lives. Earl felt tremendous gratification with the foundation's new endeavor and he could hardly wait for the facility to be completed.

Unfortunately, when the Learning Center was finally completed, Earl's cancer had rapidly progressed and he was too ill to attend the grand opening in February 2006, but he was still thrilled with what the foundation had accomplished. Although created by someone else, Earl saw this as a concept of his that had become a reality. Even after all these years, Earl still believed that anything accomplished by the foundation, or even by Tiger for that matter, was all his doing. Earl always had the tendency to take the credit for everything.

Earl was basically a good person and he thought he was always doing what was best for his son. He truly believed his heart was in the right place. However, I feel since he had been denied the opportunity to create his own legacy, especially in professional baseball, Earl chose to capitalize on his own son's success in order to provide himself with fame and recognition, which included establishing the Tiger Woods Foundation. Unfortunately, Earl's self-serving and status seeking agenda to accomplish this feat was to share the spotlight with Tiger, making sure Earl's own name would always be remembered and be permanently linked to Tiger, thus creating his own unnecessary and unmerited fame and legacy.

It's such a shame that Earl's need for recognition outweighed the altruistic nature of this venture.

Then there were times when I have wondered if Earl used the foundation and its philanthropic endeavors to create an image for both Tiger and himself in order to hide what kind of people they really were in their private lives.

21
NOT THE BEST IMAGE

THE PUBLIC AND THE MEDIA only saw Earl as a mentor, author and the man who raised and trained the number one golfer in the world. Earl was known as the "father of Tiger Woods". Earl always presented himself to be regimented, somewhat stern, very confident and well educated. In addition, Earl came across as being disciplined and very straight laced. He was also the philanthropist who helped established the Tiger Woods Foundation and the Tiger Woods Learning Center, all to benefit children.

What would people be surprised to learn most about this standup guy, this creator of the world's greatest golfer, the man who preached family values to everyone and the man who boasts that he is a role model to children throughout the world? People would be astonished to learn that Earl Woods had a secret life and was into pornography and kinky sex toys.

Yep, it's true. In fact when it came to his sex toys, he stored them in a little black bag, resembling a doctor's bag and he had dubbed it his little "black bag of tricks". These toys were like a security blanket for Earl, something to have in case he ever needed them. After all, he was getting older.

One time I even asked him if Tiger knew about his porn movies and his little black bag and Earl gleefully responded, "Well, of course, he does. He's my son, isn't he?"

I then jokingly said to Earl, "That's a little more information than I need to know about Tiger." Earl just laughed, knowing I was just a little embarrassed.

But can you just imagine what it was like for Tiger. Being the greatest golfer, number one in the world and the highest paid athlete in the history of the sport, to live with the fact that his own father was into kinky sex and porn movies? No wonder they did everything they could to keep their personal lives private and away from the media. I mean the media would have had a field day with that information.

I even remember when he took his "bag" to Hawaii with us. Earl never left home without it! Thank God this was before nine-eleven and they were not checking the contents of passenger's luggage back then. Can you just imagine?

I bet Tiger would have loved to live with those headlines.

One thing Earl did insist on, however, and which I reluctantly participated in, was watching his porn movies. He had several of his "special" movies stacked up next to his television in the corner of his bedroom. Many times when I was visiting Earl, we would be watching television in his living room and he would suddenly stop what we were watching and put in one of his "movies". I hated those damn movies, but Earl insisted that I watch them with him. Of course, I would pick up a magazine to read while Earl did the watching. I had given Earl a choice. Simply put, I read or I go home. Needless to say, I went through a lot of magazines.

There were times when I thought about how Earl would actually go out and purchase these toys and movies, since I was pretty sure his assistant did not purchase them for him. Once, I even asked Earl how he did it and he replied, "I just go in and buy them. No big deal!"

Of course, I was always curious how Earl, being somewhat well known as Tiger's father, could pull that off? Did he wear a disguise? Didn't the sales clerk or other patrons recognize him?

Then I would quietly laugh to myself when I envisioned Earl in a heavy disguise and sunglasses, sneaking up and down the aisles of the store looking for that perfect porn movie or sex toy, not realizing he was still wearing his Nike golf hat with "EARL WOODS" embroidered on the back of it. It just cracked me up when I thought about it.

22

HIDDEN FAMILY TIES

MANY TIMES EARL WOODS publicly claimed that he was an expert on golf because he raised, trained and coached the greatest golfer in the world. Earl would also continually brag about how Tiger turned out to be an incredibly perfect son and a wonderful role model for the entire world primarily because of his own excellent fathering skills. Due to his self-proclaimed ability to raise such an amazingly talented child, Earl also believed he was now an authority on raising all children.

But if he was, in fact, such an authority on raising children, then what was his excuse when it came to his relationship and the raising of his three other children from his previous marriage? Earl professed to be such a great father when it came to Tiger, but where were his so-called fathering skills and affection toward his other children? The question is, if Earl was such a great and loving father, then why did he reject his other children in lieu of Tiger?

Even though Tiger had two much older half-brothers, Earl Jr. and Kevin, and an much older half-sister, Royce, who were raised by their mother, many people were unaware of their existence, especially since Earl and Tiger tried to never discuss them in public or even acknowledge them as part of Tiger's family. From the way Earl talked, it was obvious he avoided talking about them in public because he thought they were not on the same level as Tiger. Of course, they were from Earl's past and Tiger was "the now".

Tiger's siblings did not live in their little brother's shadow. In fact, they did not even live in the same universe as Tiger. Sadly, this was a result of Earl's outright and blatant favoritism toward only one of his four children. I could understand where Earl's other children were coming from and how they went through life feeling slighted when it came to Tiger. From the time Tiger could walk and showed an interest in golf, Earl had literally devoted all of his love, time, energy and attention toward Tiger and away from his other children. After all, Tiger was different and showed exceptional promise in something, unlike Royce, Kevin and Earl, Jr.

Earl had a history of ignoring his other children. According to Earl, during the time when they were growing up, he was in the military, and although he was unable to spend very much time with them, he never really tried to put forth a sincere effort to be a father. Then Earl divorced their mother and married Tida. Soon after, Tiger was born and Earl's other children were once again set aside. I always thought it was a shame that Earl never took the time to get to know his other children as well as he did Tiger. But of course, they never possessed a talent that would someday garner great rewards for their father.

As Tiger was growing up, Earl focused solely on Tiger. He spent all of his time training and coaching Tiger, writing books about him, promoting him, and going to all of his amateur and professional tournaments. Eventually, Earl worked on the Tiger Woods Foundation, golf clinics, creating tournaments in Tiger's name, and many other projects concerning Tiger and his golf. Absolutely everything revolved around Tiger. In fact, Earl's entire world revolved around Tiger.

Throughout Tiger's entire life, Earl again did not give the much needed attention to his other children. I often wondered what Earl's relationship with Tiger would have been if Tiger had not been interested in golf, never showing any natural ability or skill in the sport. What if he had simply been a regular kid living a normal life? Would Earl have felt the same about Tiger and given him so much attention or would Tiger have been simply cast aside and forgotten and become just another statistic like Earl's other children.

Was it only Tiger's potential in golf that caused Earl to be so attached to him? Over the years, I discovered the answers to those questions. And, yes, it came down to Earl's obsession with his favorite son's talent. Earl even told me himself that if Tiger had not been such a talented golfer, he would have ended his marriage and left Tida in a heartbeat. Earl also admitted to me that he only stayed in the marriage for Tiger's sake. He believed that in order for Tiger to excel in golf, Tiger would need the security of a supportive home environment, so Earl and Tida believed it was necessary for them to stay together. Earl claimed that love had nothing to do with their decision.

Unfortunately, since Earl shared most everything with his son, Tiger grew up knowing these facts about his parent's loveless marriage. Tiger himself must have always known it was only his love for golf that kept his parents together. Too bad it wasn't Earl and Tida's love for each other that kept them together. After all, as soon as Tiger turned pro and began playing on the PGA tour, it only took Earl and Tida all of five seconds to split and go their separate ways.

Over the years, I knew Earl's other children felt rejected, ignored and set aside for the "new brother". Absolutely everything Earl did was about Tiger and Tiger's golf. And then to be cast aside and not even acknowledged by anyone as Tiger's siblings hurt and upset them terribly and I knew the rejection they felt was horrendous.

One time Earl even publicly made the statement, *"that the heart that will forever beat in my soul belongs to my youngest son, Tiger."* Now that was a painful and deliberate slap in his other children's face! Sadly, ever since Tiger was young, Earl's other children were subjected to such flagrant and hurtful comments and actions from their father and, even at times, from Tiger.

I also found it odd that Earl never had any pictures in his house of his other children. Oh, there were a couple of snapshots on the front of the refrigerator of his granddaughter, Cheyenne, and especially the one with Tiger and Cheyenne together when she was much younger, but no pictures of his other children. However, Earl did have a ridiculously abundant supply of pictures of Tiger that were always on display throughout the house. In fact, the theme throughout the entire house was all about Tiger. The walls were saturated with Tiger's awards, memorabilia and framed newspaper articles. Shelves were crowded with trophies and Wheaties boxes displaying Tiger's picture on the front and many corners were stacked high with books and magazines, each with articles written about Tiger. There were statues, carvings and engraved tables of real Tigers. The house exuded Tiger Woods.

Maybe it was simply an oversight on Earl's part, but it always made me wonder how his children felt when they came over and everything in the house was about Tiger. I'm sure this made them realize they were never going to be equal to Tiger in the eyes of their father. Everything was about Tiger and Tiger always came first to Earl.

Unfortunately, however, according to Earl, his children had given him many reasons to be disappointed and frustrated with them. No matter what his excuses were, he should never have cast them aside simply because his new son could give him more than they ever could.

What was so strange was how Tiger never once mentioned his siblings to me when he was young. Most kids would say that they have brothers and sisters and even share stories about them, but not Tiger. It was almost as though he was not allowed to discuss them. Tiger basically treated his siblings the same as Earl did, as though they did not exist. However, you cannot blame Tiger because it was Earl who instilled those negative thoughts about his other children into Tiger. I know there were times when Tiger was attending Stanford when he did, in fact, make an effort to see his sister, Royce, who lives in Northern California. However, those efforts were few and far between, thus a true brother and sister relationship was never able to be effectively established.

In the first few years when I knew Earl, he seldom ever spoke about his other children. It wasn't until Tiger had become famous that the conversations really included them. Of course, this was when Royce, Kevin and Earl Jr. decided it was time to get closer to Earl and Tiger, especially since Tiger was now wealthy. Earl had become upset with his other children because now all they wanted was his money. He felt they never really came around to see him anymore just because he was their dad. Now it was what he could do for them financially.

After Tiger turned pro and Earl and Tiger's status and wealth had been altered drastically, Earl saw dramatic changes in his other children's attitudes. His children now felt that since their father had money and their half-brother was famous and had an outrageous amount of money, it was only fair they should get a piece of the pie. According to Earl, they honestly believed they were entitled to the money because they were related to Tiger. Their selfish attitudes toward Tiger's success greatly concerned and disappointed both Tiger and Earl.

Earl had confided in me about how his children were continually pestering him, and sometimes even Tiger, nonstop for money. Earl was starting to feel that their begging had reached a point where it was getting out of hand. They wanted Tiger and Earl to buy them new cars, buy houses for them, pay for medical operations, pay for the attorney's when they got into trouble, and just give them money whenever they wanted it, whether they needed it or not.

These "children" were grown adults in their mid and late forties and were many years older than Tiger, but they still honestly believed their brother and father owed them just because they were related. After all, their little brother was now extremely successful and very rich, so why shouldn't they bask in the same wealth and reap the same benefits? I mean wouldn't you feel the same way and expect money to be given to you if your brother was Tiger Woods or someone else famous? Most people would not. So instead of constantly asking Tiger for the money, many times they chose to go through Earl directly. After all, it was actually Tiger's money that was being given to Earl, so they believed they were also entitled to it.

There was a time when Tiger did, in fact, give Royce some money. After he had turned pro, Tiger gave his sister a large sum of money so she could buy herself a house. Despite Tiger and Earl's advice to spend part of the money on the house and bank the rest, Royce chose to spend the entire amount on the purchase of the house.

A few years later, Royce realized she was out of money and could not maintain the house, so she asked Tiger for more money. After Earl and Tiger discussed her situation, Tiger told Royce he would buy the house back from her for the full amount she had paid for it. She refused Tiger's offer stating she felt he should give her an additional amount of money to pay for her expenses on top of letting her keep the house.

Frustrated with her stubbornness and greed, Tiger and Earl both adamantly refused to go along with her demands and they gave her nothing. Even though she still lives in that house today, I'm sure she received enough money from Earl's estate to now cover all of her expenses and maintain the house.

There was another time when Royce had called and asked Earl to buy her a new car. The car she wanted was very expensive and Earl had told her he was not willing to pay that much money. However, if she wanted the car that he had picked out for her, then he would buy it for her. Royce argued with Earl, telling him that she did not want the cheaper car as she wanted the one she had chosen. She told Earl she did not care how much it cost and she was expecting Earl to pay for it. Angered by her selfish and extravagant behavior, Earl refused to go along with her demands and stuck to his guns, stating he would only buy her the lesser expensive car, otherwise, no car at all.

Because of her refusal to accept Earl's offer, Royce never did get a car from Earl. Since she was not about to settle for less than what she wanted, Royce ended up with nothing. Besides, to Earl, a car was just a car and he felt she should have been grateful that he was at least willing to buy her a car at all. Earl's attitude was, "Oh, well, her loss!"

Earl's middle son, Kevin, would always ask for money and was constantly making up stories as to why he needed it. Reluctantly, Earl would send it to him. The problem was Earl resented the fact that Kevin kept asking him for money time and time again, but it hurt Earl even more that Kevin felt he had lie to his father as to why he needed it. Each time, Earl discussed Kevin's situation with Tiger, but according to Earl, it seemed Tiger just did not want to be bothered with it, causing Earl to have to handle it on his own. He could not blame Tiger because it seemed that his siblings' constant need for money was beginning to annoy him, too.

Many times after one of Tiger's half-siblings called Earl for money, Earl would call me to ask what he should do. Earl felt like he was being taken advantage of by all of them. It was a difficult position for me to be in because on one hand I wanted to tell Earl to just forget it, don't send them anything else again. I knew Earl really did not want to continually give them money. But on the other hand, I knew Earl felt somewhat obligated because he and Tiger had all this money and he thought he should share some of it with his children.

Apparently his children never bothered to think how their constant begging would affect Tiger and Earl, nor did they even care. I soon realized why Tiger no longer wanted to be involved in the money aspect of his siblings' lives. Both Tiger and Earl knew it was getting out of hand and it was just easier for Tiger to remove himself from the entire situation. Even to this day, his brothers are asking for more money, but Tiger refuses to even talk to them. I guess they burnt that bridge a long time ago.

Although it was Tiger's money they wanted, they would settle for a smaller amount from their father. Earl knew it was, in reality, his own personal problem and he should not be involving Tiger. Earl's thinking was Tiger needed to focus on his golf and winning tournaments and not be bothered with trivial things such as who and why certain people need money.

Earl Jr., (also known as Den, short for Dennison), is Earl's eldest son. He is also the divorced father of Cheyenne, Tiger's niece who just happens to be an up and coming young female golfer and who now plays on the LPGA Tour. Now, when it came to Earl Jr., it was a completely different story. On many occasions, Earl and I would discuss all of the problems Den would have at either his work, with his lack of cars and transportation, his health and even with his inability to control his life in general. Earl would explain how Den was unable to hold down a steady job and many times remained unemployed.

However, I remember when Earl decided to help Den out by purchasing a car for him. Earl called me to arrange the purchase since he knew I had contacts in the business. Through a friend, I arranged the purchase of a brand new Bright Blue Chrysler PT Cruiser. Since Den was not aware of what his father was planning, I suggested to Earl that he make the car a surprise. Earl loved the idea, especially since he had never surprised his children before with anything. So after completing the entire transaction, I made the necessary arrangements to have someone drive the car to Arizona and have it personally delivered to his son. I even wrote a large sign stating the car was from Earl. Den was shocked and thrilled with his gift, but then again, who wouldn't be.

Now when it came to Den's daughter, Cheyenne, Earl never hesitated even once when it came to providing for her. Den and his wife were divorced, but Earl still set up a special account that gave Cheyenne's mother five thousand dollars a month for her support. He also paid for all of her golf lessons, both current and future, plus an ongoing membership to a country club so she would always have a permanent course to play and practice. Like I said, Earl was generous, but only to a point. But for Cheyenne, he would do anything for her.

Tiger did not have a really large family on his father's side, however it was Tiger's niece and Den's daughter, Cheyenne, who Tiger was closest to simply because they shared the love of golf. Of course, it would only seem natural for him to feel closer to her since their golf would give them something special in common.

In Earl's own way, he loved his other children, but not in the same way he loved Tiger. There was just no comparison between those loves. Earl was convinced Tiger was beyond special, and because of those feelings, he set Tiger apart from the rest of his family.

Sadly, Earl refused to believe his other children were, in any way, being affected by his selfish behavior and his obsession for Tiger. I knew their father's obsession with their brother hurt them deeply. They were Earl's children, too, and they should have been accepted in all aspects of Tiger and Earl's lives, not just in the parts where Tiger and Earl selected. In reality, Den, Kevin and Royce were Earl's first children and they were loving Earl long before Tiger ever came along.

It had become quite obvious that there was a great deal of dysfunction within Tiger's entire family and it was also obvious that it was mainly Earl who had created much of the dysfunction. When you think about it, you can't blame Tiger for the family he had and some of the outlandish influences he was subjected to.

Sadly, Tiger and Earl never talked about the other members of their family, especially since those members did not fit the "perfect family image" which Earl worked so hard to portray for the media and the public. After all, the real truth about their entire family did not fit in with Tiger's new image.

23
MEDIA EFFECTS

WHEN TIGER WAS JUST a little kid, just barely three years old, it was Earl who took it upon himself to promote his son and put him on public display in order to expose his talent to the various media genres. Throughout Tiger's life, Earl was solely responsible for instigating and creating the publicity surrounding Tiger. Earl's relentless and continuous pursuit for news about his talented son eventually turned into the so-called "media monster".

For some reason, Earl felt it was crucial that he put Tiger in the forefront and make sure the entire world knew how great his son was when it came to golf. It was Earl who approached the newspaper and television reporters and demanded they keep an eye on Tiger and on his every accomplishment. But never once did Earl take into consideration there may be long term repercussions from this exposure and he never once thought or cared about the kind of effect it might have on his young son.

It was Earl's early and continued self-serving actions that created uncomfortable and unnecessary situations for Tiger to deal with. Unfortunately, it was Tiger who was forced to live with the consequences that Earl himself had generated. Not just as a child and into his teenage years, but more so as he moved toward his life on the PGA tour. Sadly, Earl wore blinders as he promoted Tiger, never once looking beyond the moment. The damage Earl created for Tiger would continue, as the media frenzy escalated to all new levels. And the person who benefited was Earl. The person most affected was Tiger.

Yes, Earl shaped Tiger's image by promoting him from such an early age but, in turn, Earl satisfied his own need to be in the spotlight, especially once Tiger joined the PGA tour. According to Earl, he thought he was just trying to create Tiger Woods, great golfer. However, after Tiger turned pro, Earl was convinced that it was the media who actually created Tiger Woods, "Super Star". But it was Earl who took the credit for pushing the media in that direction. Sadly, once again, Earl took credit for something he believed he had done for his son instead of accepting the fact that Tiger's "Super Star" status was based solely on Tiger's own talent and ability. The media simply took that champion spirit and ran with it.

Even though Earl spent years trying to promote Tiger as a superstar because of his Junior World, U.S Junior Amateur and U.S. Amateur wins, the media never really acknowledged him for anything more than being just a good amateur golfer. There was no fan popularity, no media hype, and no big write ups in the newspapers. Tiger was good, but he was not well known outside of the amateur golfing arena. Therefore, Tiger was not all that newsworthy, despite all of Earl's efforts.

Once Tiger became a professional golfer, the media buildup regarding his turning professional was largely thought to be just hype, simply created by his father and his agents. However, after he started winning tournaments, the media saw the chance to focus on Tiger, realizing he was a person who the public wanted to know more about. The media, along with his agents and sponsors, eventually made Tiger a household name and Tiger's popularity increased, thus shaping a new celebrity status for him. It was obvious that the more hype the media presented to the public, the more Tiger's popularity grew. Earl actually thought his earlier actions with the media had finally paid off. However, Earl just was not able to foresee the negative end result that would eventually come from it.

Other athletes have been highly successful and have received media attention, but none to the extent that Tiger received. His many accomplishments on the golf course were indisputable and definitely worthy of note, but the image was not just about his athletic ability. Tiger had now become a celebrity. His fan base had increased to all new levels as they were continually baited with the possibility of his next win. Tiger became a golfing sensation practically overnight and his popularity almost instantly traveled throughout the world. Only the media could have accomplished such a feat, and soon Tiger's name was on everyone's lips. Tiger proved himself with his incredible golfing skills, but it was the media who created the "Tiger Woods" for everyone to know with tremendous coverage and buildup. Everyone knows Tiger wears red on Sundays, but if you listen to and believe the media hype, you would expect him to be wearing a super hero costume and a red cape.

Some of the media chose to make Tiger special since he was to be the next "chosen one" when he came out as a rookie. He was to be the next Jack Nicklaus. But others were doubtful about Tiger, almost a wait and see mentality. However, unlike the other golfers who were also labeled "the chosen ones" who had preceded him, such as Ben Crenshaw, Scott Verplank, and Phil Mickelson, Tiger was the only one who was actually able to perform up to and beyond everyone's expectations. His game had actually exceeded all of the hype that had been created about him. Tiger's ongoing performances were so outstanding that it truly earned him the title of "super star" as a golfer.

Since the media was the one who created this "super" image of Tiger, the media also made it impossible for Tiger to live a normal life like the other professional golfers and other athletes. I mean Tiger is only a golfer, but for some reason, the media thought Tiger and his family were different, and their lives were now turned upside down because of all the media attention and their wanting to know more about Tiger Woods.

It was the media who wanted to give the public as much information as possible. Many other athletes are also stars in their own sport, such as basketball, baseball, or even tennis, but you don't see the media chasing them down in order to get a great story or a piece of their private lives. You never read anything about any of the other golfers on tour, except for their tournament wins. It also used to be that the media only gave the statistics of a player's performance or reported on the sport itself. Even Arnold Palmer and Jack Nicklaus did not receive so much sensationalism and they were popular and extremely talented golfers. So, why Tiger?

The media was not content with just reporting on Tiger's golf. They were after anything and everything that pertained to him, including his private life. Because of Tiger's popularity and Earl's own ego, Earl was convinced that his own private life would be invaded and examined by the media. It was Earl who truly felt he was important enough to also be subjected to the media's scrutiny, forgetting he was only the father of Tiger Woods and not of media interest. However, it was due to these misguided beliefs that Earl convinced Tiger they must both live their lives as though they were always on display. Therefore, protecting his image also ended up affecting the way Tiger had to live his life.

As Tiger's popularity grew, the more obsessed the media became and it was the media who chose to put Tiger and his life on display for the public's benefit. No matter what Tiger did in his life, it was the media who felt it was their right to report anything and everything about Tiger to the public. Tiger would, therefore, have to live with any and all of the consequences that resulted from their reporting.

The public and Tiger's fans are only interested in rooting for another Tiger win or to hope he makes it out of the fairway rough or trees with another one of his humanly impossible spectacular golf shots. But it is the media who reports to the public and it is the media who creates the image that the public sees. However, sometimes the media feels they also have the right to judge another human being, especially one so famous. They are the ones who report anything negative or positive about a player, especially focusing on the wrongdoings or any missteps. Yes, they praise the good, but they have a tendency to negatively zero in on the bad. The media actually sets the standards by which a player's performance or personal life is to be judged. All this information is reported to the public, causing the public to now judge.

Whenever a celebrity such as Tiger stumbles at some point in their lives, it seems the media is always there to be sure the person continues to fall. The problem with the media is they feel they have the right to pick out a particular person, athlete or celebrity and place him or her into the forefront for all to see with all of their coverage and reports, creating an unnecessary and untenable situation. They set this person apart, placing him in an arena when he now becomes a target for scrutiny and to be judged by everyone on the image that the media had created. This sets up the person to be the public's main focus, thus forcing the hand of the public to throw stones, based solely on what the media reported. The media feels they have the right to cast the first stone in an effort to get the public to follow. Basically, the media appoints themselves judge, jury and crucifier and so many times their reporting is far from fair.

Though so much of their reporting is based on speculation and opinions and not always on the actual facts, this targeted person must endure the wrath and unjust criticism from everyone. The media has the power to steer the public into believing whatever the media wants them to believe, either for the good or the bad. Even though their reports may be misleading, it is the unsuspecting public who relies on the so-called honest reputation of the media to present the truth.

It is also the media who continually forgets that sports figures and other celebrities are just regular people and are also only human. Lest we forget the phrase that "to err is human" and that we all, including the ones the media and the public has placed so very high on a pedestal, can make mistakes, too. After all, none of us are perfect. Unfortunately, because of Tiger's fame and success, he was placed so very high on a pedestal that it was inevitable he could eventually fall. The problem is that the media creates a particular image of a person, then, if that person does not live up to that image, the media ends up attacking and destroying their own creation. This is just the nature of the beast, and sadly, people's lives can be and have been ruined as a result of it.

A perfect example of how the media operates and can destroy an individual would be the situation that occurred with Fuzzy Zoeller. The media has a bad habit of taking a story and blowing it totally out of proportion, which is exactly what happened with Fuzzy after Tiger won the 1997 Masters tournament. Fuzzy is a jokester and meant absolutely no harm when he made a funny and innocent comment about what Tiger would be serving for his dinner the next year at the Masters as the defending champion. Zoeller said, "So you know what you guys do when he gets in here? Pat him on the back, say congratulations. Enjoy it. And tell him not to serve fried chicken next year, or collard greens or whatever the hell they serve."

When this happened, Earl told me that he and Tiger were not offended and took Fuzzy's remarks simply as a joke. Earl became angry when the media led the public to believe that Fuzzy's comment was an attack on Tiger's color and race. As a result of the media's harsh reporting, and of course, because of the initial comment itself, Fuzzy unfortunately lost his major sponsor, K-Mart, and in a short period of time, other sponsors followed. This was one of the many reasons Tiger and Earl became so fearful and cautious when it came to trusting the media and especially how they would write and report certain stories. The media says what they want by embellishing the facts, never caring what lives they have taken down.

Although Earl originally initiated the media frenzy for Tiger early on in order to help get his son's accomplishments recognized, Earl soon discovered how damaging the media could actually be, especially after Tiger turned professional and became so popular on the PGA tour. Even though Earl felt special and important when doing interviews, he realized he needed to change his approach when talking to reporters or journalists. So, in order to protect themselves and their privacy, Earl decided to play a game whenever he spoke to the media. Earl would BS any reporter who would try to get a side story from him during an interview or the ones who tried to suck up to him thinking they had befriended Tiger Woods or his father.

Earl and Tiger were both very cautious of the press and were always careful in their every word as they knew the media had a tendency to inaccurately report and misconstrue whatever they might have said or took their words totally out of context. Many of the reporters would even try to read between the lines and form their own opinion as to what Earl and Tiger were trying to say instead of quoting them verbatim.

Dealing with the media eventually became a huge game with Earl. It's funny because before Tiger turned professional, Earl did everything in his power to get the media to notice Tiger and write brief articles about him. In the early years, the press did not care when it came to reporting anything about Tiger's private life as they only wanted to report the statistics and highlights on Tiger's performance. But once Tiger proved himself on the golf course as a professional and a champion, Earl found both he and Tiger had to be extremely careful as to what they said to the media. The media now wanted to know and report absolutely anything and everything about Tiger Woods.

Earl and the agents made sure to instruct Tiger as to what to say and how to act around the media, advising him to never trust them. Tiger was also told to avoid various interviews, feeling many of them were not necessary and could cause more harm than good. Just because someone was a reporter, either for a magazine, a newspaper or even for television, did not necessarily mean they would automatically get the opportunity to interview Tiger. Tiger was extremely selective and trusted no one. In a way, you can't blame Tiger for being so careful. After all, it is his life that he is protecting.

There were even a couple of journalists who actually believed they had become Earl and Tiger's friends, thinking they were close enough to Earl, and especially to Tiger, that everything they were being told was the absolute truth. But Earl's main focus when talking to these writers was to make sure they would always write favorable reports and articles about Tiger. So, if Earl had to make a few reporters feel as though they were important, then so be it. In Earl's mind, Tiger would be the one to benefit from his contrived ruse. Earl knew exactly what he was doing and through trial and error had learned how to play the so-called media game.

Unfortunately, these journalists were completely unaware they were actually being duped by Earl, making sure he put his own slant on any story. And these journalists were gullible enough to believe everything Earl told them and they were quick to report each and every "fact" that Earl gave them. However, Earl never revealed anything to anyone, especially about their private lives. If any of these reporters and journalists had really known Earl, and were as close as they had claimed, then they would have been aware of his sense of humor and his playful wit and especially the fact that they were being played to Earl's satisfaction. Simply put, Earl got a kick out of putting one over on the reporters and watching their reactions, as though they were victorious in getting an interview with Earl or Tiger Woods. In the end, it was Earl's strange and twisted way of protecting Tiger and himself.

Since these reporters were not family or part of the Woods' close knit inner circle, nor would they ever be allowed to possess such positions, they were not privy to any real facts or information pertaining to the private part of Tiger's life. Besides, what would give them the right to feel Earl or Tiger could or would ever trust them? No matter how these reporters tried to trick Earl with friendly chit chat or doing him favors, they were still a part of the media. Did they honestly believe that Earl would confide in them and be honest about his personal life? Only in their dreams! Earl was ex-military and knew exactly how to protect himself and his son against the enemy, and to Tiger, the media was definitely the enemy.

Earl and Tiger's caution with the media, especially the tabloid segment of the media, was exemplified when Earl died and the events which surrounded his funeral. Tiger made sure the media had no knowledge of when and where the funeral was to take place, otherwise they would most likely have seen the event as just another opportunity to see Tiger and get pictures of him and to once again try to invade his privacy.

We are all aware of what the media is capable of and we know they would most definitely have taken advantage of Earl's funeral, ignoring the fact that Tiger was in mourning and distraught over his father's death. It was sad how the media and public probably never cared that it was Earl Woods who died. If you noticed, the newspapers never reported that "Earl Woods" died. They only reported "Tiger's father, Earl, died".

Also, it was strange how the reports of his death varied, since obviously the media was just reporting whatever they wanted without getting the facts straight. Some reports stated how Earl died of a heart attack and the rest reported the truth; that he died after a long battle with prostate cancer. Even in death, Earl could not trust the media to get the facts straight, showing how little you can trust what they report.

Not long ago there were a couple of other books written about Tiger and Earl. Unfortunately, the authors were journalists, and with some research, golf statistics on Tiger and a few notes from past interviews, they were finally able to compile enough information to put everything into book format. The problem is that because they were journalists, Earl and Tiger and the rest of the family, would never have revealed any personal secrets or sensitive information pertaining to their lives. If any information was given to a reporter, the information would have been slanted or controlled by Earl, Tiger or his agents, or else no information would have been given at all.

Since these writers were only acquaintances with Tiger or Earl, meeting only for interviews, they did not know Earl and Tiger well enough to be privy to any firsthand knowledge or personal information pertaining to their private lives. They were only able to write about Tiger's professional life as a golfer and his accomplishments on the course. Because of that fact, much of what these authors wrote in their books about the Woods' private lives was incorrect and most likely fabricated. Most everything was simply their opinion or speculation since they had no real facts to base their story on, thus the information they provided was only based on their theories and assumptions. I know for a fact that neither Earl nor Tiger would ever knowingly tell the media or an acquaintance anything about their private lives, especially during an interview or even during a casual conversation. As a result, the reporters end up getting only what the Woods' deem necessary.

Tiger and Earl trust no one outside of family and only a few close friends. Earl had a tendency to tell stories or slant the truth in a way that would protect himself and Tiger from the media. There was one journalist and author, however, who Earl was close to and even considered him to be a friend, and that was Peter McDaniel, who co-authored a book with Earl. Even Peter did not know everything about Tiger and Earl and their personal lives, but he definitely knew more than any other journalist in the media arena. I remember talking to Peter at Earl's funeral and then realized he was the only journalist who had been trusted enough to be invited to and speak at the services.

For Tiger and Earl, the media was partially responsible for making them feel it was necessary to change their public personas and to act differently whenever they were in the public eye, however their need to change was deemed more necessary by Earl. Because of Tiger's ranking within the golfing world and his added celebrity status, Tiger and Earl believed they were no longer private people and they were no longer entitled to that privacy. For Tiger, this was very true and justified, but for Earl, much of it was simply self-created and self-serving, again feeling he should be as important and popular as his son.

However, it was Earl's ultimate goal to protect his son from total personal exposure and having to live with and suffer the wrath from any and all media and public scrutiny and judgment. Sadly, as it turned out, Earl was actually protecting Tiger from something he himself had created many years earlier.

24

FAMILY MATTERS

ONCE TIGER BECAME a professional golfer, his life, career and responsibilities changed dramatically, especially when it came to his family. Now that Tiger was in a position of wealth and fame, he was now forced to cope with the unusual and sometimes bizarre actions and the extravagant needs of his father and mother. In addition, Tiger was trying to live his own social life separately from his professional life and the public view.

After living the single life, Tiger chose to settle down and, heeding the earlier advice of his father, found love with a woman introduced to him by a fellow professional golfer, Jesper Parnevik.

While Tiger and Elin were dating, Earl had become somewhat apprehensive about Tiger's relationship with her. After the many father and son talks they had shared over the years, Earl was hoping that Tiger had listened to his advice and recommendations and was making the right choice. Earl and I had discussed Tiger's involvement with Elin numerous times, however prior to Tiger's wedding, I remember this one particular conversation when Earl revealed his inner most thoughts to me regarding Elin.

Earl stated that Elin appeared to be a sweet person, but because of who his son was, he had these troubling doubts in regard to Elin's true feelings for Tiger. Earl confided that he was somewhat leery about her real motives and whether or not they were honest and sincere. He was concerned with the fact that she was only a swimsuit model from Sweden who was staying in the United States as a nanny for another professional golfer. Earl was afraid that her main goal was to find herself a rich golfer on tour and marry him for both his money and a permanent home in the United States. Unfortunately for Tiger, he fit into that category perfectly.

Earl told me that he hoped he was wrong in his suspicions, but in this case he honestly felt that he might not be, especially since he prided himself at reading people correctly and believed he could usually sense what someone's intentions were. Of course, the fact that Earl married Tiger's mother in a very similar fashion since she was from Thailand, probably caused him to doubt Tiger and Elin's relationship even more.

Understanding Earl's predicament, I then asked him if he was going to mention his uneasy feelings regarding Elin to Tiger. Earl assured me that he and Tiger had discussed Elin on numerous occasions. Earl told me that it was Tiger's choice and he did not feel comfortable interfering at this point, especially since their relationship was already so far along. This really seemed out of character for Earl, his not wanting to intervene, but in a way, I understood his thinking. Earl had hoped that the negative feelings he had was simply a father being overly protective of his son. Knowing how fanatical Earl could be when it came to protecting Tiger, I was hoping that Earl's doubts were totally unwarranted, but only time would tell.

Earl also voiced his concerns about Tiger's true feelings for Elin, especially when he began to think back to his own marriages. Earl had admitted that his first marriage was a huge mistake and his second marriage to Tida basically ended within the first couple of years. Even though Earl and Tida agreed to stay together for Tiger's sake while he was growing up and focusing on his golf, they simply remained friends until they eventually separated when Tiger turned pro. Earl always said that he had respect for the women in his life, but he was concerned Tiger would not see it that way and Elin would end up being nothing more than a trophy wife for him. Basically, Earl was hoping that his own past behavior did not have a negative influence on Tiger toward women, but deep inside Earl was afraid that his own history with marriage would repeat itself in his son.

Sadly, everything Earl was worried about actually became a reality when Tiger and Elin divorced in 2010.

Earl was also concerned about Tida's constant interference in Tiger's life and especially how it could affect a new wife. Earl sort of jokingly said that he would never want Tida for a mother-in-law and that he truly felt sorry for any woman who married Tiger and became her daughter-in-law. Earl explained that Tida had a way of always insinuating herself into Tiger's life, and particularly his golf career, feeling that since she was his mother, she had every right to be involved whenever she wanted. It makes you wonder if her meddling and dominating presence did, in fact, affect Tiger's marriage to Elin. You know how a mother-in-law can be, and according to Earl, Tida was no exception.

Although Earl and Tiger were extremely close and spent most of their time together, Tiger was still very close to his mother.

However, when it came to Tida, it was a completely different story. Even though Tida took wonderful care of her son and taught him many values and principles from her culture, she turned out to be a typical Thai mother. According to Earl, Tida was a loving and devoted mother, but she was extremely obsessed and very possessive of her child. Earl once explained to me that a Thai mother will always control every aspect of their child's life and basically will never let them go.

Tida has always demonstrated these traits and still does to this day, especially when it pertains to Tiger's golf. She has attended every single tournament he has ever played in and walks each hole, almost as though she is keeping a motherly eye on her son and is afraid to let him out of her sight. Tida is constantly around Tiger and because she is his mother, she has always felt that she has every right to share the spotlight with him.

When Tiger had a birthday party in Las Vegas with his own friends in his own age group, Tida made it a point to be sure that she was also in attendance. Whenever there are reporters around, Tida makes sure that she is always noticed by them. Also, if there are sponsor representatives around, especially the Nike reps, she is right there, front and center, talking to them and discussing Tiger and his business. She even expects the head honchos at Nike to walk her around on their arm. Tida will strut around like she is someone important and a well-known celebrity. She also feels she has every right, as his mother, to always accompany Tiger to every tournament, every function and every event that Tiger attends or participates in.

Earl even told me how at times she makes Tiger feel as though he was being smothered, but unfortunately Tiger cannot confront his mother and is forced to tolerate her constant overbearing and clingy behavior.

There were numerous times when Tiger had called Earl to ask for his help with Tida. Tiger would get so frustrated with his mother because she would be at a tournament or a function and she would just start talking to a sponsor representative or the media and she would end up saying some of the most ridiculous and embarrassing things, including topics that she should not be discussing with anyone, much less strangers. Tiger would beg Earl to please intervene and talk to his mother on his behalf in hopes that he could make her stop. Earl explained how Tiger was getting so embarrassed by her actions, but he didn't feel comfortable talking to his own mother about it. Sadly, Tiger felt that Tida was just getting totally out of control.

Earl would just laugh and say to me. "Well, that's Tida. She just doesn't know when to keep her mouth shut!" But when he talked to Tiger, Earl always reassured Tiger that he would have another chat with his mother and hopefully get her to stop talking to everyone.

Unfortunately, Tida did what she wanted and no matter how much Earl pleaded with her on Tiger's behalf, she was still not going to change her ways. Earl jokingly stated, "See why I don't live with her anymore?"

Isn't it strange how Tiger let his mother's actions affect him yet he never once saw anything wrong with the way his own father controlled and manipulated him. Then, again, maybe Tiger just didn't want to see it.

There were many times over the years when I truly felt sorry for Tiger, and this was definitely one of them.

I sometimes wondered if Tida's continual interference in Tiger's life would have any impact on him personally and if it would affect his ability to play golf. In fact, Earl and I were both worried that her constant presence and her smothering actions would draw him away from the many things that he truly wanted to do in his life.

In addition to being concerned about his golf, his private life and the pressures he was under, Tiger would also have to worry about what Tida was going to say or do next. Then, not only would he have to deal with any situation his mother created, but he would also have to find a way to correct it. This is why Tiger would constantly call Earl for his assistance, however, after Earl died, Tiger was placed in a position where he had to cope with his mother's actions on his own. Tiger would never admit his feelings regarding his mother to anyone else other than Earl, so I can just imagine what Tiger is feeling inside since his father is now gone.

Prior to Tiger's professional career when Tiger was younger and during one of their special father and son talks, Earl told Tiger that as soon as he became a professional golfer and joined the PGA tour, it would be Tiger's sole responsibility to financially care for his mother. Earl always knew that as soon as Tiger turned pro and was in a position to provide his mother with a new house, he and Tida would go their separate ways. It was like, okay, now you are rich, so you take care of your mother. She's not my responsibility anymore.

So when that time finally came, Tida wanted to live in a much larger house than the small tract house she lived in with Earl and Tiger, and she also wanted to drive a fancy new Mercedes, all because her son was now rich. No matter what Tida wanted, Tiger always provided. Everything she owns and every trip she takes is all from Tiger. Even the use of his private jet is always available to her no matter where she wants to go. Tiger ended up taking very good care of his mother by satisfying all of her wants and needs. To this day, Tiger still provides for her and all because this is what his father told him he had to do.

Although Tiger also provided for his father, Earl never wanted to leave the house that he had lived in for so long as he was completely satisfied to continue living there. He said he hated big houses anyway and felt they were totally unnecessary. However, Tida's requests were quite a bit more extravagant.

Being the dutiful son and doing what his mother wanted, Tiger proceeded to buy his mother a beautiful new and very large five thousand square foot house on the golf course in Tustin Ranch, California. Also, since Buick eventually became one of Tiger's major sponsors, Earl, Tida and Tiger were each entitled to a free GM vehicle of their choice each year. Each one of them would usually choose the Cadillac Escalade. And, of course, Tida's Escalade was in addition to the largest built Mercedes that she insisted on having, which Tiger always bought for her. Most recently, Tida moved to Florida to be closer to Tiger and her grandchildren. Tiger even built her a larger house than the one he originally bought for her in California and, of course, her new house is within blocks of his.

Over the years, it became quite obvious that Tida felt her son could provide for her far better than her husband ever could.

I remember when Earl called and told me that Tiger and Elin were finally getting married. I really wasn't surprised at the news since Earl had kept me apprised of the progression of their relationship. But I was curious as to the reason they decided to get married so far away in Barbados and not here in the states. When I questioned him on this, Earl explained that if they planned a wedding nearby, it would most likely become a media circus, and Tiger refused to allow anything like that to happen.

After Earl gave me the details regarding their wedding, including the when and the where, he proceeded to emphasize the fact that I needed to keep this information to myself and share it with no one. Earl said it was absolutely imperative that I keep it a secret, fearing the information could leak out to the media.

A few weeks after Tiger and Elin's wedding, Earl called to tell me that Elin had finally sent him a copy of their wedding DVD and wanted me to watch it with him. Anxious to see Tiger's wedding, I decided to go over to Earl's house that very night.

After I cooked dinner for the two of us, we watched Tiger's wedding. I commented to Earl on how beautiful the ceremony was and how hot it must have been since everyone was sweating profusely, especially Tiger and Charles Barkley. Earl mentioned that it is always very hot and humid in Barbados which made everyone extremely uncomfortable during the entire ceremony. As the wedding progressed, you could watch Elin's beautiful blond hair slowly wilt in the tropical humidity. Also, until that moment, I was not aware that Elin had an identical twin sister, and as Elin's Maid of Honor, the two of them were just beautiful as they stood side by side.

As I watched, I thought it was very sweet how Tiger showed so much love and attention toward Elin throughout the entire wedding and reception. The very simple ceremony was really quite touching and very beautiful, except for the hot humid weather. I really loved the part before the wedding when all the guys, including Tiger, got together, laughing and smoking cigars, and telling stories, but I was quite surprised to see that Earl wasn't participating in their gaiety. Earl explained to me that it was so damn hot that he wasn't feeling all that well and tried to cool off while hanging out at the bar.

Prior to Earl leaving to attend the wedding, he had told me how Tiger and Elin chose to keep the event quite small and only family and a few close friends would be attending. Earl and I got a kick out of all the articles that had been published afterwards indicating that Tiger had this huge lavish and expensive wedding with one hundred and twenty people in attendance. We even read one article that stated there were over two hundred guests at the wedding. The articles also stated that many high profile guests, including Oprah Winfrey, Bill Gates and Michael Jordan, were present. This just showed how the media was completely off base and totally incorrect in their reporting, rather in their "guessing" or "fabricating", of the actual happenings involving a celebrity, especially since the media was not even present nor invited.

The wedding was quite small and there couldn't have been more than twenty or so people there. And Oprah, Bill and Michael were definitely not there. And if Tiger supposedly spent one and a half million dollars on this wedding, as reported by the media, then Tiger would have been grossly overcharged had he not rented out the entire resort. Like I said, the wedding was small and quaint, and the reception was elegant, but simple.

During the reception, each of Elin and Tiger's parents stood at the podium and spoke about their children's union. When it was Earl's turn to speak to everyone, he talked about how very proud he was of Tiger and how happy he was for his son and his new wife. Then all of a sudden Earl leaned down on the podium, placed his head in his hands and totally broke down in the middle of his speech and just sobbed. At this moment, I immediately pushed the pause button on the remote and I turned to Earl and asked what had happened to make him cry?

Earl sadly confided to me that not only was he proud and happy for Tiger, but at that very moment the realization of the inevitable set in. He knew that his health issues would prevent him from ever being a part of Tiger and Elin's future together and from ever seeing Tiger's children, and that meant more to Earl than anything else in the world. Earl hated the fact that his illness would also prevent him from ever again sharing those special moments with Tiger, the same special moments they had shared since the day Tiger was born. He said that all of the emotion just hit him all at once and sadly, he was unable to control himself and his reaction to everything.

As Earl sat in his recliner, I moved over to comfort him and he began to cry again. This was when he told me that there was so much that he was going to miss in life and it was a life that he didn't want to leave. A little while later he wiped his eyes, shook it off and said in his calm and reassuring voice, that we all have to accept the hand that is dealt to us and this just happened to be his dealt hand.

I have always known how special and important Tiger was to Earl and Earl was to Tiger, so I had Earl make a promise to me that he would make an earnest effort to spend more time with Tiger and make the most of what time they might have left together, no matter how far apart they lived. As Earl started to cry again, he choked out the words, "I promise."

The emotions I was feeling right then for Earl made me ache inside, but the sadness and worry I felt for Tiger was even greater. I knew what the future held for all of us and I prayed that Tiger would be able to make it through the inevitable. Earl was worried about Tiger, too.

One major difficulty Tiger had to endure was having to deal with his father's various illnesses throughout the years while being a professional golfer. Back in 1996, Earl suffered a mild heart attack and then in the early part of 1997, Earl had to have heart surgery. Earl's illness weighed heavily on Tiger's mind, especially since he had just recently joined the PGA tour and was still basically a rookie. Not only was Tiger learning to cope with his new life and experiences on the tour, but he was also forced to carry the burden of his father's health.

As it would be for any son, Tiger was greatly affected as he had to face the stresses that surrounded Earl's serious illness, always worried that, at any time, he might lose his father. After all, Earl was forty-four years old when Tiger was born, so Earl had always been a much older father. Surprisingly though, in 1997, Tiger held everything together enough to win the Masters Tournament, and fortunately his father was well enough to attend and share in that incredible moment.

Since Earl's prostate cancer had come out of remission, and as his illness progressed, Tiger wanted to spend more time with his father. Eventually, Tiger had to take on the responsibility of making special arrangements for his father's in-home care. Unfortunately, this was all taking time away from his regular schedule on the PGA tour. The emotional stress Tiger was under was tremendous as he traveled between his home in Florida and Earl's home in California, all the while having to stay focused on his golf career. Unlike Earl's previous medical issues, Tiger knew this was an illness Earl would not recover from. Tiger knew he would be losing his father and best friend and he would need to prepare for the eventual outcome.

There were many times during the last year of his life when Earl had conversations with Tiger, trying in his fatherly way to better prepare him to face the future alone. There was a point when Earl actually wanted to wean Tiger from his embraces so Tiger would one day be able to stand on his own, without the support that had always been given to him by Earl.

Although Earl is now gone, the love, the lessons, and all of the memories will always remain with Tiger and they will give him strength as he himself enters into fatherhood and continues on with his life.

25

LOSING HIS FATHER

THIS CHAPTER IS ABOUT Earl's illness and eventual death on May 3, 2006. I chose to share this with you because it was a very private and difficult time in Tiger's life and without reading it, you would not be able to fully understand some of what Tiger endured throughout his father's illness and death.

I'll never forget the day Earl confided in me that his prostate cancer was no longer in remission. It had been such a long time, in fact, several years since he had been diagnosed and then was in remission, so it came as a total shock to hear the news that Earl's cancer was back. This was the day that would be the beginning of the end. It was the day that would lead to forever changing the lives of everyone who was close to Earl, especially Tiger.

Over time, Earl found himself to be experiencing more pain than usual, which began to worry him as to what extent the cancer might have progressed. It wasn't long before the pain had become worse, yet still somewhat bearable, so during this time the doctors had started Earl on radiation treatments again. Earl always kept a positive outlook and tried to never show that he was the least bit worried. He always believed with proper radiation treatments, the cancer would go back into remission. Earl believed he had beat it once before, so of course, he was hoping he would beat it once again.

One night while I was at his house, Earl and I were talking about the radiation treatments he was undergoing and how he was trying to cope with the pain and the effects of the treatment, as the cancer was now starting to spread to various parts of his body. The radiation did, however, kill the cancer behind his eye and close to his brain, but the rest of the cancer was still progressing slowly.

I remember asking Earl, "What are we all supposed to do if anything ever happens to you?" Then I asked, "Earl, what is Tiger going to do. You know what this is going to do to him, right?"

While trying to hold back his tears, Earl told me that hopefully we will never have to find out. Earl then tried to reassure me how he was going to do everything he could to fight the disease and with any luck, he would live a long and healthy life. But Earl and I both knew that luck had nothing to do with it and we also knew what the future would hold for him.

Earl had always tried to be straightforward and honest with Tiger about everything, and when it came to his illness, he tried to conceal much of the pain in order to protect him, especially during Tiger's heavy tournament season. Earl and I had ongoing conversations regarding Tiger and his concerns as to whether or not Tiger would be able to cope with his illness and with the inevitable and still focus on his golf.

I remember back to one particular conversation I had with Earl prior to the return of his cancer. Earl knew there might be a day when his cancer would return or he could have another problem with his heart. Earl was getting older and he never really knew how long he would be around. We just happened to be discussing Tiger and he mentioned he had not seen Tiger in a while. They, of course, talked all of the time on the phone, but a long span of not seeing each other had occurred. Earl explained that because of his medical issues he was trying to help Tiger become more independent and be able to function better on his own. Earl was trying to make Tiger not rely on him so much, especially since he knew Tiger had always done that in the past. Earl was aware how much Tiger had trusted him over the years as a father and he knew how much Tiger had become dependent on him for most everything. Earl knew the day would eventually come when Tiger would have to be on his own and without Earl, so Earl was trying to set things in motion to help ease Tiger into independence.

Earl had finally realized how Tiger's attachment to him was like an addiction and he was trying to take care of the problem before it was too late. Basically, Earl said that he was trying to wean Tiger so in case anything should ever happen to him, Tiger would remain strong and stand on his own without his father.

Earl was realistic in his thinking when it pertained to his age and he knew a time would come when he could no longer be there for Tiger. Earl knew he should be concerned about Tiger and he feared the closeness he shared with his son could end up harming him in the long run. Earl had created this dependency in the first place and it took this many years for him to realize the effect it might have on Tiger.

Earl's sadness and fear showed every time we discussed Tiger. Earl felt so guilty for having to put his son through all of it, even though he had absolutely no control over his illness and eventual outcome. I told Earl on many occasions to discuss his feelings with Tiger and let him know how he truly felt. I told him that Tiger needs to hear it, especially now. Earl's thinking was he wanted to alleviate some of the pressures on Tiger, especially since Tiger was still trying to focus on his golf career and win tournaments. Earl knew what Tiger was going through and, in Earl like control, he was determined to keep Tiger's career first.

I tried to explain to Earl that not everything in life is about golf and it was necessary for him to convey his thoughts because it would be those thoughts that would help Tiger get through all of it, just like they had his entire life. Earl agreed with me and saw the necessity in his being more open with Tiger.

I know Tiger and Earl continued to have their father and son talks, but I worried that Earl was not being completely open and truthful with Tiger regarding his feelings. Each time I talked with Earl, I would ask him, "Did you talk to Tiger? Did you tell him how you feel?" Each time, Earl would tell me that he had spoken to Tiger, but knowing Earl the way I did, and the way he was with

Tiger, especially always wanting to protect him and control the situation, I truly had my doubts that Earl was completely honest with his son. In the end, I hope he was, for Tiger's sake.

When I think back to all of the transformations I saw Earl and Tiger go through over the years because of their fame and wealth, I was saddened when Earl's outlook on life changed once again, however, this time it was mainly due to his illness.

When his illness was out of remission, Earl's perspective on life had become different, almost as though he was no longer concerned with the prestige and position that he had or the status and wealth he possessed. Once again, he became "just Earl", the man I had met almost twenty years earlier. At that point Earl realized life was literally too short to be concerned with such things and he spent as much time as he could trying to understand and appreciate the more important aspects of life. It was then when father and son formed a new bond, one that no longer pertained only to golf or the tribulations of life. It was simply a closeness that Earl and Tiger shared; a new bond that could not be broken, even in death.

In another conversation we had about Earl's illness, I recall asking Earl that with all of Tiger's money, why couldn't he just go to Europe or some other place to see specialists who have a better survival rate and a possible cure. After a lengthy discussion, Earl promised me he would talk to Tiger, but obviously nothing ever came of our conversation, since he never sought medical treatment elsewhere. I know the cancer was progressing, and maybe there wasn't anything the doctors could do at this point, but I just felt Earl should at least look into some alternative medical treatments that could possibly give him more options and hopefully prolong his life.

About eight months before he died and when he was still feeling somewhat good, Earl and I were sitting in his living room and out of the blue he mentioned there was one thing he never had the chance to do and wanted to do before it was too late. It was sort of a bucket list item. Earl told me he really wanted to drive up the coast of California. Earl then suggested we both go. He said, "Let's just pack our bags and go!"

I even thought about calling Tiger to see if he wanted to go or maybe just he and Earl go on the trip together, but then I remembered Earl had told me about his current schedule and I knew Tiger would be too busy, so I decided against it. I also knew if we were going to take this trip, we would have to do it soon because of Earl's health and his lack of energy. But if this was one of Earl's last wishes, by God, I was going to make it happen for him.

We finally decided we would stop in Malibu, Santa Barbara, San Luis Obispo, Pismo Beach, Solvang, Carmel, Monterey, Big Sur, and San Francisco. We were going to see it all and we would be home when we got home. Earl was like a kid getting ready to go to Disneyland, as he was so excited to finally take his trip up the coast of California. We had also decided we would begin Earl's adventure in less than two weeks.

However, as the time got closer for us to go on our trip, Earl started getting weaker as his illness was progressing faster than anyone had expected. Earl never talked about the trip again and I never brought it up. I was aware of what he was going through and how very disappointed he was, but more so, Earl soon realized that it was too late. In his heart, Earl knew our trip would never take place and he would never see the coast of California again.

Not long after that, Earl found he was somewhat unstable in his movements, especially when walking. He eventually became so unsteady Tiger was afraid that since Earl lived alone, something might happen to him, such as falling and hurting himself. This was when Tiger made the decision and insisted on having a caregiver stay with his father.

Earl was beyond pissed because he enjoyed his privacy and space and he never wanted some stranger living with him and watching his every move. Earl tried to convince Tiger he didn't need anyone to help him, but to no avail. Earl complained to me constantly before the caregiver even started working for him, but as time went on and the weaker he got, Earl was eventually forced to give in to the inevitable. The fact that Earl had to have someone live at his house at all times made him feel helpless, and for a man who had always been strong and determined, this was devastating and degrading for him. Earl knew it had to be that way, but he absolutely hated it. He hated the disease.

Over the years, Tiger had to endure Earl's many health issues, especially when he had heart surgery only a few months after Tiger had become a professional golfer. This was an extremely difficult time for Tiger. Not only was he trying to excel at his new career, but he was also faced with the many new challenges he encountered as a rookie with his busy tournament schedule. During each of Earl's illnesses, Tiger, who lived in Florida, would try to visit his father in California as often as he could. Tiger had to squeeze in these brief visits between his tournaments and sponsor commitments and still allow himself time to focus on his golf.

When Tiger first joined the PGA tour, he was not quite twenty-one years old and Earl was sixty-five. Starting out in a new career, Tiger was already carrying so much on his shoulders. Earl's heart attack and surgeries was a tremendous amount of additional pressure for someone so young to have to endure.

However, when Earl's cancer came out of remission, the many pressures Tiger had been feeling magnified to all new levels. Earl was not only sick, but he would not be surviving this illness like he had done in the past. Sadly, Tiger knew the situation was dire and he would be forced to face the future without his father. As Earl's cancer quickly progressed, Tiger found he was now the person in charge and having to care for his father. This was a role that was new for Tiger, a total reversal of how his life had always been since it was always Earl who was in control and handling Tiger's life. Tiger was put in a position where he felt obligated to abide by Earl's wishes and requests, but was forced to do what he believed was right for his father. This was probably the most difficult task Tiger ever had to master, especially since he was still trying to maintain his commitments to his golf.

Tiger had grown up quite a bit since his father's heart surgery when he was just a rookie. He was a grown man now, as he had just turned thirty years old, and had the capability of taking charge when necessary. However, when it came to his emotions, Tiger was also forced to control them and be strong for his father and his family's sake. It was incredibly difficult for Tiger to live three thousand miles away and was only able to visit when time permitted.

Frankly, I don't know how Tiger did it. How was he able to go out on the course and perform to his best ability when Earl's illness had to have been consuming his every thought? I know Tiger would play every tournament for his father, always being sure to make his father proud, no matter what the circumstances were. I admire Tiger for his strength and determination. I also knew how much he loved Earl and it was tearing him apart inside. Luckily for Tiger, he was fortunate enough to have a lighter tournament schedule that year thus enabling him to be with his father more during his last months.

When Earl's health started to diminish, his daughter, Royce decided to take a leave of absence from her job in Northern California and move into his house so she could help care for him. Earl was not pleased that yet another person would now be living in his house, but he knew he could not deny his daughter wanting to be with him.

I remember one day when I was talking to Earl, he told me about how, after his radiation treatment that morning, he had become so sick that he was unable to move. While he was resting in his recliner in the living room, he had become so extremely nauseous he began throwing up in a bucket right in front of Royce. Earl was almost in tears telling me how humiliated and embarrassed he felt because he was showing signs of weakness right in front of his own daughter and how he wished she wasn't there to witness it. Earl then stressed that he is the father and he should be the strong one.

Earl knew this was only the beginning of a very short road, and he knew there would be many more days just like this one for him. I tried my best to console Earl and let him know Royce would definitely understand, but to him, that was not the issue. He felt he was showing signs of weakness and he was so very frustrated and upset that he had absolutely no control over the circumstances as he had always been strong and able to stay in control. This man was an ex-military officer and Green Beret. He had been trained to always be the man in charge in any situation. Earl felt he was letting everyone down because he no longer had the strength or the willpower to overcome his illness. In his heart, though, Earl knew everyone would understand, but he still hated the pity they were showing. He hated the fact that his family, and especially Tiger, now had to take care of him, when it had always been his role in life to take care of them.

The last time I saw Earl, he was barely recognizable as he had lost even more weight from my previous visits. I could tell he was in even more pain than before. I saw in his eyes that he had given up; rather the cancer was forcing him to give up. Earl knew the disease now had the upper hand and he was never going to beat it. Not this time. Earl hated the disease and he knew it was taking his life from him.

This was the last time I saw Earl. He died ten days later.

The day I had been dreading came on May 3, 2006. Earl's daughter, Royce, called me around seven o'clock in the morning and she tearfully told me Earl had passed away just a few hours earlier. Royce felt I should be one of first to be notified and she also wanted to make sure I heard it in person and not through the media. We talked for the longest time trying our best to console each other. We both shared stories about Earl, some of the time laughing, but mostly we were crying. We knew this time would eventually come, but neither of us was ever truly prepared.

I also asked Royce how Tiger was handling Earl's death and she said. "He's holding up the best he can." She and I both knew this would hit Tiger hard. Even though Tiger knew his father was going to die, he still was not completely prepared for it.

Royce further commented, "You know how Tiger is. He seldom ever shows any emotion, so you really never know exactly how he's feeling."

Earl died at his home, not in a hospital, and there was only his daughter and the caregiver with him in the end. Since Earl hated hospitals, Earl wanted to be at home when he died. Earl once mentioned how hospitals are lonely places and the doctors and nurses are only nice to you because they are paid to be. So he wanted to die in his own home and have family around him. Nobody knew for sure when the end would come, as it was a day by day situation.

Later that evening, I once again talked to Royce and then to Earl's son, Kevin. Although we talked for quite a long time, never once did I sense any sadness or sorrow from him. He was cracking jokes and was very light hearted. He didn't act like his father had just passed away.

I went over to Earl's house the next day to visit with Royce, Kevin and Earl Jr. After I arrived, I asked Royce if Tiger was there as I wanted to pay my condolences to him. Seeing that Royce was upset with my question, she snipped, "Of course he is not here with the rest of the family. I'm assuming he's over at his mother's house."

"I'm sorry. I just assumed he would be here with all of you."

"Well, that's never going to happen," she said as she started to cry. I just hugged her and told her how sorry I was. She knew I understood completely.

Royce and I walked down the hall into Earl's bedroom where we found Den (Earl Jr.), rummaging through Earl's belongings and I immediately noticed that all of the bedding had been removed from the bed. It was totally stripped down to the bare mattress and then it hit me Earl had just died in that very bed. It was also shocking to see how the bedding had been replaced with Earl's belongings, all of which were strewn about and even stacked up in tall piles. All of his suits, dress shirts, sweat shirts and pants, several pairs of shoes, and even his socks were piled high on the bed. Den and Kevin were helping themselves to everything that had belonged to their father, including all of his gold jewelry. Seeing the shocked expression on my face, Den immediately justified his actions by explaining that Tida instructed them to take anything they wanted, and I guess they wanted it all. They had every right to take these items, but I thought it was quite odd they were doing it this soon as Earl had hardly been gone twenty-four hours.

I did notice, however, that everything of any great value in the house had already been removed earlier by Tiger and Tida, such as Earl's Rolex watches, the replicas of Tiger's trophies for the majors, Tiger's gold plated putters, the plastic encased Wheaties boxes, statues, crystal and figurines. I guess Tiger knew what would eventually happen if those items had been left there after Earl died.

Strangely, I noticed that Royce, Kevin and Den were not showing any signs of real emotion toward Earl's death. However, it also appeared that his children's main concern, according to the comments they had made to me, was dividing up Earl's belongings and making it to the lawyers on time to sign "the necessary paperwork". Maybe Earl had heeded my advice from our earlier conversations and decided to leave his children a tidy sum after all.

As I walked back to the living room, I passed the office area and I immediately stopped. I was surprised to see Earl's symbolic Nike hat with "Earl Woods" embroidered on it was sitting on the corner of the desk upside down with his sunglasses and keys in it. Noticing my reaction, Royce asked me if I would like to have his hat as it was the last one he had worn before he died. Of course, I took the hat without any hesitation and I have cherished it ever since.

On the large wall in the entry way was Tiger's "wall of fame" display. Every few months Earl would have the pictures rotated with others that were kept safely in the garage. Kevin and Den had decided they wanted some of those pictures, but mentioned how Tida may not allow anyone to take them. So, in order not to get caught, they backed their car up into the driveway, and they quietly snuck a couple of the pictures out of the house and placed them into the trunk, hoping Tida would never find out.

Tomorrow would be Earl's funeral.

I drove slowly down the long winding tree lined driveway toward the chapel at Fairhaven Memorial Park and Mortuary in

Santa Ana, California. As I approached the large iron gates, I was motioned to stop by several men in black suits, one holding a clipboard. He asked for my name and began scanning the list of invited guests. Finally, after verifying my name, he waved me through to the parking area. As I walked toward the chapel, there was a table where three women were seated.

As I approached the table, one of the women asked for my name, and after cautiously scanning her list, she handed me a Tiger Woods Foundation lapel pin, explaining it would allow me access to the reception. This very unusual regimentation reminded me of a check-in at a charity golf tournament. Then, the more I thought about it, this procedure was more like trying to get access to a military facility, with gates, checkpoints, lists, and checking everyone's identification. I just smiled, realizing all of this was just so typical of the Woods' family.

There were probably thirty or forty people milling around outside the chapel, all waiting to enter. Since the family was nowhere to be seen, I assumed they were inside the chapel having their private time together. After waiting about twenty minutes, the chapel doors opened and everyone formed a line as they walked in to be seated. Upon entering, I immediately noticed the closed casket positioned at the front portion of the chapel. This was when the realization set in that Earl was actually gone.

As I looked around the chapel, I noticed that other than immediate family, there was no one in attendance who really knew Earl, other than Billy Stark, his longtime friend, Peter McDaniel, a friend and author, and me. There were no friends, neighbors, or golfing buddies from the Navy Golf Course.

Everyone else were friends and associates of Tiger. As I took my seat behind the family, I noticed Steve Williams, Tiger's caddy, walk up and sit next to me. Also seated in the chapel was Charles Barkley, Mark O'Meara, John Cook, and Laird Hamilton. They were all there to support Tiger in the loss of his father.

The reverend spoke first, then Tiger, Billy Stark, and then Peter McDaniel, all giving a moving tribute to Earl. Toward the end of the service, Darius Rucker sang "Will the Circle Be Unbroken", to honor Earl. After the services were over, everyone left the chapel and went outside to watch Tiger and his half-siblings release white doves into the sky.

Then everyone who attended the funeral left the cemetery and drove to Anaheim for the reception at the Tiger Woods Learning Center. The family wanted the services to remain a secret and obviously they were successful since there was absolutely no press or even a single photographer anywhere in sight at the actual services in Santa Ana.

However, when we all arrived at the Tiger Woods Learning Center for the reception, I did notice two photographers across the street trying to get a glimpse of Tiger. Apparently they were the ones who took the picture showing Tiger, Elin and Tida arrive in their limousine and walk toward the entrance to the Learning Center. That was the only picture the media took and reported to the public.

Once inside the Center, we all shared the celebration of Earl's life. They showed a montage of pictures of Earl and Tiger on all the monitors as Josh Groban's song "You Raise Me Up" played throughout the rooms. I was sure Tiger requested that particular song to be played to honor his father, since I know Tiger felt Earl had raised him up higher than anyone ever could.

During the reception, I had the chance to talk again with Royce, Kevin and Den. From the way they were acting you could tell they just wanted to eat and get out of there. Although it was their father's funeral, sadly, other than their family, no one else knew who they were.

I saw Tiger and Elin standing nearby, and I decided to join them. Tiger and I talked for a short while, mainly talking about Earl, remembering his rigid golf lessons, all of us playing golf together, the trip to Hawaii, and so much more. I then told Tiger I was very proud of him because of his composure and strength he had shown in order to get through this unfortunate time.

I could tell Tiger was holding in his emotions. He was trying to maintain the calm and focused image that had been drilled into him for so many years. He was acting somewhat stoic and reserved as though he was afraid to show his true feelings and emotions, especially since he was in a somewhat public place and in the presence of others.

However, when we talked, he seemed more relaxed, almost like he wanted to cry. Just looking into his eyes, I was able to see the emptiness and heartache that was consuming him and I knew he could break down at any moment. Tiger was showing less confidence and was even revealing signs of vulnerability. Tiger lost his best friend, his confidant and lifetime advisor. Earl was Tiger's compass throughout life, and now Tiger will have to travel the roads alone and find his own direction. Although Earl was gone, the father and son bond had not been broken. Earl once told me that relationships don't end, they simply change. I hope Tiger remembers that.

After Tiger and I talked, I started to cry and I looked up at him and asked, "What are we going to do without Earl?"

Tiger gave me the longest hug, and then softly said, "I really don't know." We both knew from that very moment, our lives would forever be changed.

26
PRIMED TO FALL

TIGER WAS BORN INTO this world to be just a normal kid, but it was Earl who decided to take Tiger's life and run with it. Out of the four children Earl was father to, for some unknown reason, it was Tiger who he chose to dedicate himself to and finally become a real father. Of course, it could be the fact that Tiger was the only one of his children who had the ability to provide the fame, recognition and wealth that Earl believed he had been deprived of in his own life many years earlier.

With Earl's dedication and devotion came a need to control and dictate every part of Tiger's life. From this came Earl's over the top obsession to do whatever was necessary to push Tiger to greatness. Many times Earl had claimed that he and Tida were loving and concerned parents who were raising Tiger with solid family values, but I knew it was also Earl and Tida who placed the many high demands and expectations on Tiger throughout his life. Although Earl's heart was supposedly in the right place, his well-intended actions resulted in causing Tiger to become the person who Earl thought he should be instead of letting Tiger be true to himself.

Even as a pro, Tiger had his father, his agents, his sponsors, and even his mother telling him what to do, how to act and what was right for him instead of letting Tiger decide what was truly right for himself. It was obvious to me that Tiger was put in a position where he had to do what they said, live the values they told him to live by, abide by the schedules they created for him and live the life they carved out for him. Wow, now that is what I call a lot of control! And on top of that, it was almost as though Tiger was forced to believe in everyone else instead of believing in himself.

According to Earl, Tiger was expected to put his trust in all of his advisors because they supposedly knew what was best for him. After all, they were experts in their fields of business and Earl was sure they would definitely have Tiger's best interest at heart. There were many times when Tiger's advisors would share their ideas and opinions with him, but it was Earl who would force Tiger into a position where he felt obligated to go along with whatever they suggested, even though at times he disagreed with their advice and recommendations.

These people dictated much of Tiger's life and with this kind of control, I often wondered if there was another side of Tiger, one that had been aching to come out for many years and wanting to break away from the rigidity of his life. This made me question if it was possible that Tiger was tired of living the squeaky clean life and having to always present the role model image and celebrity that had been created for him. After years of doing what everyone else expected of him, maybe Tiger just wanted to finally be himself.

I remember back in the early years when Tiger simply wanted to play golf and be the best golfer on tour. He wanted to break records and win as many tournaments as he could. After Tiger became successful on the PGA tour, Earl even told me how Tiger really didn't care about all the money or even the celebrity status. It is true, however, that Tiger wanted the glory for winning and, of course, the prize money; but he never really wanted all of the obligations that came with it. After all, when Tiger initially started playing on the PGA tour, the money for winning was not all that great, but Tiger was still willing to accept it, just as so many other golfers before him.

But, of course, in Tiger's case, he started off as a rookie with huge contracts from many sponsors. When it came to his sponsor endorsements, Tiger was extremely fortunate, especially since no golfer had ever been offered such lucrative contracts. The money he was given was an amount that was never imagined nor was it ever predicted in the early planning stages of his career. So, was all of the money worth Tiger giving up his soul and who he really was just to placate everyone else?

When I think back to the way Earl had raised Tiger, in a way I can somewhat understand why Tiger has made some poor choices which ended up redirecting his life. Although Earl was his best friend and they shared so much, in reality, Tiger had been subjected to a lifetime of Earl's obsessions and fanatical behavior, resulting in Earl controlling almost every facet of Tiger's life. The effects on Tiger were tremendous, especially Tiger's addictive dependency on his lifelong friend and advisor: his father.

Until Tiger moved away to college, Tiger's parents were always around him almost to the point of being suffocating. Very seldom was he ever alone and he seldom was allowed to shine in his own light. Even after he turned pro, his parents continued to be a constant in his life. Think back to the "Hello World" TV announcement, every tournament Tiger played in, the Tiger Jam concerts, golf clinics, television appearances, his news conference admitting to his infidelity, and the list goes on and on and on. One or both of his parents were always there. Not just once in a great while; they were there every single time.

In comparison, you hardly ever see the parents of other athletes constantly hovering around their child, especially to the extreme that Earl and Tida always were. I understand they had to be around when Tiger was a kid, but he was thirty years old when Earl died. There were many times when Earl and I would discuss why he and Tida felt it was necessary to continually be in Tiger's life and Earl would simply respond with, "We just want to be there for Tiger. He needs us and we have to protect him." Earl called it love. Many would call it interference and control.

I remember when Earl was trying to "wean" Tiger from his hold so Tiger might eventually be able to stand on his own. This occurred shortly after Earl's cancer was back and when he realized just how closely involved he had been in Tiger's life since the day he was born. Knowing how much Tiger relied on his guidance and advice, Earl was afraid of what might happen to Tiger when he would no longer be around. Sadly, it took Earl's illness for him to finally accept the fact that Tiger always had a dependency on him and to recognize the situation he had created. Because of this new revelation, Earl finally became concerned for his son's future.

Earl had confided in me that he knew the time had come when he needed to cut Tiger loose and away from his hold. Earl did his best to make this process happen, but unfortunately, Tida objected to Earl's theory as she never felt it was necessary to back away from her son. She was, and still is, a dominating mother and will always refuse to release those responsibilities. So to this day, Tida continues to insinuate herself into every part of Tiger's life and is constantly around him, no matter what.

After Earl's death, Tiger was left having to cope without his father and his best friend. New lessons would have to be learned, a new direction would have to be mapped out and the choices Tiger would make would now be made alone and without the benefit of his lifelong advisor.

Unfortunately, for Tiger, the damage had already been done. A lifetime of Earl's control and manipulations, where Earl pulled all the strings, would leave a scar on Tiger's life and his mental outlook. Earl may have put Tiger in the fast lane for his career, but he was the road block when it came to Tiger being a normal person. Tiger would continue his life, still reeling from the effects from his father's dominance. It would be like a new beginning for Tiger; a beginning where he could finally find himself and learn who he really is, or rather, who he wants to be. But this would not happen overnight as it could take years for Tiger to finally find himself and be at peace with who he has become.

A few years after Earl's death, I heard rumors that Tiger was having an affair. Then the allegations were splashed all over the news, tabloids, magazines, late night talk shows, and every other media venue. Knowing the way Earl had raised Tiger, I simply refused to believe any part of the breaking scandal. What they were saying was impossible and I honestly believed there was no way in hell that Tiger would ever be unfaithful to Elin. Even though everyone was positive the stories were true, I continued to staunchly defend Tiger. However, if I had been a betting person, I would have lost big on this one.

A short time later, Tiger held a press conference on national television and confessed his wrongdoings. I felt like such a fool for defending him. I could not believe that Tiger publicly admitted to his transgressions. However, I think I was even more shocked that he felt it was necessary to broadcast his admission of guilt to the entire world and wondered if Earl was turning over in his grave at that very moment. My immediate reaction was to question Tiger's motives, wondering if he was really sorry and wanted forgiveness or was his statement created solely for the edification of the media and public. After all, during his confession, Tiger had admitted that because of his status he believed he was invincible and above it all and thought he could get away with breaking the rules of morality.

Still stunned by what I heard, I just sat there after it was over and thought about how Tiger had used those women and was unfaithful to his wife. No matter how I tried to digest the news, none of it was making any sense to me. It did, however, make me realize how much Tiger had changed due to his fame and wealth and how his attitude toward life had been so drastically altered. So much of Tiger's actions I blame on Earl because of the poor values Tiger was taught over the years.

For reasons known only to Tiger, he fell off course and was unfaithful in his marriage to Elin. With total disregard for the consequences, not only did Tiger forget about his marriage vows, but he also closed his eyes to who he was and what he represented. Tiger abandoned the image that his father had so carefully crafted and worked so hard to maintain for him and the role model that he had dedicated himself to be.

But when I look back, I can't fully blame Tiger. In a way, Tiger's fall was always in the making especially because of his upbringing and the dubious influence he was subjected to growing up. Tiger was only doing what he was taught and living by the mixed set of values that had been instilled in him. Tiger was repeating what his parents did in their own marriage. Earl and Tida were not great role models and they failed to set the best examples for their son. Therefore, because of Earl and Tida, Tiger was primed for an eventual fall whether it was in his personal life or in his career. What his parents forgot to realize is you can push a person only so far and then they will eventually break.

Nevertheless, it was still Tiger's choice to ignore his image and the position he held in the golfing world by having an affair.

Well, actually, according to the media and all the women who came forward, I guess we are supposed to believe that Tiger all of a sudden had multiple affairs over a short period of time. After all, I am sure the media has always been one hundred per cent honest and correct in all of their reporting!

After Tiger's affairs were made public, I began to wonder if his father's first marriage to Barbara and his leaving her for his second wife, Tida, had any lasting effect on Tiger. I honestly do not believe it was "monkey see, monkey do". It was more like, "do as I say, not what I do" and if you choose to "do", definitely don't get caught. Ultimately, it was still Tiger's choice.

Tiger is his own person and knew in his heart exactly what he was supposed to do. But because of the secrecy Tiger was taught to maintain throughout his personal and professional life, I know we will ever have any of the real answers since Tiger will never reveal anything pertaining to his private life and no portion of it will ever be made public. People who have written articles or books about the scandal are simply speculating on what they think happened, but in reality they know absolutely nothing. They can try to create a scenario for the benefit of the public, but they will be wrong. They still know absolutely nothing. Tiger, or anyone in his camp for that matter, will never reveal anything. And, it is Tiger's right to keep it private.

For all we know, Elin was not the perfect wife and Tiger was pushed away like so many husbands are by their wives and vice versa. Maybe their marriage was already on the rocks as indicated by Earl early on in their marriage. Even prior to Tiger and Elin's wedding, Earl had his suspicions regarding their union. But in the end, only Tiger and Elin know the truth about their marriage, none of which is our concern nor is it our place to judge. Thus, we will never know the truth.

When you think about it, why should we even care what he does in his private life? It definitely does not change who Tiger is as an exceptional and talented athlete. And if his actions do change our perception of Tiger, then the weakness falls on us as being judgmental toward others without knowing fully any of the why's and how's.

When it comes to Tiger's marriage, I knew Earl's history in his own marriages might eventually have some effect on Tiger. Earl freely admitted to me how his first marriage was a mistake from the very beginning, especially since many family members had initially advised him against it. Earl wanted out but then his first son was born. In his second marriage, Earl claimed his love for Tida ended shortly after they were married and wanted out, but then his son, Tiger, was born.

Earl was always open and honest with Tiger when it came to his feelings for Tiger's mother, so Tiger was completely aware of Earl and Tida's broken and unloving relationship. According to Earl, Tiger was young and was so close to his mother and attached to the "solid" family life which they were trying to exemplify, that a divorce could cause unexpected ramifications and Tiger's values would be greatly affected.

However, in reality, Earl always said it was all about Tiger's golf. As soon as Tiger turned professional Earl and Tida separated, however, still leading the public to believe they were together and in a happy marriage. According to Earl, Tiger's values were most definitely affected because of his parent's "pretend" relationship. Earl and Tida would always appear as though they were together at every tournament, every function, and anything that involved

Tiger. They duped the public and media into believing they were still a solid loving family for Tiger's sake and for his "image".

Sadly, Tiger's parents never set the perfect example for their son when it pertained to marriage. In many ways, Earl and Tida's actions and values were far from being role model material.

Although Earl had numerous discussions on this topic with Tiger over the years, I often wondered if Tiger listened to the values Earl was trying to teach him or was Tiger more influenced by witnessing the lack of solid values and instability in a marriage which Earl actually demonstrated. The fact that Tiger knew his parents were in a loveless marriage must have had a tremendous effect on Tiger's own views on marriage. Also, it is quite obvious that Tiger's knowledge of Earl's past history with women and relationships had a strong influence on his own love life and attitude toward women. Of course, maybe the "do as I say, not what I do" part just did not stick with Tiger.

There is one other thought that had come to mind about Tiger's poor choices. Since Earl was a controlling father and placed such high expectations on Tiger, especially with the demands to be perfect and to live up to the "role model" image, was it possible this is what caused Tiger to lose himself and forget who he really was? Because of Earl, Tiger was forced to carry so much on his shoulders throughout his life that you might say Tiger was possibly pushed to his limits. Since everything about Tiger had to be perfect, one questions if the stress and changes in his life ruined his marriage and caused him to stray. After all, now that Earl was gone, Tiger no longer had to worry about disappointing his father or letting him down.

I believe losing Earl and not having him to confide in and seek advice from was not necessarily an underlying factor behind Tiger's ill-fated choices. I know Tiger lost his father and his best friend, someone who he had shared a tremendous bond with his entire life. But the problem I have is I just do not believe Tiger was so weak that he allowed his father's death to have such a long term effect on him. Tiger's affairs were three and a half years after Earl died. I mean, if Tiger was going to go off the deep end and do something reckless and foolish, he would have done it shortly after Earl's death, not years later. When you think about it, Earl's death really had nothing to do with any of Tiger's decisions.

Earl's death should not be used as an excuse for Tiger having an affair. There are so many other problems Tiger had that should be factored in, such as the strict and controlled environment in which he was raised by two dominating and dictating parents, the pressures he was under as a golfer, and the possibility of an unhappy marriage. To everyone on the outside, Tiger appeared to have had a great life, full of love, attention, wealth and fame, but they were unaware that Tiger's life may not have been what it seemed. Tiger may have been suffering the repercussions from the constant exposure and extreme life he was forced to live, mostly thanks to his father. One might wonder if after Earl's death, was Tiger feeling lost or was he finally feeling free.

Remembering Tiger at the funeral and seeing such a void in his eyes when we talked, in my heart I knew he might someday stumble, but I never imagined he would fall this hard or this far. Tiger walked from sadness in a way that only he knew why and possibly it was a way of healing for him.

Contrary to what some people may think, Earl was not a womanizer and should never be considered as such. The true definition of a womanizer is a man who has "multiple" affairs with many women at one time. Earl never did this and his own actions should not be likened to that of his son as some other have stated.

There was a large difference between Earl and Tiger. Tiger's alleged multiple short term affairs were solely sex driven and without any benefit of friendship and emotional support. The women involved in Tiger's life were with him simply because he was rich and famous and nothing more.

It was also strange how Tiger was reportedly dating only strippers and, for a lack of a better word, "loose women". He was not having an affair with a soccer mom he met at the grocery store or a nice girl he met at a golfing function. According to the press, Tiger apparently met these women not only in nightclubs but in lower class bars and strip joints. I thought it was convenient when all of a sudden so many of these women came out of the woodwork, just in time to claim their "supposed" affairs with Tiger. Where were they six months earlier? And we are to believe these women, why??

Do I believe Tiger had an affair? Yes. Do I believe there was more than one? I honestly do not know. Do I believe the parade of women who were brought out by the media? I believe these women about as much as I believe the story about the three headed alien baby from another planet!

Let's remember Tiger is known for frequenting high class nightclubs in Las Vegas, New York, the Bahamas and many other exclusive locations and his appearance in these clubs would not be out of the ordinary. It would seem totally out of character for Tiger to go elsewhere. What I don't understand is when Tiger was supposedly out and about at these "less than classy" venues, not one person ever noticed that the famous and very well-known Tiger Woods was in their presence.

I'm sorry, but it is truly hard to believe that not one person recognized the famous Tiger Woods. Not one patron or employee ever grabbed their cell phone or camera and snapped a picture of Tiger. No one could ever convince me that all of the people in these establishments wanted to allow Tiger his privacy and not one single person in the club was interested in taking a picture of Tiger Woods for themselves or for the benefit of selling it to the tabloids for a very large sum of money.

Oh, wait, I know what happened! All of their cell phones and all their cameras were confiscated at the door when they entered the club, just in case some high profile celebrity might decide to come in that night. Yah, right! And that's really going to happen! Also, I am sure most of these "women" were loyal and trusting and extremely concerned about protecting Tiger's privacy. They only came forth when the story was finally broken, simply out of a sense of duty to the public. And if you believe this, I have more pictures of the three headed alien baby for sale.

Another question I have is where was the media during all these many "public" escapades of Tiger's? Not doing their job, obviously. Is that why they were only able to speculate on what supposedly happened and they had to "create" so many stories about Tiger? It's as though they made up so much of the scandal afterwards in order to compensate for what they did not see. It's funny how the media jumped on the bandwagon with each and every woman who came forward. Their actions made me wonder if these women were simply set-ups. Maybe the media had to make something up just to save face.

With Tiger's busy schedule, practicing and playing in all of his tournaments, spending time with his family, and his many business and sponsor commitments, just how in the world did he ever find time for "all" of these women? The only answer I can come up with would require cloning.

I know if Earl was alive, Tiger most likely would not have had an affair. Or at least he would not have been caught. However, when I think about it, if Tiger had chosen to have an affair while Earl was still alive, I know that because of the way Earl controlled Tiger's life and did everything humanly possible to protect and defend his son, the affair would have been handled in an entirely different manner.

Earl would have had Tiger respond with a statement denying the allegations much sooner, almost immediately, thus preventing the scandal from ever surfacing to the magnitude in which it ultimately did. Earl would then most likely have advised Tiger to lay low and never hold a press conference and never, ever make an admission of guilt in public. In addition, Earl would never have allowed Tiger to participate in the any sex therapy sessions. But then again, it was never proven that Tiger actually participated in any sex therapy sessions at any rehab center. It was the media who led the public to believe there were photos of Tiger at the facility.

Of course, those photos were not clear enough or close enough to actually identify that it was indeed Tiger.

Earl would never have allowed any part of Tiger's private life to be revealed, stressing it was definitely no one else's business, especially the media. At this point, Earl would have instantly hit the press strong in order to silence any news, after which Earl would go into his typical defense mode for his son. Because of his intensely protective nature, Earl would have been on the attack and would have jumped on the press straightaway, showing Tiger as a victim of the media, which in effect, he was. Earl would then blame the media for the injustice that was happening to his son because of the sensationalizing nature of their constant reporting. Earl would even go so far as stating if Tiger was white, the media would not have been as interested in what Tiger had done. It's unfortunate that Earl's reactions would have been the result of his always believing that everyone was out to harm his son in one way or another.

It is so very sad that Tiger's life had to change so much after Earl's death. Tiger was indeed a victim in so many ways, not just from the media, but from his entire upbringing. Earl did have some good qualities, but when it came to Tiger, Earl's obsessive behavior stood out above all the rest. I'm sure that even to this day Tiger is still unable to recognize his father's manipulations and obsessions and just how much Earl's actions truly affected him and his life. I hope the day will come when Tiger is fortunate enough to finally realize what he had to endure at the hands of his father.

However, Tiger would most likely never admit to it especially since he would then have to look at his father's memory in an entirely different light. But you can't blame Tiger because much of who he is today is simply a result of Earl's many misguided and self-serving intentions.

27

DESTROYING THE IMAGE

AFTER EARL'S DEATH, it was obvious the lives of everyone who loved Earl had been affected in one way or another, especially Tiger's. For Tiger, losing his father was devastating as it would be for anyone who has lost a parent. Knowing the closeness Tiger and Earl shared, I continued to worry about his ability to carry on, not just in his golf, but in his personal life as well. After Earl's death, Tiger found it difficult at times to focus on his golf game and maintain the frame of mind that is necessary to win a tournament. With Tiger's discipline and fortitude, he was able to remain strong, and from that, his game continued to stay on track, but unfortunately his personal life did not.

Sadly, Tiger's personal life took a devastating hit when his affairs were made public, thus creating a worldwide scandal. No matter what Tiger's reasons may have been for having an affair, even multiple affairs, it was his own personal and private business. Many believed it was totally wrong that the media chose to have continuous coverage regarding his affairs and his personal life, thus escalating the scandal to such an extreme level.

Why did the media feel there was such a need for the public to know about absolutely everything in Tiger's life and to also create so many untruths and rumors about Tiger? Never once did they take into consideration the effect their reporting would have on Tiger and especially his family, nor did they even care. This is the problem with the various forms of the media today as they simply want a story, no matter how they get it, who it hurts or what the outcome of their report might be. The reporter will do whatever it takes to get the story and to get their name in print.

Due to the fact that Tiger makes an obscene amount of money playing golf and he is extremely popular with the public, the media, therefore, took it upon themselves to determine the public had "the right to know" absolutely everything about him in regard to his private life. The media also believed it was their right to scope out and bring these stories to the public's attention, although many of the stories were unfounded and most definitely were not entirely true.

Of course, we all know about how the media operates and the reporting of Tiger's situation was quite typical of them. Was Tiger's affair really an event that should have been broadcast around the world? NO! This was not a reality show with multiple episodes. Tiger is only a golfer. Popular yes, but he is still only a golfer.

Instead of people or the media having the compassion and understanding for another human being and to take it upon themselves to fully understand what could have caused a person's downfall, they have a tendency to become judgmental. It is such a shame that no one chose to be more empathetic and believe Tiger might have been going through a personal hell after the death of his father or to simply say Tiger is only human, so what if he made a mistake. Who are we to judge?

Who are we to place someone such as Tiger on such a high pedestal, much less the morality pedestal? I don't remember Tiger ever volunteering or vying for the title of role model for the world. His father may have wanted and believed Tiger should fill that position, but it was the media and the public's perception of Tiger that created this part for Tiger to play. They envisioned Tiger in this role and crowned him with that distinction. Tiger never asked to be given this responsibility, thus he should not be judged based on that position or on his morals. Tiger only wanted to be judged on the merits of his golf game and nothing more.

Those who judge suddenly act as though they are better than the fallen person because they believe they would have never made that particular mistake themselves, thereby forgetting about their own shortcomings and indiscretions. Tiger was a targeted person and was instantly removed from the pedestal on which he was once placed. In other words, we will keep the person on the pedestal if they continue to be good, but if they do anything wrong or something we do not like, we will take them down, even if their wrong doing has absolutely nothing to do with why we put them on the pedestal in the first place.

I would love to know how many people were so quick to judge and then condemn Tiger for his transgressions when, in fact, they, too, had either cheated on their own spouse or partner or were living a not so squeaky clean life. But isn't it strange that we are not nearly so quick to judge ourselves as we are when we are judging others?

If Joe Blow down the street had an affair, no one would have cared one bit, and certainly not the media. Why should it be any different just because a person is well known? I mean, if Phil Mickelson, Arnold Palmer, or even Jack Nicklaus had done the very same thing as Tiger, would the media have publicized it the same or would the public have even cared? Of course not!

There have been many prominent golfers and star athletes in other sports who have cheated, divorced, married and remarried and the media did not seem to care about any of them. Nothing these people ever did in their personal life, good or bad, right or wrong, was ever considered a major story. So, why did they pick on Tiger?

Simply put, it was because Tiger was being persecuted for violating his perfect "role model image" and not for the act itself. If you think about it, Tiger would never have been in the news so much and it would not have created such a sensationalized "scandal" if it had not been for his so-called image. If it had been someone else, like popular professional golfer John Daly, the incident would have gotten no more than fifteen seconds of airtime, if that, and probably no tabloid coverage at all. People would simply say, well, that's John, and not another word would have been mentioned on the subject.

The problem was that everyone expected Tiger to live up to his squeaky clean image that had been created and strongly promoted by his father, his agents, his sponsors, and the public, thus leaving him no room for error. Basically, Tiger was being forced into a position of having to live his life according to the standards set by everyone else and it was those standards that prevented him from being the person he may have wanted to be or to live his life according to his own choices.

If Tiger Woods had not become a golfer, but instead was just a normal person who just went to college, got married, lived in middle suburbia, and worked as a computer programmer, and then had an affair, or several for that matter, nobody would care. But he would still be Tiger Woods. Worse yet, if Tiger had turned professional on the PGA tour, but was not as successful as a player or as popular with the public, and if he had these affairs, would anyone care or would it be a national media event? Of course not, but he would still be Tiger Woods.

It was Tiger Woods, the person, who did wrong. But it was Tiger Woods, the image that was attacked.

The simple fact is Tiger's affairs drew more media attention than the affairs of Bill Clinton, John Edwards, Rudy Giuliani or any other high profile celebrity or political figure. Of course, Bill Clinton was only the President of the United States and running a country. Obviously, a professional golfer must be more important and more newsworthy and warrants more public ridicule and judgment than the President. Besides, if Bill Clinton had an affair today, who would care? Would it make any more headlines than the back page of the society section?

See what happens when you are no longer in the limelight? Just imagine what would happen if Tiger had another affair today. Would anyone even care? Of course not, because he has already been pulled down from his pedestal to a level where he is now just a normal person. He is no longer worthy of public judgment and criticism.

Something that has always amazed me was the fact that during Tiger's entire professional career, starting from the time he was twenty years old, there was never one single time when the media ever saw or reported an incident involving Tiger doing anything wrong, much less with women. I remember when Tiger was one of the most eligible bachelors in the world prior to his wedding to Elin, yet there had never been a hint of scandal or wrongdoing. It seems strange how during Tiger's scandal, the media decided to report that Tiger used to be a wild playboy during his bachelor days. But, if this was the case, then why didn't the media ever see or report anything back then when Tiger was single? I guess we are to assume there just wasn't anything all that newsworthy about Tiger! So, why now?

It is also a known fact that the media's reporting can apply so much pressure to an athlete, or anyone else for that matter, and often these actions will actually interfere with their ability to perform. In regard to Tiger, the media went overboard with their constant reporting of his affairs and his divorce to the point where he was unable to have any peace of mind, thus preventing him from focusing on his game and career. This caused Tiger to remove himself from golf for twenty weeks, eventually resurfacing at the 2010 Masters Tournament.

You can tell that the media still wants Tiger to be a great golfer, but their constant invasion into his private life continues to affect his ability to play, and unfortunately for Tiger, the effects could be long lasting. If people truly cared about Tiger as a person, a living human being, they would remember back to all the years when they reported great things about him and simply give him a break. More recently they could have shown some compassion instead of using him as a whipping post.

Of course, Tiger has not done himself any favors with his secrecy. Because of his attempts to keep his private life a secret, in a way, Tiger actually fueled the media's attention. If Tiger had just been more open and had acted like one of the guys, as most of the other golfers and athletes do, there would not have been anything to write about. Basically, Earl's philosophy on maintaining the image by keeping secrets backfired and set Tiger up for the fall.

After Tiger made his televised admission of guilt regarding his affairs and asked for the public's forgiveness, Nike tried to gain sympathy for Tiger by coming out with a television advertisement featuring Earl talking to Tiger. During the Masters Tournament, I was in the kitchen and all of a sudden I heard Earl's voice coming from my living room. As I walked to the television, I was thinking, "What in the hell is going on. That's Earl talking."

Then when I saw the ad again and heard Earl's exact words, I immediately thought there was no way in hell Earl would have ever said anything like that to Tiger. And Tiger would never have stood there looking like a beaten puppy when his father spoke to him. The Earl I knew, and I did know him well, would have said something like this: "What in the hell were you thinking? You sure f_ _ ked things up now!" This would have been followed by a two hour lecture, not a gentle mentoring session as Nike would like you to believe.

Earl was not a Buddhist Monk who spoke softly. He was an ex-Green Beret in the Army. BIG DIFFERENCE!!

Nike used the words in the ad that came from a previous interview with the "public image" of Earl. The public image was the person who tried to impress people with his mentoring skills. The "real and private" Earl would have spoken in an entirely different manner, more like he was pissed off. He would not have shown horrible anger, but his tone would have been harsh and disapproving, displaying much disappointment in his son.

I even remember the comment Earl once made to me about how everything Tiger does throughout his career, good or bad, affects the Woods family. Earl told me if Tiger ever forgets who he is and stops trying to be a good person, Earl would be very displeased. If Tiger did something to embarrass or disappoint Earl and his family, Earl would be terribly upset and he would be forced take charge of Tiger's actions and correct the situation. One of Earl's favorite sayings was, "For every cause, there is an effect." This incident and the related scandal most definitely caused major effects for all of them.

Nike used the "public" image of Earl because this was the only persona the public had ever seen. Throughout the years, the public knew Earl only as the father of Tiger Woods. The public was led to believe, not just from the media, but also from all the books Earl had written, that he was a great mentor and teacher. Nike tried to capitalize on this image in their advertisement. But the image they showed was not the real Earl and not the real father of Tiger Woods.

Since the scandal first broke, the media, various writers and authors and even the public have devoted unbelievable amounts of time and energy trying to find out why Tiger had these affairs and exactly how many women were involved. They have come up with countless theories as to why Tiger chose to break away from his marriage to Elin and destroy his role model image. For some unexplained reasons, these people were driven to seek answers

These people also tried using the assumption that Earl was a womanizer. In their minds it was obviously like father, like son. But then according to their theory, I suppose if Earl had been a bank robber, Tiger would have robbed banks, too. Frankly, using this type of logic is just plain lame and a far stretch from the truth.

When considering how Tiger was raised and how he became a victim of his father's obsessions and manipulations throughout his entire life, I hope people can understand why Tiger is who he is today. Whether or not the way Tiger was raised had anything to do with his having an affair would be strictly speculation on my part. Tiger is the only person who has the answers; therefore, no one will ever know the real truth. More importantly, why should we care? Tiger is not the first person or celebrity to ever give into temptation and I guarantee he will not be the last.

It was the media, the journalists, the writers, and especially the tabloids who continued to keep the public focused on the scandal. Basically, Tiger was on trial by tabloid. What they don't understand is maybe the public just wants Tiger back playing golf and winning tournaments. What is so wrong is that on one hand everyone is forcing Tiger out of golf with all of the unnecessary reporting and then on the other hand they state that they want Tiger back. Sometimes you can't have it both ways.

Let's be honest. Tiger doesn't have to ever return to golf. Yes, Tiger wants to compete because that is his nature. But Tiger has enough money to last him several lifetimes, so there is no real need to play golf just for the money. Tiger just wants to play because golf is who he is.

However, when he plays golf, Tiger knows he is subjecting himself to the continuing wrath of the public and the media, thus affecting his ability to perform to his own standards, which is trying to be the best. Maybe it's time for everyone to forget Tiger's so called image, so we can get that fist pumping brash winner back to the game of golf. Golf just is not the same without him, and sadly, it was the media and Tiger's fear of non-acceptance from the public that pushed him away.

Back in 1996 when Tiger turned pro and joined the PGA tour as a rookie, he came out as just a golfer. When Tiger became the world's most popular athlete, he was still just a golfer. The person who the fans and the world came to love and admire was Tiger, the golfer. Even though he had an affair, Tiger was still just a golfer.

So why should his private life change who he is. To everyone, he should still be just a golfer. Sadly, the media and the public forget Tiger is just a person, "not an image", and what he does in his private life should not affect how we feel about him as a golfer.

Tiger is still a great athlete, one of the very best, and what he did was his private business and it should not affect the way we feel about his playing golf. If Earl was still alive, he might not condone what Tiger had done, but he would hope people would recognize Tiger is still only a golfer and we should judge him only on that ability.

After all, Tiger fell from grace, not from golf.

28
DON'T BLAME TIGER

QUITE OFTEN EARL USED the phrase "cause and effect". He would always say, "For every cause, there is an effect", and then go into a very long dissertation as to what he meant and then give his many versions. Earl basically raised Tiger with this expression, telling him no matter what he did, whether it was in his golf or in his personal life, there would always be some type of an effect. Tiger learned to focus and think things through simply by looking at his cause and then making sure he was aware of the eventual effect.

Regrettably, Earl did not always abide by his own words of advice and the cause and effect theory when it came to his son. There were many times when Earl did not think about the effect that his own neurotic behavior and off kilter principles would have on Tiger. For example, throughout Tiger's life, Earl's main focus was all about Tiger's golf and making sure he became the best black golfer. Earl had become so preoccupied with his son's talent that Earl was not necessarily focusing on the actual needs of his child. Earl was, at times, a good father and was able to pass on certain lessons that would be valuable to Tiger. However, the way Earl and Tida actually raised Tiger and the hypocritical values they tried to instill in him were not always in their son's best interest. Sadly, throughout Tiger's life, Earl was only using Tiger for his own personal agenda and it was Tiger who ended up paying the consequences for his father's selfish actions and obsessive and controlling behavior.

You cannot really blame Tiger for the way he was raised. Most kids are smart and very impressionable and Tiger was no different. In fact, at times Tiger was a very obedient son and he trusted, respected and believed everything Earl told him. From everything I saw from Tiger and Earl, Tiger grew up idolizing his father and was always mesmerized by everything Earl said or did. It was Earl who said:

"Tiger actually gains strength from me and my presence."

Earl's actions and behavior were the reasons I always likened him to a cult leader; someone who would persuade unsuspecting and vulnerable people to follow his self-righteous and holier than thou path with total acceptance and obedience.

Actually, most of us grew up believing everything our parents told us and even worshipped the ground they walked on and we looked up to them for inspiration and as role models. After all, our parents are supposed to love us and protect us and always have our best interest at heart. We just naturally trust that they would never do anything to harm us. Unfortunately, we are shaped and influenced by our parents from both the good and the bad and what we learn ends up having long term effects on our mental outlook, personality and character throughout our life. Tiger was no different. Tiger loved his parents, but grew up conflicted with their teachings, demands and expectations. He eventually reached a point where his feelings and his sense of loyalty began to collide.

As Tiger grew and became even more successful in golf, Earl continued to push his son while manipulating and controlling more and more of his life. Sadly, Earl was pushing Tiger for all the wrong reasons. What Earl did not understand, or rather refused to believe, was Tiger did not always share his thoughts and visions. Even according to Earl's own admission, Tiger just wanted to play golf and get the joy and satisfaction out of playing and being a winner. Tiger did not need or want everything else. Tiger had his own dreams and aspirations. Tiger wanted to be a champion, but he did not need to be a "star" or "celebrity".

It was Earl who took it upon himself to steer and push Tiger toward stardom. Tiger did not necessarily need to be the best. It was his father who demanded that Tiger had to be the best, no matter what. Earl believed the way he had trained Tiger would cause him to be a stronger golfer, which was true. However, Earl ignored the fact that teaching his child that it was acceptable to be arrogant and feel superior to others could have a negative effect as Tiger grew up. Is Tiger arrogant? Yes, but this is who he was programmed to be. The focus Tiger has makes him a true winner, but this seems to also have the effect of making him appear aloof, unapproachable and even disinterested. Tiger did, in fact, emerge a true champion, but at what cost to his character.

Earl thought he was simply showing love for his son by being such an integral part of his life, but in effect, Earl ended up dominating Tiger's life, causing Tiger to give up his identity and his independence. Only as an adult and after he moved away from his parents, was Tiger able to begin to gain some semblance of independence. Until Earl's death, Tiger still continued to rely on his father's advice and direction prolonging his dependency on his father. However, it wasn't until after Earl died when Tiger was able to demonstrate his own independence without interference and judgment from his overbearing father. Unfortunately, Tiger's identity and brash and arrogant personality remained the same, thanks to the many years of Earl's continued strong influence and manipulations.

The negative effects of Earl's teachings eventually surfaced in Tiger's adult life. More harm than good came from Earl's life lessons and the examples he set. Sadly, Tiger was the one who ended up having to deal with the repercussions, which included a scandal, the end of his marriage, and a threatened golf career. Tiger's relentless desire to compete and his refusal to show pain resulted in a leg injury which could have ended his career. Also, his indiscretions in his private life created the scandal that destroyed his carefully crafted image.

However, once the scandal had died down, Tiger's troubles continued as he faced the end of his marriage. Tiger was now forced to deal with the breakup of his marriage, a custody battle over their children, and the financial penalty that would result from his infidelities.

Although Tiger and Elin had only been married for about five years, Elin was very fortunate that she still received a hefty settlement, rumored to be one hundred million dollars. Luckily for Tiger, the amount he ended up giving to Elin could have been much larger considering in most divorces involving tremendous wealth, many wives can receive up to fifty percent of their husband's current and future earnings. In Tiger's case, he got off cheap.

I remember Earl telling me how Tiger made sure to have Elin sign a prenuptial agreement prior to their wedding and I am sure this resulted in Elin receiving the amount she did. Tiger's divorce also reminded me of Earl's earlier skepticism about Elin's motives when it came to Tiger. He truly believed there was a possibility Elin was only after Tiger for his money. Well, based on her actions where she bulldozed her twelve million dollar mansion in Florida that she purchased after her divorce, maybe this time Earl was actually correct in doubting his daughter-in-law. Then again, she did go from swim suit model to nanny to wife and mother to multi-multi-millionaire, thus showing that wealth does have an effect on people.

On the other hand, Earl had often worried that perhaps Elin was only a trophy wife to Tiger. And with Earl and Tida's loveless relationship and what Tiger saw growing up, it is possible that Tiger may be incapable of fully understanding the true nature of marriage and family.

Many more changes came to Tiger including the end of his relationship with his swing coach, Hank Haney, and his caddy, Steve Williams. Both of these people were crucial to Tiger and his career, so once again, adjustments had to be made in Tiger's life to compensate for loosing these people. Tiger did, however, remain with his agent, Mark Steinberg, when Mark opted to leave IMG, the agency that Tiger first signed with when he first turned professional. Although Mark was Tiger's second agent while at IMG, a friendship had formed between Tiger and Mark, and out of loyalty, Tiger decided to follow Mark to his new marketing agency. Besides, Mark has made a tremendous amount of money for Tiger over the years, so why would Tiger change agents at this stage of his career.

Since the scandal had subsided and so many changes were being made by Tiger in his life, one might wonder if he was also trying to change the once created image that was so prevalent for so many years in his career. The image Earl believed was necessary for Tiger to have in order to be successful is now being replaced with a more friendly and approachable persona. Since the role model image that was so carefully crafted for him has now been dispelled, it now appears Tiger is trying to adapt to a new humanized personality, one that may sway his fans back to his corner.

However, there are times when I wonder if Tiger's actions are only an act or is he really trying to overcome a lifetime of Earl's manipulations and control. Even if he is sincere in his efforts, I wonder how successful Tiger will be considering his upbringing and the tremendous influence Earl had on him throughout his entire life. Just maybe, Tiger finally realized that he is a real person and not a made up image. Maybe he is trying to stand on his own without the crutch his father so selfishly provided. Then again, maybe people are finally realizing Tiger is, in fact, a real person, with real feelings, and he is not this made up image of a golfer who they placed so very high on a moral pedestal. Hopefully, everyone is in acceptance with who Tiger really is; an extremely talented and tremendously successful golfer. Period!

Yes, Earl helped and encouraged Tiger with his golf and he was proud of Tiger for his talent. And yes, Earl was a good person, which I can personally attest to. But when it came to Tiger's golf, Earl was completely over the top and totally out of control. He made comments about his son which were bizarre and eccentric, at times even embarrassing his son. Earl truly believed his son was so perfect that he could cure everything wrong in the entire world. Earl once publicly stated,

"Tiger is refreshing. His graciousness, poise and character are manifested in all that he does. His purity and his philanthropic attitude is exactly what this country and the entire world needs. We all need reassurance that we are good people and Tiger will bring that goodness to everyone."

What a load of crap! Sadly, these are the type of publicly made statements that Tiger had to live with.

In Earl's quest to also push his son to stardom, Earl became obsessed with a vision of his own, which was seeing himself finally allowed to be in the spotlight. It was almost like an addiction for Earl. Once he had a taste of fame and recognition, he just could not stop and from there Earl sadly became irrepressible in his behavior and his need to be known as someone important. Stardom was not Tiger's dream; it was the dream of his father which he expected Tiger to fulfill. It was Earl who pushed Tiger to be the best and convinced him that he had to be the best. Earl had his own self-serving agenda and chose to capitalize on his son's tremendous talent, taking advantage of the fame and wealth that would come with that talent, only to satisfy his own personal needs and desires. After all, if Tiger had not been a great golfer, Earl would not have been recognized as someone important, meaning the "father of Tiger Woods". So in order for Earl to be noticed and form his own celebrity status, Tiger *had* to be the best. Tiger *had* to be the perfect son.

Earl's influence was extremely penetrating on Tiger and I blame Earl for making Tiger the smug and arrogant person he has become. With a less demanding upbringing and a more normal childhood environment, I sometimes wonder what kind of person Tiger would have turned out to be.

When it comes to his talent and success in the world of golf, Tiger is simply amazing. He is relentless in his pursuit to win. Nobody can dispute that statement. But when it comes to his real world, the one that does not revolve around golf, it was there where I had always hoped Tiger would be a little more sensitive and even more caring.

I did see a glimmer of that side of Tiger when he was a kid and at times while he was growing up. But sadly, Earl's influence on Tiger was innately strong and Tiger grew up believing that he was, in fact, perfect and that he was actually better than everyone else. When Tiger walked around with his head held high, he was not doing it out of self-pride. Tiger was actually feeling he was above it all, so his stature was just demonstrating that fact even further.

So once again, you can't blame Tiger for who he has become. Blame Earl Woods who always made the claim that he was the sole person who "created" Tiger Woods.

Many times I have thought about what if Earl had simply allowed Tiger to be just a regular person with normal aspirations, even those of being a champion, then maybe Tiger would not be facing so much destruction and sadness in his life and have the overwhelming need to continually be perfect.

Tiger grew up fearing his father's disappointment and disapproval. Maybe if Earl had raised a child who loved to play golf instead of a golfer who had to be perfect, Tiger's personal and professional life may have taken a considerably smoother direction without the need for excessive pressure and stress. If Tiger had been allowed to simply grow up without so many demands and expectations from everyone, just maybe Tiger would have ended up more secure and content with himself.

Then again, maybe Tiger will never be truly content with anything, thanks to his father.

29
HIS STRUGGLE TO RETURN

WITHOUT HIS FATHER'S usual guidance and direction, Tiger was now forced to cope with the changes that were taking place in his life as a result of some reckless and costly choices, some of which were his to make and some others were made for him. The consequences from Earl's earlier method of raising his son were now starting to create havoc in Tiger's life. Ironically, however, Earl spent his entire life trying to make sure Tiger was accepted by everyone. Not just as a person, but also as a golfer of color. And then in an instant, Tiger destroyed that acceptance, leaving the entire world to doubt him as a person and as a golfer.

Tiger's golfing career was drastically altered due his knee surgery and his not being able to play golf for eight months. Then, of course, his career was also affected because of his much publicized scandal. As a result, Tiger was forced to endure all of the criticism and scrutiny that was being thrown at him, not only from the media, but also from his fellow golfers and the public. When Tiger made his comeback, just imagine how difficult it was for him to go out and play golf for the first time after everything blew up. He now had to face his many accusers and set aside his embarrassment in order to return to the sport he once dominated.

Frankly, this had to have taken a lot of guts to make his first appearance in such a public setting. However, if anyone was able to cope with the stress and pressure of returning to golf under such uncomfortable and stressful conditions, it would be Tiger. I knew Tiger had the courage and fortitude to overcome such obstacles. As a child there was very little room for emotion, but the feeling of being invincible ran rampant. Even so, I still felt bad that Tiger had to experience such unhappiness and turmoil in his life. After all, from the way he was raised, Earl primed Tiger for a fall.

Tiger could have simply walked away from his career, removing the stress and pressures that he knew he would have by playing golf again. After all, it is not like he needed the money, right? And he had already broken almost every possible record there was, except of course, beating Jack Nicklaus's record of eighteen major championship wins.

So when you think about it, what else was there to motivate Tiger to return to golf? Could it be all of the people who were against Tiger and judging him for his indiscretions? Absolutely not. Simply put, golf is in Tiger's blood. Golf is all he knows. Golf is his life and has been since he was two years old. But more importantly, Tiger just has to compete. Earl trained Tiger to be the best and to always win. This is why he keeps coming back.

So, you can't blame Tiger for wanting and needing to go out and once again face the challenge of trying to conquer the "green monster", also known as a golf course. Setting his apprehension and feelings aside, Tiger made a choice to return to golf, even though he was still concerned about his earlier knee injury. Since Tiger had always been taught by his father to never show pain and to never quit, no matter the reason, there would be a possibility that he could cause more injury to his healing knee.

However, because of the way Tiger was raised to always push himself and to never show any weakness, his attitude was still to go out and win. To Tiger, he would not and could not fail. He had been told all of his life that he was the best and that there is no defeat for him. After all, he is Tiger Woods.

Then, of course, with all of the changes occurring in Tiger's life and his not being able to perform to his fullest expectations on the golf course, Tiger decided it was once again time to change his swing with yet another coach, Sean Foley.

Ever since Tiger was little, he always wanted to be the best. Of course, he was taught by Earl that he could always be better. I could fully understand his need to make adjustments to his swing as he grew and his body size and strength changed. However, when it came to the swing he had from the time he joined the PGA tour, I could never understand his need for such drastic changes.

I remember in 2004 when Tiger changed his swing coach. He decided to leave Butch Harmon and switch to Hank Haney. Once again, Tiger decided this was the right time for him to change his swing, hoping the adjustments he made would improve his length, accuracy and overall performance.

I asked Earl, "Why in the world would Tiger want to change his swing again. I mean that swing has earned a lot of money for him over the years?"

Earl just laughed and decided to use a cute analogy just for me. He replied with, "Linda, a swing is like a basic black dress. You wear it and wear it and then one day you just get tired of it. Then you decide that you want a new little black dress. Well, Tiger is tired of his black dress and wants a new one."

I just stared at Earl, laughing at him, of course, and sort of understanding what he was trying to explain. I then asked, "But if it ain't broke, why fix it? Why change to something completely new? Besides, it's not like his swing has worn out, right?"

Again, Earl just laughed, "It's the little black dress thing. Tiger thinks the new one will be even better than the old one."

At this point, I decided to leave well enough alone and hope that Tiger's choice was indeed going to improve his game, because if it doesn't, Tiger will most likely be in a world of hurt. His entire career and golfing talent is based solely on his swing and without that, his ability to win tournaments will be tremendously affected.

Earl chimed in once again by stating, "Don't worry. You know this is not the first time he has made changes to his swing and it most definitely will not be the last. You know how Tiger is. He has to be perfect in every part of his game."

"Yah, but he's pretty close to perfect now, right? So why does he have to change anything?"

Earl sighed, "Pretty close to perfect isn't good enough. He has to have total perfection."

Then I thought about Tiger's need for perfection, knowing full well that it was Earl who pushed Tiger to be perfect and made Tiger think he had to be absolutely flawless in order to succeed and to be accepted. I also remembered back to the many times when Tiger was younger and would demonstrate such frustration and anger as he strived for perfection. It was sad that a father would put such huge expectations and demands on his son, not thinking about any future repercussions that might ensue. Tiger was only human with human emotions. Besides, nobody is ever completely perfect.

Because of this mindset, Tiger had never been emotionally prepared for any type of defeat, either personally or professionally. Earl had pushed Tiger so hard in order to be victorious over others that he never once thought it might be necessary to explain the true definition of defeat to his son. The problem was Earl never considered defeat to be losing a tournament in which Tiger had hoped to win. In those instances when Tiger lost a tournament, Tiger had not been defeated; Tiger simply did not play up to his expected standards of performance. Therefore, Tiger just did not win. There was always an excuse or a reason why Tiger lost, and it was never because he had been defeated by any other golfer.

Tiger was also conditioned by his father to believe that he was incapable of failing at anything. Earl's belief was his son cannot and will not fail. It was simply not possible. It had always been programmed into Tiger that he was perfect and to be perfect, you cannot fail. Those seeds were planted many years ago and Tiger grew from those words thinking he was invincible and would always be better than every other golfer. Tiger believed he would always conquer and would never be defeated.

However, Tiger did face defeat and it was from his own doing. Tiger ended up suffering loss after loss which covered a two year span. This just does not happen to Tiger Woods. For the first time since he started playing on the PGA tour, we watched as Tiger struggled on the golf course, unable to perform, not only to his father's earlier expectations, but also to his own. Sadly, Tiger was disappointed in himself and he also knew that he had disappointed everyone else. After all, he had a reputation he was expected to uphold.

Throughout Tiger's struggles, everyone still took it upon themselves to judge Tiger and then to place those unbelievable expectations on this one golfer who just happens to be human, and far from being perfect. It was because of Tiger's absence from golf that all eyes were on him, expecting, rather demanding perfection. But no matter how hard Tiger tried, and he did try, he just was not able to pull it all together to make a win. In the end, you really can't blame Tiger for trying. Personally, I admire him for his many attempts and for trying to put the past behind him.

As it turned out, there were many people who were also saddened that Tiger could not triumph. Yes, they were expecting, but more so, they were hoping Tiger would once again go out and be a winner. In reality, no one truly wanted Tiger to fail. However, there were some people who, after the scandal, had judged Tiger harshly prior to his return and when he did play in his first tournament, fans in the gallery literally turned away, denying Tiger their once given support. Of course, Tiger not only felt the pressure, but he also felt their rejection. Tiger had to be strong in order to shield himself from all of the negatives and overcome the gallery's display of silence. Tiger knew he had to do whatever it took to be perfect, believing that his perfection would again earn him acceptance.

Unable to succeed in his many attempts, Tiger temporarily pulled away from golf, only to return for another shot at a win. Tiger once more gave it his all and came close to a win on a few occasions. Never once losing sight of achieving his goal, Tiger continued to put forth an earnest effort as he again sought out dominance.

Tiger eventually did emerge a winner at his own World Challenge Tournament in December, 2011, at Sherwood Country Club in Thousand Oaks, California. Although he had won this tournament many times before, this particular tournament win was extra special for Tiger, since not only was it his first win in two years, but it also sponsors the Tiger Woods Foundation. The win may not be sanctioned by the PGA tour, but to Tiger it was truly an important moment in his life as he proved to himself and to everyone else that he can still be a winner. In his mind, Tiger believed he was finally back.

Tiger then went on to win three more tournaments in 2012. Tiger won at Arnold Palmer's tournament at Bay Hill Country Club, Jack Nicklaus' tournament, The Memorial, and the AT&T at Congressional. Once again in 2013, Tiger flourished with five wins and receiving the 2013 PGA Tour Player of the Year Award. His wins that year included the Arnold Palmer Invitational, the

Farmers Insurance Open, the Players' Championship, and two World Golf Championships, namely the Cadillac Championship and the Bridgestone Invitational.

There are many people who don't really consider Tiger as truly being back until he wins a major, but what other tour player has won eight tournaments in two years and regained his number one ranking, albeit for a short time?

Then the unthinkable happened. Tiger injured his lower back while playing in one of the tournaments, causing him tremendous pain each time he took a swing. Tiger's performance continued to be poor, especially for him, during all of the tournaments he attempted to play. Tiger found he was unable to control most of his shots, including his once incredible short game,

The problem was that since Tiger had been taught to play with an injury and to always make sure to not show any pain, Tiger continued to struggle through each tournament, and in many of them he failed to make the cut. The more Tiger tried to play, the more he suffered, eventually causing him to withdraw from the sport he once dominated in hopes his injured back would heal.

Unfortunately, his injury led to surgery, and to this day he has not yet returned to professional golf. With the past behind him, everyone seems to be in complete anticipation of his return in hopes to have Tiger back on top once more. However, win or lose, many simply want to see Tiger play golf again.

Tiger is the epitome of golf and he has been for the last twenty years. Yet, there are, of course, some naysayers who feel Tiger is done playing golf and can no longer perform. They feel he is too old to be a real winner, so why should they invest themselves in someone who can never again be a champion. Many of these cynics predict that Tiger will never again win a major nor will he ever get back his number one ranking.

It is quite obvious they don't know the real Tiger Woods. If Tiger can physically play golf again and play without any type of injury, then Tiger can and will win.

Tiger has the focus, mindset and superior talent to comeback once again. Will he be number one again? Possibly. Will he win another major? Possibly. After all, Jack Nicklaus won the Masters at forty-six years old. Even Phil Mickelson won the British Open at forty-three. When it comes to golf, age has nothing to do with it and if you don't believe that, remember Tom Watson almost winning the Open at sixty years old. All it takes is Tiger to believe that he can win.

In a way, Tiger's life has come full circle. Tiger grew up with a controlling father who did everything he could to push his son to greatness, mostly for all of the wrong reasons. All the while, Earl was priming Tiger for an eventual fall.

However, since the once fan favorite has not graced the golfing arena with his presence for quite some time, Tiger is the one who now needs to push himself back and into the sport that he so desperately needs to be a part of. Tiger doesn't need to be a superstar or to be placed on a pedestal. Tiger just wants to play golf and win.

During Tiger's last run of tournaments before he had to quit due to injury, you could see a portion of the former brash rookie aching to come out. You could see how badly Tiger wanted to exert his excitement on his great shots by using his old signature fist pump, but stopped short. This made me wonder if the years of control and discipline and the need for "the image" was beginning to fade.

This also made me think back to the ten year old kid who was striving for perfection, and who was cocky, playful and had a nasty little temper. That kid is now all grown up, but he is still just Tiger.

Printed in Poland
by Amazon Fulfillment
Poland Sp. z o.o., Wrocław